From The
Horse's Mouth

❖

Dr Wynne's Diaries

FROM THE
HORSE'S MOUTH

❖

DR WYNNE'S DIARIES

Dr Wynne Davies
MBE., FRAgS.

Gomer

Published in 2015 by
Gomer Press, Llandysul, Ceredigion, SA44 4JL

ISBN 978 1 78562 036 2
ISBN 978 1 78562 037 9 (ePUB)
ISBN 978 1 78562 038 6 (Kindle)

Printed and bound in Wales at
Gomer Press, Llandysul, Ceredigion
www.gomer.co.uk

FOREWORD

When I read Dr Wynne's first book, I realised that there was very little mentioned as to how or why he got so involved with the Welsh Pony.

I am delighted that this interesting and amusing diary has come to fruition, which reveals so much of his life, passion, interest and success over the years.

The Hon Dame Mrs Shân Legge-Bourke DCVO

ABBREVIATIONS

BDS British Driving Society

BSJA British Showjumping Association

BSPS British Show Pony Society

ch champion

ch* overall champion

f. foaled in

FO Fayre Oaks

FS Foundation Stock

g- great

gns guineas (£1.05)

hh hands (four inches)

HOYS Horse of the Year Show

M&M Mountain and Moorland

NPS National Pony Society

PofW Prince of Wales

RASE Royal Agricultural Society of England

RB&B Russell, Baldwin and Bright (auctioneers, now Brightwells)

RW Royal Welsh Show

RWAS Royal Welsh Agricultural Society

RWPoW Royal Welsh Prince of Wales

Welsh section A Welsh mountain pony (under 12 hands, 121.9 cm)

Welsh section B Welsh pony (under 13 hands 2 in, 137.2 cm)

Welsh section C	Welsh pony (Cob type) (under 13 hands 2 in, 137.2 cm)
Welsh section D	Welsh cob (no height limit)
WHP	Working Hunter Pony
WPB	Welsh part-bred (12.5 per cent registered Welsh)
WPCA	Welsh Pony and Cob Area Association
WPCS	Welsh Pony and Cob Society
WSB	Welsh Stud Book
x	by
y-o	year-old

CONTENTS

1932–1939

I was born at Ceulan Stores, Tal-y-bont, Cardiganshire, on 19 March 1932, the third child of Evan Samuel Davies and Janet Mary (Williams). Ceulan Stores was rebuilt between 1935 and 1937 and renamed Central Stores. While the work was being carried out, the business carried on in the warehouse (later to become Hillside House). Although my father had no formal training in architecture, he planned Central Stores, a most complicated building, constructed on two levels in the southern end, three in the northern end, six bedrooms and three staircases. The shop fittings were of exceptional quality, bought by my grandfather in London and sent with doors, fireplaces and other fittings by rail to Tal-y-bont.

My father was very interested in art, particularly horse paintings, and bought several here and there over the years. There must have been something in the genes, because to everyone's surprise, I passed the Central Welsh Board School Certificate in Art with credit. Our son David is competent at painting and sculpting, and his daughter Miriam was top student in her year in her Fine Arts degree, and was awarded First Class Honours.

There were stables behind the shop which housed the cob that pulled a flat cart delivering animal feedstuffs, hay seeds etc. as far afield as Cwm Einon and Borth (a round trip of 16 miles). The cob mare, which I remember, was Polly, registered name Ceulan Chessie, sired by the well-known Llethi Valiant. Presumably, the famous Seren Ceulan lived there before my time. They were turned out to graze in Cae'r Efail, a field in the middle of the village next to the blacksmith's forge, currently the site of Davmor Garage, or in Cae Lletyllwyd, about a mile from the shop, where I spent many hours of my childhood with various mares and foals.

My father, Evan Samuel Davies (Evie, 1899–1972) was born in London. He joined the Welsh Pony and Cob Society in 1915 and became president in 1955. Evie's father, Samuel Morris Davies (1864–1949), was born at Bachystarn Farm, Farmers, Llanwrda, the fifth child of Evan Davies (born in 1832) and Rachel (Morris, they were married in 1855), who died when she was only 34 years of age. Evan Davies subsequently married Mary in 1868 and they had six children of their own. Most of the eleven children remained in the Crugybar area as farmers or farmers' wives. Child number ten, Richard (born in 1880), stayed on to farm Bachystarn, followed by his daughter Lizzie (Thomas) who died in 2000 and her grandson, Mansel Lewis, Pentwyn Farm, is a leading farmer in the Crugybar area now.

There was not enough work on the farm for more than one son, and the eldest daughter Lisa (born 1856), went to work in Tondu, near Bridgend and married John Davies (1854–1930) of Tondu Farm, and they had seven sons. This was a remarkable family. Four of the sons went to Oxford or Cambridge universities. It was a rare occurrence in those days for a farmer's son from Wales to enter either (although my mother's brother went to Cambridge) – for four brothers to do so, it must have been unique. David (born 1882) became headmaster of Bargoed Grammar School and Oswald (born in 1893) started British Crop Driers in Lincolnshire. Alec (born in 1897) was a consultant in Harley Street and Eddie (born 1895) was a Captain Adjutant by the age of 21, became British Ambassador to Ceylon, and would send tea parcels to his relatives in Wales during the war. Of the other three sons, John (born in 1885) carried on at

Tondu Farm, Sam (born in 1890) was a construction inspector of schools and Evan (born in 1883) went to the Baptist College and became a missionary.

My grandfather, S. M. Davies, bought Ceulan Stores and married Mary Jane Reed (born at Braichgarw, Tal-y-bont, in 1865), whose cousins were the Hughes family of Tynrhelig Farm, Tal-y-bont and Felin Gyffin, Dole and the Davies families of Llwyngronw Farm, Penrhyncoch (Richard), and Tyncwm Farm, Capel Dewi (Tom). SMD and his wife then bought a draper's shop in Battersea Park Road, London, leaving Mary Jane's sister, Catherine Anne, to look after Ceulan Stores. It was common practice in those days for Cardiganshire families to set up businesses there, housing their cattle in central London and selling milk, butter and cheese.

My father and his sister Rachel (Riggie) spent their childhood in London, but would escape to Tal-y-bont for their holidays, and they also went to school there for some time. My father was happiest at Tanyrallt farm, home of the famous Tanyrallt Stud of hackney horses and ponies. SMD would regularly buy a pony and trap at Tal-y-bont and drive it to London, a journey of 220 miles, which would take him four days, the usual stopping-places being Kington, Bromyard, Witney or Oxford.

Mary Jane Davies died in London at the age of 63 years in 1929. The shop in Battersea was bombed in 1942, and grandfather and Riggie were evacuated to Central Stores. The government compensated homeowners who were bombed with about £50 per house. My father's cousin Polly (Llwyngronw), who lived at nearby Charlotte Street, survived the blitz, and when her daughter Megan (Richards) died in 2004, the property was sold for £3.4m! Megan left a bequest in her will that the whole family (about 60 in number) would be paid travelling expenses (some from as far afield as Canada), and accommodation for a weekend reunion at the Marine

Hotel, Aberystwyth. A photograph of the group appeared in the *Cambrian News*.

Polly's sister Lizzie (James) and her husband also went to London. Their son, Dr Brennig James, was a GP in Marlow and was the first person to fly a glider without oxygen in the Himalayas. Both families often visited us at Tal-y-bont. The Richardses always drove an Aston Martin, which created much interest in the village. A second cousin was (Sir) David James, Pantyfedwen, who had a childhood illness and spent some months with my grandparents, father and aunt at Battersea Park Road.

My father got his first Welsh pony in 1914, which was the 12.2hh white short-tailed pony of cob-type Seren Ceulan, foaled in 1910 and bred by Lewis of Tyngraig, Tal-y-bont. Her sire was the 13.1hh chestnut Total (John Thomas, Tre'r-ddôl, my maternal grandfather's uncle) and her dam was Aeronwen Ceulan (f. 1905) bred by L. R. Lewis, Ffynonddu, Clarach, daughter of Ffynon Queen (f. 1900) by Eiddwen Flyer II. Ffynon Queen was a prize-winner at Tal-y-bont, Aberystwyth and Machynlleth in 1903. The *Welsh Stud Book Volume III* shows that Ffynon Queen won the WPCS silver medal at Tal-y-bont Show in 1903. She was one of the first 23 ever to be issued WPCS medals in a list which included famous names such as Prince of Cardiff, Llwyn Prince of Wales and Greylight (exported to Australia for £1,000 in 1911).

Seren Ceulan herself won two second prizes for my father when he was just 15 years old at the Tal-y-bont Show in 1915, followed by two first prizes and the WPCS silver medal at Tal-y-bont on 6 September 1916. The certificate was signed by David Davies (president), J. Marshall Dugdale (chairman), Charles Coltman Rogers (vice-chairman) and John R. Bache (secretary). The Tal-y-bont Show was held in 1915 and 1916 despite the country being at war. At the 1916 show, the winners did not receive any cash prizes. Wounded soldiers attended the show, and £127 was donated to the

Red Cross. No show was held in 1917 or 1918, but it re-started in 1919.

Seren Ceulan did her stint pulling the cart from Ceulan Stores while my father was off in the Army in Germany in 1917. When my father returned in 1920 he re-started showing Seren Ceulan, and she won more medals at Tal-y-bont shows in 1921, 1922, 1923, 1924 and 1925, and at Aberystwyth Show in 1926. She competed further afield in 1925 in the Royal Welsh Show at Carmarthen where she was second, and a member of the Cardiganshire winning group. Her crowning moment of glory came at the 1928 RWS in Wrexham, where she won the brood mare class of six exhibits (five of which had been national winners), the WPCS silver medal for best mare or filly, the Royal Welsh Agricultural Society Prince of Wales' championship medal and the RWAS Dragon medal for the county group. Seren Ceulan died in 1930 and Captain Howson wrote an obituary for her in the RWAS Journal, calling her: 'a pony of that grand old-fashioned order for which her native country has so long been famous. Full of substance, yet full of quality withal, and abounding in free swing action.' He noted that her dam, Aeronwen Ceulan, was still alive and going strong at Tyngraig Farm.

When one considers that Seren Ceulan worked most of her life and had only five years off to have foals, it is amazing that her blood is to be found in many present-day top studs of sections A, B and C. Three of the foals were exported – Ceulan Aven Bun (f. 1924) to the USA, Brenin Cymru (f. 1925) to Argentina, and Ceulan Comet (f. 1926, Royal Welsh champion four times) to Australia. Ceulan Kitty (f. 1921) was lost without trace, leaving only Ceulan Silverleaf (f. 1929 and reserve champion at the 1932 RW) to continue the strain. Ceulan Silverleaf herself had ten foals. The first two – Ceulan Silver Belle and Silver Gem (f. 1934 and 1935) – were exported to the Italian count Idelfonzo Stanga, and Ceulan Cora (f. 1948) and

Ceulan Carol (f. 1953) to the USA. Silver Belle and Silver Gem were sired by Grove Sprightly (Royal Welsh champion nine times 1930–1939), which would entail my father walking Silverleaf four miles to Llandre GWR station and six miles the other end from Church Stretton station to Dinchope farm, Craven Arms.

One of the most influential of Silverleaf's progeny was Ceulan Revelry (f. 1943) by Ceulan Revolt. He was a consistent winner inhand and harness for Mr Tom Lewis of Merthyr Tydfil, then spent five years as a premium stallion on the Gower peninsula, where he produced Royal Welsh winners (sections A and C) for Mr Colin Davies (Cefn Stud) and Mr Donald Morris (Bryn Stud). The senior brood mare at Ceulan Stud, Miskin, recently was Ceulan Cariad (f. 1988, twice RW winner, died in 2014) and descended from Ceulan Silverleaf in five generations.

Silverleaf's 1938 foal was sired by an Arab stallion, Incoronax (bred by Lady Wentworth) at the time when section B of the WSB was being formed. The foal was registered as Ceulan Silver Lustre. She became a legend, and the name 'Lustre' has continued for three-quarters of a century. The 2013 Welsh National section B champion, the Dutch-bred Valeur Dancing Fairy Lustre is, unbelievably, only three generations from Ceulan Silver Lustre, and a fourth-generation descendant, Thistledown Sheer Lustre, was female champion at the 2014 Royal Welsh.

Silverleaf's last foal was born on St Valentine's Day 1951. She was sired by our 1947 and 1952 RW champion, Dinarth What Ho x Ceulan Silverleaf, and was named Ceulan Valentine. Valentine remained at Ceulan all her life, originator of the Ceulan 'V' family. The stud had many representatives of her daughters Ceulan Venus (f. 1961) and Ceulan Vanity (f. 1963), the last being Ceulan Vienetta (f. 2003), which was sold in 2006. After being ridden for ten years, Ceulan Valmai (f. 2001) returned to Ceulan in 2015 to carry on the 'V' line.

My parents were married in 1925 after my father returned to Tal-y-bont from Germany. My mother Janet (born 1900) was the second child and eldest daughter of Lewis Oliver (L. O.) and Annie Williams, who lived at Frongoch, Tre'r-ddôl. They had five children. The eldest was David Oliver (Rev D. O. Williams, MA Cantab), then my mother, then Laura (Mrs Jack Morris, Loughton, Uncle Jack being a son of Brynrodyn farm, Borth), Cassie (Mrs John Gwilym Evans) and Josephine (Mrs Cecil Jones, whose husband was vicar at Eglwysbach and Ruthin). Cassie died soon after her son Billie was born, and Billie was brought up by his grand-parents at Frongoch. His daughter, Mrs Anne Jones, has the Frongoch Stud. L. O. and Annie Williams had a butchery business at Frongoch and a large stud of Welsh ponies, cobs, hackneys and Shire horses (with stallions at stud), and employed full-time grooms. The 1923 stud card includes the Shire stallion Wedding Bells, the Welsh pony stallion Cream Bun (second at the 1923 RWS when owned by my grandfather, and champion in 1925 when owned by Dinarth Hall), which my mother drove to a four-wheeled show wagon, and the hackney King Simon, son of Copper Belle, which my grandfather bought from Sir Nigel Colman and which my mother drove to win several harness competitions. The Frongoch farm accounts ledgers give descriptions of all the mares served by these stallions and the stud fees paid.

My grandfather also owned the Brickyard and Glanmorfa farms, situated between Tre'r-ddôl and Borth. During the First World War, my mother ran the farms while her older brother David was at Cambridge University studying to become a Wesleyan minister. He was subsequently based at Rugby, Skegness, Warwick and Northampton among other places. My mother was the first female driver of a motor car in north Cardiganshire. She used to relate how, on one foggy night, driving on the long straight stretches over Borth bog, she ran over a drunken walker whom she could not then find, because he was under the car! In those days, the cars were very high off the road. So she reversed, got the man onto his feet and sent him off in the right direction. The man lived in Tre'r-ddôl, and he was never told about the incident – he lived to a ripe old age.

My grandfather was brought up at Clettwr Hall, Tre'r-ddôl, a house built by his father, Captain David Williams MIMechE, a manager of mines in north Cardiganshire, and previously at Pateley Bridge, Yorkshire. That was where my grandfather met my grandmother, a member of a well-known Yorkshire family, the Summersgills. Captain David Williams lived at Clettwr Hall for about twenty years after retirement. During most of this time, he was a member of Cardiganshire County Council, reportedly always coming out top of the poll at the elections. He also owned successful racehorses, of which I have no details, sadly. He died in January 1918, his wife Jane having predeceased him three months previously. Jane was a member of the Tre'r-ddôl Thomas, London House family. Her brother John Thomas, a corn miller, owned the Welsh pony stallion Klondyke which was bred by another John Thomas (John Thomas, the carrier) who lived nearby. John Thomas won first prize with Klondyke in a class of stallions from far and wide at the Welsh National Show (now Royal Welsh) in 1905 and sold him that day for £120 to Mr W. S. Miller of Forest Lodge, Brecon, who owned the largest stud of Welsh ponies in the country at that time.

My father, writing about the ancestors of the famous Coed Coch Glyndwr in the 1968 WPCS Journal, did not believe that the two John Thomases of Tre'r-ddôl were related to each other. Years later, I received the *Showing World* magazine Lifetime Achievement Award at the Horse of the Year Show, and a report of the award appeared in the *Cambrian News* and in *Ardwynian* magazine, together with information that the ponies I currently have at Ceulan are descended from those owned by John Thomas of Tre'r-ddôl. A copy of the *Ardwynian* found its way to Australia where it was read by David Rowlands, senior director at the Australian Government in Canberra, who informed me that John Thomas (the carrier) was his great-grandfather, and that he was, in fact, a cousin of John Thomas (the miller). He supplied me with a copy of the will of their grandfather William Thomas (1849), showing that he had three sons and five daughters. One son, William, was bequeathed the house, land, stock and crops, another son, Lewis, got £100 and my grandfather's mother Jane got only 2s 6d (12.5p) – perhaps because she had married a captain who had enough money to build Clettwr Hall! It was nice to discover an Australian second cousin that I didn't know I had. He has since investigated the fortunes of a tree which I planted at Cefn Onn Parc, Romsey, Victoria in 1984 and found that it has flourished well and is now quite large.

The catalogue of the 1905 Welsh National Show (the second show) records that my grandfather was second in class 33 for two-y-o Welsh cob fillies or geldings, and my grandmother fifth in class 34 for yearlings. How wise not to compete against one another in the same class! An interesting prize won by my grandfather was first at Machynlleth Show on 24 August 1910, where all exhibits had to be offered for sale to the government's Remount Department at a price not exceeding £40. This class was judged by Prince Francis of Teck, brother to Queen Mary. Since an annual agricultural wage in 1910 was £37, I imagine my grandfather would have been very happy to accept £40 for his first prize-winner.

My grandfather's older brother David returned to live at Clettwr Hall after serving as a medical officer in the Boer War in South Africa from 1899 to 1902. The *Cambrian News* of 16 August 1901 carried two columns relating Dr Williams' experiences in South Africa. On one occasion, he trekked for thirty miles, crossing three drifts by himself with an oxen ambulance through Boer country.

The family also owned the farms Cae'r Arglwyddes and Lletylwydin, and most of the houses in Tre'r-ddôl village. Dr Williams served as a GP in Tre'r-ddôl, Taliesin and Tal-y-bont until his death in 1948, originally going on his rounds on horseback – later, he was chauffeur-driven. He was also medical officer for the Royal Welsh Agricultural Society, and his photographs in the RWAS Journals group of officers are the only ones I have of him. It was said in his obituary that he never sent bills to patients who could not afford to pay. He was responsible for bringing electricity to Tre'r-ddôl and Taliesin, and perhaps the income from this enterprise made up for the lack of income from his medical work. What was my great-aunt Jane Evans' Aberleri Farm in Borth is now the site of the Borth golf course and caravan park. When her daughter Marie left school, she became housekeeper to her uncle David at Clettwr Hall and after his death, she went to London and married an industrial chemist, Dr Joe Lloyd-Evans.

I started attending Tal-y-bont primary school in 1937. The headmaster was Mr Harry Evans, who lived at Caerdova, next door to Central Stores. While the shop was being rebuilt, we lived at Brynhyfryd and as a shortcut to walk to school, a temporary plank was placed over the river Ceulan. Tegwyn Owen, who lived opposite the shop, often related how I slipped off the plank and he jumped into the river and rescued me, otherwise I would not be here to write these reminiscences!

Harry Evans was an expert mathematician, and an amazing number of my contemporaries went on to follow university courses in Mathematics, Physics and Science. He also had a dedicated support staff, such as Miss Lillian Edwards from Taliesin, and Tal-y-bont pupils invariably headed the secondary school entrance examinations. Mr Evans' son Gareth Wyn Evans was the third Ardwyn pupil to receive a state scholarship (1939), and later became Mathematics lecturer at Swansea University.

Since my primary school years coincided with the Second World War, there were regular rehearsals of evacuating the school and retreating to hide under the bushes at Allt-y-crib in the event of an air raid. One night, three bombs were dropped about two miles from Tal-y-bont village, one at Pwllglas and two at Rhydyronnen. Luckily, they exploded on farm land and did not cause any damage to persons or property. The village hosted many evacuees and their teachers, and this was the first time I had to speak English – my Tre'r-ddôl grandmother, although she never spoke Welsh, understood the language quite well.

The other mare which lived alongside Ceulan Silverleaf at Tal-y-bont during the pre-Second World War years – and died there aged 29 in June 1962 – was the red roan mare Coed Coch Serliw (f. 1933: Revolt x Coed Coch Seren by Grove Sharp Shooter). Miss Margaret Brodrick of Coed Coch held a sale of 38 ponies at her farm on 28 August 1937 and Mr S. Walton of Leeds bought 35 of them for £1,099. Mr Walton's family contacted Miss Brodrick stating that, although there was not a problem financially and they had paid for the purchases, they had no land to keep animals, so they paid Miss Brodrick to keep them for two weeks until a second sale could be arranged. Top of the first sale at 63 guineas was Serliw, who had won at major shows, and was in foal to Coed Coch Glyndwr (f. 1935: Revolt x Dinarth Henol by Llwyn Satan), who later became one of the five most influential sires ever in the breed. Mr Walton paid 45 gns for Glyndwr. At the second sale, my father bought Serliw and was under-bidder on Glyndwr, which Miss Brodrick bought back for 30 gns and sold him to Lady Wentworth for £400 in 1944. Serliw duly produced a colt foal, Ceulan Revolt, in 1938, who had the distinction of being the first foal ever sired by Glyndwr. Serliw won many prizes for us, including the female championship and reserve overall to Tregoyd Starlight at the 1949 RWS at Swansea. My father also bought the 13hh bay gelding Richard (bred by Mr Llewellyn Richards of Criban) in the second sale, on which my brother David won many riding and jumping prizes.

1940–1949

Tal-y-bont was the largest village in Cardiganshire, and had three Nonconformist chapels plus the modern St David's Church. Nearly everyone attended Sunday services held in the morning and evening with Sunday school in the afternoon. My family were members at Bethel Congregational chapel, where the minister was Rev Fred Jones, one of a well-known south Cardiganshire family of poets known as 'Bois y Cilie'. He remained minister there until his death in 1948. The Sunday school trip was an annual event, and as many as three buses would leave Bethel for a day in Rhyl or Barry Island. A 'gymanfa ganu' (a hymn-singing assembly) would be held on the first Wednesday in May in alternate years in Bethel and Seion, Aberystwyth, where the organist was Prof R. M. Davies, whom I later came to know as Professor of Physics at UCW Aberystwyth. Shortly after I left the university, R. M. Davies died (in February 1958) aged only 55. There was a very impressive organ at Bethel, and well-known organists would come to give recitals. The pumping of the organ was very hard work, and two strong young men would be allocated this duty at monthly intervals. After Rev Fred Jones' death, the minister at Bethel was Rev Morlais Jones, who was a very friendly man, and until I went to live in south Wales in 1957, I was a member of the Bethel 'noson lawen' group, and we gave concerts as far away as Llansannan.

Only a few yards from Bethel was Tabernacl Baptist chapel, and when the windows were open in the summer, we could hear the Tabernacl hymn-singing. The minister at Tabernacl was Rev W. J. Gruffydd, who won the bardic crown at the National Eisteddfod in 1955. There was much celebration in the village when he returned home with his crown. With dwindling membership, Tabernacl closed in 1991. Up a steep hill in front of Central Stores was Nazareth Methodist chapel, which had a stable behind it, and Mr Jenkins, Erglodd Farm, would drive his pony and governess cart over twice on a Sunday, leaving the pony stabled while the service was on. Another member of Nazareth was Mr J. M. Jenkins, Cerrigcaranau Farm, a very successful breeder of Welsh Black cattle and a member of the WPCS who bred cobs and ponies under the 'Caran' prefix. His Caran Black Bess (f. 1914 by Trotting Jack) won the WPCS medal at Tal-y-bont Show in 1919. Mr Jenkins celebrated his hundredth birthday in 1984 and died aged 102.

The Post Office in Tal-y-bont had been located near the village square for 30 years or more, and the postmistress was Miss Griffiths (Lizzie Post). When she retired in 1941, my father became postmaster, and the Post Office was moved to Central Stores. My father was assisted by his sister Riggie, who converted the warehouse into a residence called Hillside. In 1970 my older sister Kathleen (Mrs Richards) took over as postmistress, and after our father died in 1972, Kathleen and John carried on at Central Stores until John died in 1975. The shop was sold in 1976 and my mother, Kathleen and her daughter Janet moved into next-door Bryn, where my sister continued as postmistress until 1989.

In 1943 I passed the scholarship examination to Ardwyn Grammar School, Aberystwyth. The top pupil that year was another Tal-y-bont pupil and my best friend John Morgan, who lived at Tanyrallt. John was set on a brilliant career in the Royal Air Force and had reached the rank of Lieutenant when he was killed in a helicopter crash in Borneo in 1965. My contemporaries at Ardwyn included Lord John Morris, former Welsh Secretary and

Attorney General (my father was best man at the wedding of John's parents of Penywern Farm, Tal-y-bont, before the family moved to Aberffrwd), and Lord Elystan Morgan, Bow Street (former under-secretary of state at the Home Office), who travelled on the same school bus as me and spent a lot of time with his school friends at Tal-y-bont.

My other two closest friends from the village were John Watkin, Tyrrell Stores, who became a Congregational minister at Rhydymain, Morriston and Llandudno, and Ian Hides from the White Lion Hotel. After a gap of sixty years, I met up with Ian at the wedding of his nephew Mark Harries (son of Christine Hides) to Amanda Price Jones of the Synod Stud in 2004.

After such a good grounding at Tal-y-bont school, I got a very good report at the end of my first year at Ardwyn, with first-class examination marks in Science, Mathematics, English Language and Literature and Art, with second-class in French, History and Latin, but only third-class in Geography – never my strong point, and one of the reasons why I married a geographer was to make up for my shortcomings! We were given the option of French or Welsh, and I chose French because the Ardwyn deputy headmistress was Dr Ethel Jones, a former lecturer at the Sorbonne University, who lived with her family at Tal-y-bont and travelled on our school bus. By the time I reached Matriculation in 1948, I had dropped French and passed with credits in Welsh Language and Literature, English Language and Literature, Mathematics, Physics, Biology and Art, and distinction in Chemistry.

My first two years coincided with the end of the Second World War, and we were regularly notified of former pupils who lost their lives. Altogether, 57 former Ardwyn pupils died on active service between 1939 and 1945, including some from my home village.

When I started studying Chemistry in the third form, the teacher was Mr Isaac T. Jones, who had retired from Pentre

Secondary School in the Rhondda Valley, but had been brought out of retirement owing to the shortage of teachers during the war years. Mr Jones terrified all his pupils and, when I later lived in the Rhondda Valley, I was told that he had terrified everyone at Pentre as well. Mr Jones was a stop-gap appointment until Mr Bobby Lloyd returned from the war and instilled an interest in chemistry in the school almost overnight. It is amazing how many influential chemists started their careers under Mr Lloyd at Ardwyn. Mr Lloyd lived until the age of 89, passing away in January 2008, a much-loved and respected figure in Aberystwyth.

Other teachers whom I remember well are Mr Maurice Chapple (Physics), Mr Beynon Davies (Welsh) and Mr George Rowlands (English). The Headmaster was Lt Col D. C. Lewis who was my Mathematics teacher in the sixth form. He was the commanding officer of the local Home Guard and Mr Rowlands was company commander, and he later became mayor of Aberystwyth in 1955.

My brother David Maurice was six years older than me, and was already in the sixth form when I entered Ardwyn. David had a brilliant school record, was a member of the soccer team and was awarded the Samuel Exhibitioner Scholarship of his year to enter the Royal Veterinary College, which had been evacuated from London to Reading owing to the war.

My younger sister Anne (Jenkins, whose husband Gwilym wrote *Ar Bwys y Ffald*, his life history at Tynygraig and Tanrallt farms) did better than me in the Ardwyn entrance examinations in 1945, when she gained top marks for the whole school. Ardwyn was divided into four houses for competition purposes – Arfon (blue), Ceredigion (red), Gwynedd (green) and Powys (yellow), and the various trophies in the Main Hall (for athletics, rugby, football, cricket, eisteddfodau and so on) would bear the coloured ribbons of the house which had won them that year. Because David was in Arfon, so were Ann and I. My main contribution was winning the boys' solo competition three times! All through primary and secondary school, I thought my name was Edgar Wyn, which appears on all my certificates. It was only when I was applying to university and had to refer to my birth certificate that I realised that I was actually registered as Edgar Wynne (note spelling).

The captain of Arfon and head boy when I went to Ardwyn was Harry Hallam, who was a friend and mentor to everyone. I would meet up with him again when he was a world-renowned professor of Physical Chemistry at Swansea University. His early death in 1977 robbed Wales of a leading scientist.

At the age of seven, my brother David won sixth prize in the children's riding pony section for riders under 12 years of age at the 1933 Royal Welsh Show at Aberystwyth, riding The Imp. He also won the special award for the best rider in the class, receiving a most complimentary report in the RWAS Journal. Other competitors in this class were Sam Morgan, Parc Stud, Lampeter, riding Shandy Gaff (fifth), the future Sir Meuric Rees, Tywyn, riding Biddy (seventh) and Lady Auriel Vaughan, daughter of show president the Earl of Lisburne, riding Megan (eleventh). David won several more prizes on various ponies at local shows, and competed in showjumping, racing and gymkhana classes. When he came home on vacation from the veterinary college, he would ride and drive his favourite stallion, Ceulan Revolt. In May 1946 while he was at Reading, he was asked to ride the hack Pretty Jane at Windsor Horse Show for Swansea auctioneer Mr Roland Jenkins (father of Carey Knox and Martyn Jenkins), who had two horses entered in the same class. David was very amused when he beat the owner, who said: 'Obviously, I gave you the wrong horse'!

One of the first agricultural shows to be held after the war was at Aberystwyth in August 1945, where there were only two judges – Mr Meyrick Jones of Mathrafal (Shires, Welsh ponies, cobs and harness) and Mrs Nell Pennell of Bwlch (riding ponies and hunters). Mr Jones awarded the Loxdale Cup for the best pony or cob to Ceulan Silverleaf, then the two judges combined to judge the best horse or pony in the show for the Western Mail Cup. The cup was won by Ceulan Silverleaf with the Shire reserve, followed by the ridden hunter, then the hackney in harness. Later in the afternoon, Mr Jones suffered a stroke and was taken back to Bicester by ambulance. He never really recovered and passed away in 1950. It stated in the show schedule that the Western Mail Cup would be won outright, but by 1946 the show committee had changed its mind, the cup had to be returned and was then offered in rotation to cattle, sheep and horses!

The Lampeter Show followed on 21 September, where the judge was Captain T. A. Howson, Ruabon (secretary of the RWAS and WPCS 1927–1951) and entries turned up in great numbers, not having been able to show for the previous six years. The Welsh cob mare class consisted of 13 exhibits, which contained some of the most famous names in the history of the breed. The top eight were placed in the following order: Meiarth Welsh Maid (RW champion 1947, 1949, 1950, 1954), Dewi Princess, Parc Welsh Maid (dam of Parc Lady), Dewi Rosina (RW ch 1951, 1953), Oakford Charming Bess, Dewi Black Bess (RW ch 1935), Sheila (RW ch 1952) and Daisy Gwenog. The class for Welsh pony mares consisted of eight exhibits led by Dyffryn Rosina (RW ch 1956) and Queenie (RW ch six times between 1947 and 1957). The class for Welsh mountain ponies had twelve exhibits; it was open to any sex (at Aberystwyth Show it was for mares or geldings only) and was won by David showing Ceulan Revolt, who went on to win the WPCS medal for the best exhibit in the section, with Meiarth Welsh Maid reserve and Dyffryn Rosina second reserve.

Ceulan Silverleaf produced Ceulan Blue Vision (filly, 1941), Revoke (colt, 1942), Revelry (colt, 1943) and Reveller (colt, 1944) all by Ceulan Revolt. My father approached his friend Sam Fennell (groom to Lord Howard de Walden of Chirk Castle) to try to purchase Lord Howard's pony coach to drive Revolt, Revoke, Revelry and Reveller as a team, but the coach was not for sale. When my father lived in London, he would accompany Mr Fennell on the coach with bay leaders by Wentworth Windfall and chestnut wheelers by Wingerworth Eiddwen every Sunday morning around Hyde Park.

In 1945 my father sold Ceulan Revoke to Mrs Dorothy Gilbert of the Reeves Stud, Penn, High Wycombe, and thus began a life-long friendship which included the purchase, in 1947, of Ceulan Silver Lustre, her two-y-o son Reeves Golden Lustre by Ceulan Revoke, her yearling filly Reeves Crystal by Ceulan Revelry and her filly foal Reeves Nantgarw, also by Revelry, all four for £100. They were purchased on the condition that they could be registered with the purchaser's 'Reeves' prefix rather than the customary breeder's prefix. Golden Lustre had been handled a little, but the other three had never been touched, and Silver Lustre was now nine years old. It was a major manoeuvre to drive four loose ponies along the main A487 road from Tal-y-bont to Llandre railway station, but fortunately, in those days motor cars were rare, and they were loaded into the railway horsebox without incident. What happened when they reached their destination I was never told but, to my amazement, Silver Lustre won a class a few months later (after her foal was weaned) at the Beaconsfield and Penn Show ridden by Geoffrey Carter, with whom we are still in touch.

Every year between 1946 and 1951 Mrs Gilbert commissioned a whole train to transport about 20 horses and ponies and her riding clients from High Wycombe to Llandre. They would stay at the Black Lion Hotel and spend a month riding in the Cardiganshire hills and competing at a few local shows. She usually included a spare pony or two, and I would accompany them most days. Two sisters who came every year for a month were Gillian (now Mrs

Baverstock) and Imogen (Mrs Smallwood), the daughters of Enid Blyton, the world's most famous author of children's books, which have sold over 400 million copies.

In 1946, because of my brother's ill health, my father only competed at Tal-y-bont Show, where he won the championship with Ceulan Silverleaf. The show was reported in *Horse and Hound* of 14 September by Dalesman (Mr C .N. de Courcy Parry), stating that 'the owner [my father] has bred some of the best Welsh ponies in the world, and he has at present two stallion ponies that cannot be beaten.' Mrs Gilbert, he said, 'had some very well-schooled ponies, and all were very well turned out and smart, so that a lot of us became apprehensive that all the awards would find their way from Wales to Buckinghamshire.' Mrs Gilbert entered up to five in some classes; she was a very strict riding teacher of the old school, and the standard of riding, especially amongst the children, was something we had not witnessed previously at Tal-y-bont Show.

In July that year I travelled with my father, who was judging at the Shropshire and West Midland Show (prize money of £6, £3, £1), where the three classes were won by Dinarth What Ho (stallion), Coed Coch Serog (mare) and Craven Toscanini (youngstock). The dam of Serog was Coed Coch Sirius, who was a maternal sister to Serliw, and Sirius had been sold as a foal in the second 1937 Coed Coch Sale for 10 gns. She later became dam of Coed Coch Siaradus who, in my opinion, was one of the greatest mares of all time. What Ho was owned by Miss Nora Mathieson, and came to Ceulan on livery the following year. He was overall RW champion in 1947, male champion in 1952 and winner of the harness class every year until his death in 1953. Because Miss Mathieson (who had bred some of the best Welsh mountain ponies since 1923) hadn't paid any liveries or showing expenses for two years, she offered us What Ho in lieu, and that is how we came to own him. We also went to

Bodedern, Anglesey on 20 August, where my father judged all the light horse classes.

A circus visited Aberystwyth in June 1946 and several of us from Tal-y-bont went there on the bus. Two days later, I was desperately ill with a temperature of 105 degrees and delirious, and this lasted for about a week. By then, 220 people had the same illness, which was diagnosed as typhoid fever, and they were taken to Tanybwlch mansion, which was turned into a makeshift hospital, where four people died. Visitors were not allowed in, and could only see their family through windows because typhoid was so infectious. It transpired that the person selling ice-cream at the circus was a typhoid carrier. I missed a term of school, which meant that I had to repeat the year, and sat my Central Welsh Board School Certificate in 1948.

The Criban Stud held a sale on 5 November at Brecon Market, and we went there with John Berry of Betws-y-Coed, who often stayed at Central Stores along with many other pony breeders. My father bought a dun mare, Criban Rally (daughter of the famous Criban Socks), for 30 gns and John Berry paid 20 gns for a filly foal, Criban Golden Spray, which created great excitement, since most of the other foals sold for between two and five guineas.

1947 was a very sad year for my family – a real *annus horribilis*. My grandmother Annie Williams died on 30 January. My grandfather never really settled after that, and he passed away the day before Christmas the same year. But the saddest event of all was the death of my brother David, three weeks after his twenty-first birthday on 30 April – a glittering light extinguished in the prime of his life. It took very many years for my parents to overcome their grief – if they ever did – but my father attended a few shows to distract himself. We visited the Shropshire and West Midland Show on 21 May, where Mr Holden's stallion Tregoyd Starlight was champion and Mr Tom Jones Evans' mare, Craven

Lymm, reserve. On the way home we called in on Tom Jones Evans at Dinchope Farm, Craven Arms, and I took a photograph with my Kodak Brownie camera of the 29-y-o Grove Sprightly (he died in 1949) held by housekeeper Mrs Gladys Meredith with his trophies behind, a photograph which has been reproduced many times in my books. Mr Tom Thomas judged at the Lampeter Show on 19 September, where Mr Roscoe Lloyd's Dewi Rosina won the WPCS medal. A photograph which I took of the section C mares Dyffryn Rosina, Queenie, Dulas Doll and Teify Pride is, I believe, the only one in existence of Dyffryn Rosina and Dulas Doll. That was 68 years ago, and I am still snapping away!

My father judged at three shows in August, starting with the Pontypridd Horse Show on 2 August. We travelled on the bus to Pontypridd (my father never drove in his life), and were met by his great friend Mr Matthew Williams of the Vardra Stud (his grand-daughter Diane was bridesmaid at our wedding in 1961), and stayed with the family over the weekend. Mr Williams transported us to the show with his ponies in the trailer behind and carrying Vardra Charm, who was champion and Vardra Nance reserve! Unlike today, when it would be considered unethical for a judge to award prizes to animals they have bred, the circuit was so much smaller back then that it was inevitable. All the exhibitors and judges were great friends as well, because we saw each other so often.

Next was the Cardigan Show on 13 August, where the winning Welsh cob mare was Verwig Bess (dam of Teify Welsh Maid RW ch 1955* and g-g-dam of Honyton Michael ap Braint RW ch 1967*) owned by J. H. Davies of Bigni Farm, Verwig. Other exhibitors included S. O. James, Tyhen, Beulah, and the Misses Taylor and Saunders-Davies of Llanarth, breeders who would become household names in the Welsh Cob world. The farmer's or tradesmen's turnout was won by Mr and Mrs Jones of Blaenannerch, Aberporth, accompanied in the trap by their 13-year-old son. When

Where it all began – Central Stores, Tal-y-bont, Aberystwyth

My grandfather's home. Clettwr Hall, Tre'r-ddôl

My grandparents S. M. and Mary Jane Davies, her sister Catherine Ann and my father and Aunt Rachel (Riggie) as children

My grandparents L. O. and Annie Williams and their children (from left) Janet Mary (my mother), David Oliver, Josephine, Laurie and Cassie

S.M. Davies with one of the ponies and traps he would drive from Tal-y-bont to London

The exceptionally gifted Tondu family

Seren Ceulan (f. 1910) at Tal-y-bont

My brother David on Ceulan Silverleaf (f. 1929) in Cae'r Efail in front of the smithy

The Cardiganshire group at the Royal Welsh Show 1925 (from left: Seren Ceulan, Kerry Queen, Ormond Welsh Comet, Ormond Satisfaction)

David riding The Imp, Royal Welsh Show 1933

My primary school days

My parents Evie and Janet Davies with their grand-daughter Janet Richards

(from left) Miss Margaret Brodrick with Criban Waaf, Revel Betty and Revel Coquette; Mr John Jones with Coed Coch Pansi, Trysor and Serog; Mr Arthur McNaught with Coed Coch Morfa and Ceulan Serene and Mr Shem Jones with Gatesheath Moonlight, 1948

Dinarth What Ho and my father at the Royal Welsh Show, Swansea 1949

One of Mrs Gilbert and friends' visits to the Black Lion on a specially-commissioned train

Dinarth What Ho winning the harness class, Llandeilo 1953

The Chemistry department at Aberystwyth University 1956 (I am front row, second right)

With my father in the WPC display at the Royal Welsh Show, Machynlleth 1954

With my much-loved harp

Receiving my PhD, Bangor University 1957

Miss Brodrick and Mr Shem Jones in the water at the RWS, Aberystwyth 1957

With Mr William Simpson of the USA, May 1957 at the Dyrin Stud, Sennybridge, where Mr Simpson bought seven mares (four with foals at foot) and seven fillies

Our 'noson lawen' musical group with the Rev Morlais Jones (left) and accompanist Miss Ruffina Owen (centre front)

Llandaff Technical College staff football team 1960 (I am front row, second from left)

Our wedding day, Hebron Chapel, Ton Pentre, 1961

Ceulan Farm in 1962 when we moved in

Ceulan in snow, 2010

handing out the first prizecard to the lady, my father had rather a long discussion with Mrs Jones and, when I asked him later what it was about, he told me that she was the former Miss Isaac from Tre'r-ddôl, who had been my mother's best childhood friend. The son Richard (Dic), who was born at Tre'r-ddôl, later became one of Wales' most important and best-loved literary figures, and was appointed archdruid of the Gorsedd of the National Eisteddfod of Wales in 2007. Sadly, he died in 2009 before completing his term.

In 1942 my father had repeated his usual walk to Llandre station, and thereafter from Church Stretton to Dinchope Farm, Craven Arms, this time with Serliw, to be mated to Craven Tit Bit. Serliw produced a very smart filly named Ceulan Serene but, with the war raging on, not much attention was paid to the ponies.

After the war was over, interest resumed and, mainly due to the ambassadorial efforts of Miss Brodrick, who travelled all over continental Europe and also to the USA, there was a possibility that the export market might open up again. Miss Brodrick had an order for nine mares to go to Mrs Charles Iliff of Arnold, Maryland, USA. She contacted my father about Serene, who was of great interest to her since her dam was Coed Coch Serliw and she was in foal to Eryri Gwyndaf (f. 1940: Mathrafal Tuppence x Coed Coch Shonet), the stallion we had at Ceulan in 1947. My father asked £80 for her, and Miss Brodrick offered £100, which he gladly took, and she went off with another eight in January 1948. Serene duly produced a colt foal registered as Severn Sure Shot, who became a very influential sire in the USA. It is customary in the USA to regard the person who puts the mare in foal to be the breeder, so consequently, E. S. Davies and Son had the honour of being the breeders of a great American sire.

Because this consignment created much interest in the USA, more orders followed for Miss Brodrick, and she and John Jones would travel Wales and beyond to replenish their stock. If Miss

Brodrick was travelling to south Wales (she had much admiration for the ponies on the Gower peninsula and around Brecon), she would contact my father and offer me a day's outing, and my father would have to provide a sicknote to cover my absence from school. These were delightful journeys in Miss Brodrick's old-fashioned upright Standard car, with her elkhound Jan sitting on your lap in the back. Once – fortunately, I was not with them – the steering wheel came off while they were travelling down Penglais Hill in Aberystwyth, and the car hit the hedge and overturned. Miss Brodrick and John Jones were taken to hospital, but miraculously were none the worse for their escapade. It was a great education for me to listen to John Jones summing up the good and bad points of the ponies which they were offered. To my childhood mind, Miss Brodrick was like royalty – she was a very kind lady. Her letters were always charming. In one, she thanks my mother for the cherry sponge tea, and apologises for having eaten what was intended for Sunday!

By 1947 it was a lorry (converted from a car bought from Mr Morgan, Pwllglas) which was used to deliver animal foodstuffs from Central Stores around the farms, driven by John Richards from Fedwfaen, Aberhosan. He and my older sister Kathleen married in August 1956. The ponies were transported to shows in a cattle lorry owned by Jack Jones, Ynystudor, Tre'r-ddôl. In 1950 a new chassis EJ 9857 was bought in Birmingham, and wooden detachable sides for the ponies or for foodstuffs were constructed by Lloyds Sawmills, Crugybar. I joined the WPCS as a life member in 1948 and by 2008 I was the 'father of the house', although there are older members who joined later.

Since his teens, when he spent all his spare time at Tanyrallt Stud, Tal-y-bont, my father's other passion was the hackney horse and pony. The post-war years were the heyday of hackneys – there would be harness classes with twenty or more exhibits at the Royal Welsh, and similar numbers in the in-hand classes at the breed shows at Derby. Nowadays, the hackney breed is an endangered species, and double figures have not been achieved in-hand or harness at any show for the last twenty years. I would accompany my father and his best friend, Mr Tom Wood Jones, a butcher of Great Darkgate Street, Aberystwyth, to the breed shows and sales at Crewe and, in those days, I knew all the exhibitors and the names of all the exhibits. Mr Wood Jones owned the magnificent stable block at Plas Tanybwlch, which later burnt down, though no animals were lost. There was a collective sale of 38 hackneys at Manley's Repository at Crewe on 3 September 1948 and Mr Wood Jones secured the top lot, the 10-y-o hackney pony stallion Broompark Sir John for 1,275 gns, which, according to the Retail Price Index, would give a figure of £39,000 today. Mr Wood Jones also privately bought the stallion Bossy for a reputed £4,000, and these two won the harness championships at all the major British shows for the next ten years. They were stabled and exhibited by Mr Jimmy Black at Reading, and the cost of keep, transport to shows, expenses etc., would have been enormous.

There was no Royal Welsh Show in 1948 due to petrol rationing, so we decided to try our luck in a major English show, and took Coed Coch Serliw to the Cheshire County Show on 14 July. Tregoyd Starlight won the stallion class from Coed Coch Seryddwr, who later became famous as the sire of Coed Coch Madog and was exported to South Africa. Serliw won the mare class (and was reserve champion) from Craven Bright Sprite (who had won at Shropshire in May) and Coed Coch Mefusen (who had produced Madog the previous year and Meilyr at foot, and was sold to Canada later in the year). Coed Coch Sidan won the youngstock class, and her dam Coed Coch Seirian was Serliw's only foal at Coed Coch before my father bought her.

Thankfully, other shows in Wales went ahead as usual, and our team of ponies battled it out with those from other major exhibitors. At the first show at Pontarddulais on Bank Holiday Monday, What Ho was second to Eryri Gwyndaf (the stallion we had at Ceulan the previous year), and Serliw won the mare class. Serliw also won at Aberystwyth (and reserve to Dewi Rosina for the Loxdale Cup for overall Welsh) and at the Radnorshire Show at Rhayader. At the North Breconshire Show, Mr D. O. Morgan awarded Serliw the female medal, What Ho the male medal and reserve for the WPCS medal to Serliw – a very successful day for Ceulan. At the Montgomery County Show in Welshpool in September, Serliw won her class with stiff opposition from Captain and Mrs Brierley, Mr Dick Swain of Crossways, Lady Margaret Myddleton of Chirk and Lady Kathleen Leighton of Loton Park, Shrewsbury. Children's riding ponies attracted numbers of fifteen and more in each class, the winners being Mrs Agnes Hepburn of Sutton Coldfield with Coed Coch Powys, and Sheelah and Tony Brookshaw of Market Drayton riding Govan, some of the best British ponies, and ones that we would not normally encounter at south Wales shows. Two days later at Beulah Show on the Epynt mountains, Serliw and What Ho both won their classes with Serliw champion.

Because my father was judging at Brecon Show on 18 September, the last battleground for us was Lampeter Show the previous day, where the judge was again Mr Matthew Williams. Serliw won a big class from W. J. Jones' Criban Leading Lady (daughter of Criban Rally which we bought on the 1946 Criban Sale) and What Ho was second to Craven Tit Bit, but won the WPCS medal, since Tit Bit and Serliw had already won medals. Reserve for the WPCS medal was the four-times Royal Welsh champion cob Meiarth Welsh Maid who had beaten some famous names in her section, such as Polly of Hercws, Peggy of Hercws, Parc Welsh Maid, Hercws Bright Star, Meiarth King Flyer, Eirlys Gwenog and Oakford Charming

Bess. What Ho won his harness class from Ceulan Revelry and Bolgoed Peep O'Day, daughter of the great producer Grove Peep O'Day (f. 1919). The hackney harness classes were very well supported, and won by Mr Tom Wood Jones' Broompark Sir John from Warwick Nipper, owned by Mr Stanley Turner from Earlswood, Warwickshire.

The 1949 show season opened again with the National In-hand Hackney Show at Crewe on 23 April. There were 78 exhibits present in 21 classes, and in the catalogue I wrote comments on each one. Sir Nigel Colman's brilliant black hackney stallion, Black Magic of Nork, was supreme, with John Sword's pony stallion Craigweil Mischief reserve. The Hackney Harness Show was held at Reading on 23–25 June. This saw the emergence of the brilliant six-y-o mare Holywell Florette driven by Mrs Cynthia Haydon for W. T. Barton to be supreme. The pony champion was Bossy, driven by Jimmy Black (uncle of Mrs Haydon) for owner Mrs Harcourt-Wood.

We decided to try our luck at an English show again, and Serliw (with colt foal Ceulan Stardust at foot) travelled to Cheshire County, where she won from Coed Coch Siaradus (winner at Shropshire and Bath and West) and Serliw won a championship shield with the winning stallion Craven Titbit reserve. Coed Coch Sidan (now in the ownership of Lord Kenyon) was youngstock champion.

The first show in Wales where we exhibited was Aberystwyth on 3 August, where Dewi Rosina won a class of 14 cob mares, most of whom had won elsewhere. Coed Coch Serliw won the mountain pony mare class and Dinarth What Ho was second in the stallion class of eleven exhibits to Eryri Gwyndaf. What Ho reversed the tables on Gwyndaf in harness, where they were first and second, followed by Ceulan Revelry and Whitehall Knight. Prize money of £20, £10 and £5 attracted large entries in the hackney harness classes from as far afield as Leeds and Cornwall.

A noteworthy Royal Welsh Show was held in Swansea, where the judge for Welsh ponies and cobs was Captain T. A. Howson, who had retired from being secretary of the RWAS and the WPCS, the new secretary being Mr Arthur George. The cob mare Meiarth Welsh Maid won the George PofW Cup with the stallion Llwynog-y-Garth reserve. The famous Pentre Eiddwen Comet made his first RW appearance (3-y-o) and won the youngstock class. Welsh ponies of riding-type and cob-type shared the same section but had separate classes. The strongest class (13 exhibits) was for riding-type youngstock, won by Gredington Bronwen. Mrs Cuff's Criban Heather Belle won the riding-type mare class, Queenie won the cob-type class from Dyffryn Rosina and Piercefield Lady Lilian (dam of Lyn Cwmcoed), and Welsh Echo won the cob-type stallion class where, strangely, Criban Victor (later seven-times RW section B champion) was third.

Welsh mountain ponies turned up in unprecedented numbers. Coed Coch Meilyr (RW male champion the following year) won the yearling class and Criban Golden Spray the 2–3-y-o class. Fourteen of the top reigning mares appeared, and we won it with Coed Coch Serliw, from her daughter Coed Coch Seirian and Mrs Cuff's Craven Bright Sprite and Craven Good Friday. Because Captain Howson had bred Councillor R. J. Jones' 11-y-o stallion Craven Titbit, the stallions were judged by Mr J. J. Borthwick, Chairman of WPCS Council, and he placed them: first Tregoyd Starlight, second Craven Titbit, third Dinarth What Ho, fourth Eryri Gwyndaf, fifth Ceulan Revelry and sixth Craven Daylight (owned by Mr Edgar Herbert, who sold him to Fayre Stud). Captain Howson judged the championships, with Tregoyd Starlight winning the second Tom and Sprightly Cup, and Serliw reserve. What Ho won the harness class and was reserve to Broompark Sir John for the magnificent gold Geoffrey Bennett Trophy for the harness championship, judged by Mr Bennett. Finally, there were district classes confined to Glamorgan, Pembrokeshire, Carmarthenshire and Cardiganshire. There were five mountain pony classes judged by Captain Howson, when What Ho won the stallion class and Ceulan Stardust (Tregoyd Starlight x Coed Coch Serliw) the foal class. Altogether, Ceulan won so many prizecards that the front of the lorry was completely covered. My sister Ann and I stayed nearby with Councillor R. J. Jones, Whitehall Stud, grandfather of Mr Hugh Thomas, CBE, DL, Chief Executive of Glamorgan and 1999 President of RWAS.

Apart from wins for What Ho and Serliw at Machynlleth, that show is remembered for two other reasons – Brenin Gwalia won the Welsh cob stallion class, and the photo I took of him that day with the archdruid John Roderick Rees was painted by Mr Aneurin Jones, and is featured on the cover of my book *Ceredigion Champions*. What Ho won the harness class and I also took his photo being driven by my sister in the show wagon, which we had had made by Pickering Brothers of Liverpool the previous winter. The show wagon was six inches too long to go across our lorry, but rather than buy a wider lorry, we had the wagon shortened. It is the only wagon in the world where the rear axle is mid-way along the back platform, and as such is easily recognised. Mr Alfred Williams judged the Tal-y-bont Show on 7 September, where Serliw won the mare class and the Western Mail Cup (outright, for the third time, for the best light horse in-hand, under saddle or in harness). Serliw was also champion at the Montgomery County Show the following day.

In August 1949 my father had an enquiry for a Welsh cob mare with a colt foal from Tom Carruthers, Otago, New Zealand (who had imported the Welsh cob stallion Grove Welsh Dragon in 1924). At the Cardigan Show the previous year, he had awarded first prize to a four-y-o chestnut mare Llwynpiod Maid, owned by Dan Morris of Llwynpiod, and he recommended her to Mr Carruthers. Her colt foal was by Deinol Welsh Comet and she was covered again. Her sire was Meiarth Royal Eiddwen, and she was the third generation of Llwynpiod breeding with dam Llwynpiod Blackie (f. 1941) and g-dam Llwynpiod Bessie (f. 1927). We went to see her in October, a price of £120 was agreed, and we proceeded with the export and veterinary arrangements via the London firm of Dalgetty and Co. Mr Morris wrote on 17 December asking for early payment since he wanted to buy some cows! The shipping was arranged for 10 January 1950 on the *Port Phillip* from the Royal Albert Dock, London. A ten foot by eight foot wooden crate was constructed for the mare and foal, and the cost of shipping to New Zealand was £360. The rail carriage from Cardigan to the Royal Albert Dock cost £14, but Dalgetty demanded a reduction because the journey took 32 hours, and they almost missed the ship. Llwynpiod Maid and her colt foal arrived safely in New Zealand in March but, sadly, Mr Carruthers had died and never saw her, though she left her mark on Welsh cob breeding in New Zealand.

1950–1959

I entered the University College of Wales, Aberystwyth, in 1950 when the principal was Dr Ifor L. Evans, a former Fellow of St John's College, Cambridge, who had been in post since 1934. He retired in 1952 and was replaced by Goronwy Rees, who was principal for only four years, resigning after press revelations of his alleged connections with spies Guy Burgess and Donald Maclean, who left Britain for Russia. Goronwy Rees was replaced as principal just before I left in 1957 by Dr Thomas Parry, Librarian of the National Library of Wales at Aberystwyth. There were some very famous professors there, including Sir T. H. Parry-Williams (Welsh), Gwyn Jones (English), Reginald Treharne (History), R. I. Aaron (Philosophy), R. B. Forrester (Economics), Charles Clements (Music), Llewelfryn Davies (Law), E. G. Bowen (Geography), Lily Newton (Botany) and Professors Nichols, Ellison and R. O. Davies (Agriculture). T. Maelgwyn Davies was the registrar, and Arthur ap Gwynn the Librarian. Student President in 1950 was Gwilym Prys Dafis (later Lord Prys Dafis), whom we met up with later when we lived at Miskin and he lived at Tonteg, and our children attended Gartholwg Welsh primary school together. Tuition fees were £10 per term for Arts subjects and £12 for Science, and hostel fees were £95 per annum.

The president of the college was Dr Thomas Jones CH, who resigned in 1954 at 82 years of age and died the following year. He had been cabinet secretary to four prime ministers. In his book about his childhood, *Rhymney Memories*, he writes that his grandfather, Benjamin Jones of Gwynfil, Llangeitho, travelled the Welsh cob stallion Cardigan Comet as far as Herefordshire and Gloucestershire. Dr Thomas Jones' son Tristan Jones (his sister was Baroness Irene White, MP for East Flint 1950–1970), director of *The Observer*, visited us at Ceulan in 1966 looking for a Welsh cob foal whose pedigree could be traced back to Cardigan Comet, and bought the foal (Llangybi Seldom Seen x Meiarth Modern Maid), which we registered as Gwynfil Comet. When Mr Jones died in 1990 he had arranged for his coffin to be drawn through the streets of St Nicholas-at-Wade by a Welsh cob descendant of Cardigan Comet.

Having passed my Higher School Certificate with credits in Chemistry, Physics and Mathematics, I was exempt from the first-year course and started with subsidiary second-year courses of Physics, Chemistry and Mathematics, a total of 11 hours lectures and 12 hours practical work a week, so I was kept quite busy. The next year was known as the final grade in Physics and Chemistry (eight hours lectures and 15 hours practical). For Honours Chemistry, it involved six hours a week of lectures, and we were expected to devote our whole time to practical work in the laboratories. With so many practical sessions, there was not much time for anything else. but I did manage to become involved with the Welsh Society, made many friends amongst music students, and had harp lessons from Alwena Roberts. I reached the finals of the 'cerdd dant' (counterpoint melody) solo at the Inter-college Eisteddfod, which was held in Bangor that year.

Chemistry had always been my main academic interest from my days at Ardwyn, and from the beginning, it was my aim to follow the Honours Chemistry course. The Chemistry department was situated away from main college at the Edward Davies Chemical Laboratories on the Buarth, a very impressive building which had been opened in 1907 by Mr Asquith, the Chancellor of the Exchequer. The cost of this building was £23,000 – a very generous gift from David Davies of Llandinam who (as Lord Davies) was president of the college from 1926 to 1944. The Professor of Chemistry during my student days was C. W. Davies, who had been on the staff since 1920. Electrochemistry was his speciality, and he was one of the original scientists to investigate ion-exchange and water softening. Professor Campbell James retired in 1944 after forty years on the staff, but lived locally and was a frequent visitor. His retirement interest was studying the effects of the local lead mines on river pollution and the problem of 'plumbosolvency', which he investigated for the Ministry of Agriculture.

With two branches of chemistry – inorganic and organic – requiring good memory, which I didn't have, I concentrated on Physical Chemistry, which required more reasoning, and my previous Physics and Mathematics studies held me in good stead. The other Physical Chemistry lecturers were Dr Mansel Davies and his colleague Dr Orville Thomas (both experts on spectroscopy), and Dr C. B. Monk, who had been doing research work with Professor Davies at Battersea and decided to follow him to Wales. Col Hudleston, who had been on the staff since 1920 and died in 1954, was the inorganics lecturer and for organic chemistry, it was Welsh-speaking and friendly John Bowen, Scot Dr Sam Graham, who died soon after I had left in 1957, and Bill Williams, an ex-RAF Aberystwyth Chemistry graduate. Bill Williams gave over 800 lectures and spectacular demonstrations of chemi-luminescence and the Faraday effect torch all over Wales and beyond to 10–12-year-old schoolchildren until 2011, when he reached the age of 91 years. For this, he was awarded the MBE in 1997. During the war years, the chemistry lecturers and students from University College, London, were evacuated to Aberystwyth, including Professor Christopher Ingold, who returned to London (where he died in 1970), and, joined by Professor Ted Hughes from UCNW Bangor, revolutionised the understanding of the fundamental mechanisms of organic chemistry.

The funding for my research work between 1954 and 1957 came from being a demonstrator in the practical classes for the degree students. I enjoyed this, as it was an avenue for getting to know them, since the chemistry laboratories were rather isolated. I opted to do research under Dr Monk and, since much of it involved reaction kinetics, with reactions which could not be left once they were started, and sometimes taking readings overnight, I was grateful that Dr Monk was a bachelor, lived in lodgings and often spent nights in the laboratories! He was a pipe smoker and grew his own tobacco, both in the laboratory and afterwards at his retirement bungalow near Clarach. This did not seem to cause him any ill-effects, and he enjoyed good health, living alone until his death in 2005 aged 95.

The subject of my research was 'Spectrophotometric and Kinetic studies of Complex Salt Solutions', and I received my PhD degree at a graduation ceremony at the University College of North Wales, Bangor, on 19 December 1957. There were only 58 students graduating that day, compared with over 4,200 students who graduated in July 2014 at Cardiff Metropolitan University, where I later worked for thirty years. A former Tal-y-bont teacher informed me that I was the third person from Tal-y-bont to receive a PhD after Emrys Gwynne James, O.B.E., who went to work with Semi-conductor Manufacturers Ltd., and David Trevena, who became a Reader in the Physics Department, UCW, Aberystwyth.

There were about twenty chemistry research students during my time. They included Iolo Wyn Williams (Professor of Education, UCNW, Bangor), Bill Jeremy Jones (Professor at Aberystwyth, later Head of Department and Dean of Faculty, Swansea), Bill Pritchard (Reader at Imperial College, London) and Graham Loveluck (a minister in Anglesey and married to Llio Rhydderch, leading harpist in Wales at that time). Then there was Bryan Morgans, originally from Maerdy, Rhondda, is a top industrialist in Canada who still comes to visit us regularly, Douglas (Bob) Bale (from Aberkenfig, industrialist with ICI who worked a lot overseas, and sadly died just after retirement in 2001, his wife Shirley having predeceased him the previous year), Tony Hamilton Jones (HMI, Cardiff who, until his disability, was an active member of the Cardiff branch of the Aberystwyth Old Students' Association, and died in 2015). Graham Williams was an Ardwyn pupil who returned to the Aberystwyth staff in 1966 from the National Physical Laboratory, Washington, became Professor at Aberystwyth, later Swansea, and Terry Williams from Pontrhydyfendigaid was best man at our wedding, whose wife Betty was a sister to Charles Arch, who was senior commentator with me as at the Royal Welsh Show until 2013. My friends Robert Hefin Jones from Blaenau Ffestiniog and David Griffiths from Tenby left after their initial graduation to pursue research work at Battersea Polytechnic. Bob Jones became an HMI for Wales and was given two years' sabbatical leave (1967–1969) to organise the investiture of HRH The Prince of Wales at Caernarfon.

Terry Williams was the first one to be involved with radio-chemicals at Aberystwyth, and until the Soddy Radiochemistry Laboratory was built in 1958, it is doubtful if the facilities were adequate. In the winter of 1956 Terry set off in Dr Monk's car, driven by Bob Bale, to collect a radioisotope from Harwell. The car hit some ice near Talgarth and went through a hedge, but they were able to get it back onto the road and continue their journey without further incident. Had it occurred on their way back, and the isotope had escaped from the boot of the car, Talgarth town may have had to be evacuated! Terry used the radioisotopes for electrochemical studies. This was a period before health and safety regulations came into force. We were continually pipetting up carcinogenic substances by mouth, safety glasses were unheard of, and many chemists of the day lost fingers through explosions. A major expansion to the Edward Davies buildings was completed in 1962, the addition being about twice the size of the original building.

Professor C. W. Davies retired in 1960 and was replaced by Professor (later Sir) Trotman-Dickenson who left in 1969 to become Principal of UWIST, Cardiff. Swansea-born Professor John Meurig Thomas came from Bangor to be head of chemistry until 1978, when he was called to the University of Cambridge, after which he became Director of the Royal Institution of Great Britain in 1987 and was knighted in 1991. Bill Jeremy Jones took over as head of the department, and Graham Williams was also a personal professor. It was a source of disbelief and great sadness to generations of former students when the University of Wales announced that it was closing the Chemistry department, and that the buildings would be taken over by the Arts department. Professors Jeremy Jones and Graham Williams transferred to Swansea, from where they retired.

With about 1,200 students (900 men and 300 women) in a town with a population of 4,000, Aberystwyth University was a good place to get to know everyone, as one person in every four you met was a fellow-student. I tried to spend as much time as I could outside the department and, in my last year, I met Ruth (Williams), who was in her first year reading Honours Geography. Ruth's maternal grandfather (also E. W. Davies!) was a native of Trefor on the Lleyn Peninsula in north Wales, and had been ordained minister at Hebron Baptist Chapel, Ton Pentre, in the Rhondda Valley. Ruth's uncle, the Rev Griff Sorton Davies, was minister of Bethel Baptist Chapel, Barry, and her cousin, the Rev Ifan R. Williams was later minister of Ainon chapel, Ynyswen, Treorchy. The family surname of Sorton can be traced back to Randolph Sorton, who lived in Plas

Gelliwig (location of the 1950s film *Johnny Jones*) near Nefyn in the seventeenth century. We have continued the name Sorton with our children and grandchildren, and also the children of Ruth's brother, Roger. Ruth's paternal grandparents were from Lampeter farming families, close to Bachystarn, where my grandfather was brought up, so they may have known one another. It is strange how history creates connections. In the 1925 RWS photograph of the Cardiganshire winning group of Welsh ponies, my father E. S. Davies, is on the left with Seren Ceulan, while on the right is S. O. Davies, Dyffryn Farm, Silian, Lampeter, with Ormond Welsh Comet. Sixty-four years later, in 1989, Dai Davies, Gwarffynnon, Silian (grandson of S. O. Davies), married my niece Gwen Jenkins, grand-daughter of E. S. Davies. Ruth inherited her interest in ponies and horses from her farming ancestors, and during her university holidays she ran the Hafodawelon Riding School in Aberystwyth while the owners (Eric and Elizabeth Carson) went on holiday. Mr Carson was clerk to Ceredigion County Council.

The long summer university holidays fitted in well with the dates of shows – perhaps that is why I decided to pursue a career in education rather than follow the majority of my colleagues into the chemical industry! Every year from 1950 to 1954, I spent two or three weeks at the Revel Farm, Talgarth, with Emrys and Dinah Griffiths, whose hospitality was legendary. Emrys would ride up into the Black Mountains most days to check on the stallions, mares, foals and sheep, an expanse which went as far as Hay-on-Wye, Llanthony Abbey and Abergavenny, a distance of 20 miles. There was always a pony there for me to ride with him, and sometimes we rode into the mist. Emrys' advice should I ever got lost was to leave it to the pony to find our way home. These hill farmers led a unique way of life not always understood by lowland breeders. One breeder, who had sent a visiting mare to be covered by a premium stallion, telephoned to say that he was coming to collect her the following day. He had to be stopped, since we could go up into the hills many times without seeing her, and even then we might not be successful in getting her down to the catching pens. When I was buying ponies for the USA in 1956, Emrys sent me particulars of a filly which he had for sale, but admitted that he had not seen her for two months. The filly was eventually located near Abergavenny, on the other side of the Black Mountains, and two months later she was in the USA. Emrys had an uncanny recognition when it came to ponies, presumably as a result of spending many hours a day, most of the year, shepherding on the mountains. I accompanied him to Cui Stud in late summer 1954. After the sudden death of Mr Willie Richards, his widow Betty, who had not had much to do with the ponies, was left with 180 ponies to be recognised and catalogued for an auction to be held on 1 October. Emrys would not have seen all of the Cui ponies, but was of enormous assistance to the brothers Llewelyn and Dick Richards, especially when it came to which stallions had sired the foals, and in most cases he was able to confirm with the shepherd the mares which had run with a particular stallion the previous year.

There were various groups of ponies on the same mountain owned by farmers who had grazing rights – the Greenow, Stephens, Wall, Brown, Jenkins, Price, Watkins and Holland families – and they all helped one another when it was time to round up the ponies or the sheep. In 1951 and 1952 Ceulan Revolt (f. 1938) was awarded premiums to run out on the mountain, his best-known progeny probably being Revel Fair Maid (f. 1952), a foundation mare for the Weston Stud. He was then sold to Eppynt Stud and awarded a further three premiums, then sold to Criban and Will Thomas (Will Coity Bach, breeder of Criban Biddy Bronze), from whom I bought him back in 1958.

A two-y-o bay colt which Mr Griffiths bought in 1949, and who died that year after covering four mares, was Pendock Playboy

(Bowdler Blue Boy x Craven Tosca). His 1950 foals were Revel Light (out of Winestead Larina who died on 2 July 1952 while I was there), Revel Playtime (out of Winestead Zenia), Revel Springsong (RW ch 1957) and Revel Fun. Revel Playtime was dam of Revel Pinup, champion at the 1955 Brecon Bicentenary Show, when the trophy was presented to Mrs Dinah Griffiths by HM The Queen. I was very impressed with the dark bay Revel Light, and in 1952 we caught him (he had never been haltered before), and washed him ready for the Brecon Show. Revel Light did not take too kindly to being handled, and on the night before the show, he escaped from the orchard, heading back for the mountain. Luckily, he was stopped in the field next to the mountain, re-caught, and succeeded in winning a rosette which, I believe, was the only time he ever competed in the showring. I tried to buy him in 1952, and was told that he was not for sale, but that I would be given first refusal. It took me fifteen years to persuade Mr Griffiths to sell him to me and he arrived at Ceulan on 10 September 1967. In the meantime, I had bought some of his progeny, such as the 1961 filly foal Revel Siesta, dam of Ceulan Sprite, the originator of the 'S' family at Ceulan. It was while I was staying at the Revel in 1952 that we were warned to expect a loud explosion when Glanusk Park was blown up, and we heard it ten miles away. Emrys Griffiths had the reputation of being a difficult person to strike a deal with, but I think I got to understand his philosophy. If he asked you £150 for a pony, it was no good you offering £140, as he would not accept it. However, come Christmas time, he would send £20 each to the children, so at least he would have received what he considered the pony to be worth!

The first show for us in 1950 was the Three Counties Show at Leominster on 10–12 June, where the judge was Captain Howson, and he was very well-supported in terms of entries. Eryri Gwyndaf won the stallion class with What Ho second, and Coed Coch

Siaradus won the mare class, having been champion at Shropshire and Cheshire, and overall supreme Mountain and Moorland mare at the National Pony Show. Eryri Gwyndaf was champion, with What Ho reserve and Siaradus third. Because Gwyndaf had already won a WPCS medal, this went to What Ho, who also won the harness class.

The Royal Welsh Show held at Abergele on 26–28 July was full of drama! Mr Jack Havard judged the Welsh cobs and section Cs, where the champions were Meiarth Welsh Maid (for the third successive year) and Queenie (first time overall champion with another three to come). Mr Matthew Williams judged the section Bs (champion was Coed Coch Siabod, his first time, with another one and two male championships to follow before he was exported to Australia), and the section As, where the championship order was Tregoyd Starlight (stallion), Coed Coch Siaradus (mare), Coed Coch Meilyr (Gredington, two-y-o colt), Revel Delight (yearling) and Brierwood Honey (three-y-o filly). The mare class was full of famous names: Coed Coch Siaradus, Craven Moonlight (ch at RASE), Coed Coch Pioden, Vardra Sunflower, Coed Coch Sidan, Dovey Twilight, Criban Leading Lady (Glascoed Stud), Trefesgob Stardust, Gwyndy Penarth Relight (Witherley) and Llwyn Mwci (Glascoed). Tregoyd Starlight had also won the district stallion class, the top five foals were all sired by him, and his two-y-o son Coed Coch Meilyr had won the youngstock class. Then news circulated that Tregoyd Starlight had failed the veterinary inspection on the grounds that he was a cryptorchid (rig), and seemingly had been so all his life, but this had never been spotted in previous veterinary examinations. The RWAS protest committee met on 28 July and Tregoyd Starlight's winnings were cancelled. Coed Coch Siaradus won the Second Sprightly Championship Cup, Coed Coch Meilyr won the WPCS male championship medal and Eryri Gwyndaf, Dinarth What Ho and Ceulan Revelry were promoted in the stallion class.

August was a busy month, competing at eight shows – we must have been gluttons for punishment, often competing on consecutive days! The Pontarddulais Show was traditionally held on Bank Holiday Monday (7 August), a long way to travel for prize money of £3, £2 and £1. The judge was Mr D. O. Morgan, Parc Stud. We knew What Ho was a favourite of his, and he duly won the stallion class from Eryri Gwyndaf and Ceulan Revelry and four others, and he also won the harness class. Two days later was the Aberystwyth Show, whose conscientious secretary was Mr Emlyn Lewis the blacksmith, and he would write individual letters with copperplate handwriting inviting entries. Consequently, we had present Miss Brodrick and Lord Kenyon with their section As, and Mr Portlock of Solihull and James Black of Reading with hackneys. Mr Tom Ryder of the Marfleet Stud, Hull, author of many brilliant books on hackneys, judged the harness class, where What Ho won from Ceulan Revelry and Bolgoed Nipper, and a welcome newcomer fourth in the form of the lovely bay mare Craven Lymm, who put up a brave show for her first harness showring appearance.

The following day Thursday we were off again, this time north to the Oswestry Show, where the judge was Mr Douglas Meredith who, with his wife Gladys as housekeeper, was running Dinchope Farm for Mr Tom Jones Evans, who passed away two months later. What Ho won the stallion class and Serliw was taken out on a rare showring appearance at 17 years of age, and won the mare class from her grand-daughter Coed Coch Sidan. Serliw had at foot a filly foal, Ceulan Serenade, the first of her three sired by What Ho. On Saturday 19 August we took What Ho to the Radnorshire Show, held at Presteigne that year, and he won the stallion class and harness class. The RASE champion Craven Moonlight won the mare class for Mr Llewellyn Richards from Craven Bright Sprite and Criban Sweetly, owned by Mrs Cuff of the Dowland Stud, who later moved to live at Presteigne from Badminton. Mr Richards also won the youngstock class with Criban Bantam, who was to become a well-known sire for the Blanche, Dyrin and Synod studs. It was always good to go to this show since it was the only one where Mr Tom Powell of Cefnpenarth, Penybont, would compete. Mr Powell had been a member of the WPCS since 1915 (he died in 1954), and was largely responsible for organising the Penybont Common Premium Stallion scheme for forty years. Penarth Dainty, who won the filly class, ended her days with us at Ceulan in 1970.

Next, it was to Llanilar Show on Wednesday 23 August, where What Ho was first, and third in his class was Revel Brightlight, which we had leased for the year. The next day, we were off again, this time to Llandeilo where, with Mr Matthew Williams judging, Eryri Gwyndaf won the Evan Jones Cup (to be won three times) for the second time. Luckily, he didn't win it the following year and we won it outright in 1954. What Ho won the harness class again. Two days later, we were off to the North Wales Show at Caernarfon, and with judge Mr D. O. Morgan, What Ho won the stallion class from Coed Coch Meilyr, Coed Coch Serenllys and Coed Coch Socyn, that was later senior stud stallion for the rest of his life at the Stoatley Stud in Sussex. Coed Coch Pioden won the mare class of eight entries. Standing fourth (and beating entries from large studs with grooms) was a young schoolboy with his pony, Polly, which he had bought for 10 shillings – this was Eifion Williams of Tyddyn Bach, Caeathro, who judged at the RW in 2009. What Ho won the Championship Cup which had been presented by Mrs Armstrong-Jones, mother of Lord Snowdon.

Standing last in this class was a three-y-o colt owned by Mr Owen Ellis of the Hendre Stud. He was straight off the field, in poor condition and ungroomed. We were offered him at £25 but decided not to buy him, which was the biggest mistake we ever made with any pony. Miss Brodrick bought him, intending to send him to South Africa, but he improved so much in such a short time that she sent Coed Coch Pibydd Moel instead. When we saw this colt at the Shropshire Show in May 1951 (where he stood second in the stallion class to Eryri Gwyndaf) we thought he was very special, and my father offered £250 for him. But by this time, he was not for sale, and he was Coed Coch Madog, who was RW male champion in 1951, and went on to win this award another eight times.

What Ho won next in-hand and in harness at Machynlleth Show on 30 August. There was no stallion class at Tal-y-bont Show on 6 September, and Serliw was brought out again and won the Western Mail Cup outright for the third year in succession for the best light horse in the show. This cup had been competed for since 1930 and had been won mainly by hackney exhibitors, including Mr Robert Black of Reading, Mrs Henriques of Southport and Mr W. S. Miller of Bridge of Earn.

Then there remained only two more shows – Lampeter and Breconshire on 15 and 16 September respectively. Mr John Jones, Coed Coch, judged Welsh cobs and ponies at Lampeter, the only time to my knowledge that he ever judged. Dewi Rosina was the champion cob, with Meiarth Welsh Maid reserve. Eryri Gwyndaf won the section A stallion class, and Craven Lymm won the mare class. Mr Jones awarded the WPCS medal to Craven Lymm followed by Dewi Rosina, and Eryri Gwyndaf and What Ho won in harness. The following day at Brecon, What Ho was second again to Gwyndaf with judge Mr John Berry, and won the harness class, his ninth for 1950.

Following the death of Mr Matthew Williams of the Vardra Stud in January 1951, a sale of his ponies was arranged for 6 April at Gowerton Market with auctioneers T. E. Jenkins and Son. It was a dreadful day and no member of the family was certain of the pedigrees of the ponies. Lots 7, 8 and 9 were three fillies, two years old, not registered, and never been handled. According to the catalogue, all three were sired by Vardra Sunstar – lot 7 out of Vardra Nance (she made 10 gns to Mr Emrys Griffiths), lot 8 out of Brown Sugar (lot 5, 13hh) by Royal Pom TB was very small, and made 32 gns, also to Mr Griffiths, and lot 9 out of Vardra Moonshine Foundation Stock made 20 gns to Miss Brodrick. Lot 7 was registered as Revel Nance section A (Vardra Sunstar x Vardra Nance), and mysteriously, three months later was section B champion at the Royal Welsh Show! Lot 8 was registered as Revel Choice (Vardra Sunstar x Vardra Charm), and was section A champion at the 1961 RWS, and bred a whole host of champions at the Revel e.g. Revel Caress (f. 1957, sire Revel Springlight, RW ch 1963), Revel Cassino (f. 1966, sire Clan Pip, RW ch 1976, 1977). Lot 9 was registered as Coed Coch Nans FS1, and produced exceptional stock at Coed Coch, some of which were sold at high prices. When the son, Mr Tom Williams, resurrected the stud at Holme Lacy, Hereford, in 1969, he bought some descendants of Revel Choice. When Tom died at the age of 56 years in 1974, a sale was held of his 30 ponies, but two were kept, and they and their descendants have lived at Ceulan for forty years to keep the 'Vardra' prefix active.

In 1951 we competed at 11 shows – I suppose it was a case of 'make hay while the sun shines'. What Ho was on the crest of a wave, and show secretaries would contact my father to encourage him to attend, saying that his presence attracted spectators – he was a Welsh phenomenon. The RWS was held on 25–27 July at Llanelwedd, which became the permanent site in 1963. Miss Brodrick won both the championship and reserve with Coed Coch Siaradus and Coed Coch Madog. What Ho won a strong harness class where the judge was Mr Horace Smith, riding instructor of HM The Queen. We won second prize to Coed Coch Symwl (RW ch 1960) in a 15-strong class with a grey three-y-o filly Ceulan Cora (Eryri Gwyndaf x Ceulan Silverleaf). Cora was sold to top the September 1952 WPCS Sale at Shrewsbury at 75 gns to the Duchess of Rutland, who sold her to American William Simpson in October 1955.

A new trophy, the Cwmrhaiadr Cup, was offered at Machynlleth Show on 4 August, and was won by What Ho (won outright in 1953), and he also won the harness class from Mr Douglas Evans' Ceulan Serenade (Eryri Gwyndaf x Coed Coch Serliw) and Mr Wood Jones' Caran Revolt (Ceulan Revolt x Caran Daisy). Two days later, on Bank Holiday Monday at Pontarddulais, What Ho was champion in-hand, Ceulan Cora was reserve champion and What Ho also won in harness. Two days later we were back in the fray again, this time at Aberystwyth, where What Ho won the Lion Royal Cup from Mr Roscoe Lloyd's Dewi Rosina (brood mare) and Mr John Thomas' Oakford Black Bess (barren mare), and What Ho won the harness class judged by Mr Tom Ryder.

There was then a well-deserved rest before Llandeilo Show on 23 August. The show committee was in the habit of appointing well-known horse authorities to judge, rather than specialist judges for various sections. These judges would then judge Welsh ponies and cobs, pony breeding and riding classes, in-hand, ridden hunters and harness. What Ho won the Evan Jones (breeder of the famous Greylight) Cup, which had been won the previous two years by Eryri Gwyndaf, but Gwyndaf did not find favour this time and stood last in the stallion class. One first prize winner that day in the riding pony breeding section was Mrs Pennell's yearling colt Bwlch Valentino, who later became the most famous riding pony sire of all time. Two days later at Caernarfon, What Ho was reserve champion to Madog for the Armstrong-Jones Cup, with the noted Coed Coch Pioden third, and What Ho won in harness. What Ho won an outright cup for the best horse or pony in the show at Llangeitho and the Llidiardau Cup (which he won outright in 1953) at Llanilar. With Serliw having won the Western Mail Cup outright (three years in succession) at Tal-y-bont, the *Western Mail* replaced it with a perpetual cup, which What Ho won, while Ceulan Cora won the WMP mare or gelding class. The brood mare class over 13.2hh was open to cobs or ponies, and it was won by Lord Kenyon's grey mare Silver (registered as FS WSB section B), making one of her very rare showring appearances. Silver made a very important contribution to the section B breed. Her daughter, Gredington Milfyd, was RW champion in 1958, 1962 and 1963, and her g-daughter Gredington Blodyn won RW champion in 1971. Blodyn's son, Baledon Squire, was RW champion in 1978, and her g-g-daughters Rotherwood Honeysuckle won in 1970 and 1978, and Rotherwooxd Lilactime in 1981. Then Honeysuckle's son, Rotherwood State Occasion (f. 1979), topped the WPCS section B sire ratings nine times between 1985 and 1994. Looking at Silver at Tal-y-bont Show that day, one could not have envisaged that here was a mare that would change the course of the Welsh pony section B. What Ho then rounded off the 1951 season by winning in harness at Lampeter and Brecon.

1952 started off with the Criban Sale of 65 ponies on a very wet day outdoors at Tal-y-bont-on-Usk Market on 2 May. Top of the stallions was the seven-y-o Vardra Sunstar, with which Mr Richards had won second prize at the previous RWS, and he went to Mr Tom Parry of Gurnos Stud for 74 gns. Another prize-winner, the five-y-o Criban Bantam, made 70 gns to Mr David Reynolds of Blanche Stud. Top of the sale at 76 gns was Criban Opera, who went to breed well at Mrs Hope's Ready Token Stud. A three-y-o filly, Criban Activity, sold to Cusop Stud for 48 gns, went on to win the ridden class at the RW five times and was later a successful brood mare. The two-y-o Criban Topsy went to Miss Pam Horton of the Hinton Stud – Topsy later achieved great fame as the mount of the young Hayley Mills in the film *Tiger Bay*.

Two other sales were held on consecutive days. The first was of 50 Coed Coch ponies sold at the Home Farm on 26 September, and the next a collective sale of 80 ponies at the North Wales Horse Repository at Wrexham. Four mares were sold to Mrs Mackay-Smith, USA, who had imported Coed Coch Seren from the 1937

Coed Coch Sale. These exports to the USA gave breeders much encouragement. Criban White Wings was bought to go the USA for 32 gns, but the veterinary surgeon did not consider her to be in good enough condition to travel, and she was sold to Mr Tommy Evans, Tanlan. White Wings produced the noted Tanlan Wennol in 1953, and died when Wennol was three months old. Wennol was hand-reared by Mrs Evans and went on to live for 32 years. The section B yearling colt Coed Coch Berwynfa was bought back at 45 gns to carry on and produce a whole host of champions at Coed Coch.

Mr Wilding-Davies bought the stallion Craven Daylight for his Fayre Stud, also at 74 gns. At the 1952 shows, What Ho came out fitter than ever despite his 20 years, living out at Tre'r-ddôl on the edge of Borth bog all winter and covering 15 to 20 mares a year. At the RWS on 23–25 July at Caernarfon with Mr Frank Preece judging, we were expecting very strong opposition from the large entry in the catalogue, so perhaps I put in an extra effort! There was great rejoicing among the Ceulan ranks when we beat the great Coed Coch Madog (only five years old) into second place. Coed Coch Siaradus won a large mare class full of well-known matrons, where her dam Coed Coch Sirius was seventh. Siaradus won the Second Sprightly Championship from What Ho and the winning yearling filly Hogen Cymru, owned by Lampeter auctioneer Dafydd ap Gwilym Jones. Hogen Cymru was sired by What Ho and bred by my father's cousin, also named Evan Davies, out of his Gwen Tafarn Jem, a bay mare that was later to produce Dovey Prima Donna (RW youngstock champion 1959) and Ceulan Madam Butterfly (champion in Denmark and Sweden). We bought Hogen Cymru for William Simpson in 1957. What Ho also won the harness class and the Tom and Sprightly Cup open to the Welsh breeds and hackneys judged by popular applause, using a clapometer. What Ho was such a favourite with the Welsh spectators that he always had a good chance of winning this award whenever he qualified to compete (confined to champions and reserves).

We then competed at another ten shows, the next being Aberystwyth on 2 August and with judge Mr John Berry, What Ho managed to beat Madog again. Mr Berry was joined by the cob judge Mr D. O. Morgan, and What Ho was adjudged champion, with the cob mare Sheila (RW champion that year) reserve. What Ho won in harness from Ceulan Reveller, which we sold as a foal to Scotland (1944) and was bought back by Mr Wood-Jones, who sold him shortly afterwards to Mr Willie Richards of the Cui Stud. Lord Kenyon won the mare class with Coed Coch Sidan from Coed Coch's own Coed Coch Pelen. Pelen's colt foal (by Madog) won the foal class. He was Coed Coch Planed, who later became a famous champion for Gredington, and RW male champion in 1954.

The Pontarddulais Show was always two days after Aberystwyth, and What Ho won the WPCS bronze medal for champion in-hand and also won in harness. The long-established United Counties (Carmarthenshire, Pembrokeshire and Cardiganshire) Hunter Show held at Carmarthen staged Welsh classes on 15 August, and What Ho won in-hand and in harness. With such a distinguished history, it is tragic that this society was discontinued at the end of the century. The list of past presidents included Viscount St Davids, Earl Cawdor, the Earl of Lisburne, the Earl of Coventry, Lord Glantawe, Lord Kylsant, Lord Ystwyth, Lord Dynevor, Lord Merthyr and many more dignitaries.

The Cardigan Show on 23 August was held on the County Grammar School grounds, and What Ho was again champion. At Llangeitho on 27 August, What Ho won another outright cup for the best heavy or light horse, and also won first in harness. Llandeilo Show on 28 August continued their selection of judges from distinguished British horsemen and women, and this time it was Miss Sybil Smith of the Cadogan Riding School, Maidenhead, and Mrs Joan Gibson of Oakham, Rutland, who judged every horse class in the show. What Ho won the Evan Jones Championship Cup for the second time and also won in harness. Mr Davies, Blaenpistyll, who had won with his cobs at pre-war RW shows, judged Tal-y-bont Show on 3 September, and What Ho was overall champion light horse in-hand, also winning in harness again. Similarly at Llanilar Show on 10 September, he put another notch on the Llidiardau cup for best pony or cob and won in harness.

The final shows, held on consecutive days, were always Lampeter and Brecon. What Ho was champion in-hand and first in harness at Lampeter and again at Brecon. Third to What Ho in the stallion class at Brecon was Ceulan Reveller, now owned by Cui Stud. Because What Ho had won a WPCS medal at Pontarddulais, the Brecon medal went to the winning mare, Craven Bright Sprite, and the reserve was the yearling filly Craven Sprightly Light, owned by Fayre Stud, champion at the Royal of England Show and exported to Australia in 1960.

1953 was the coronation year of HM Queen Elizabeth II. As Princess Elizabeth, Her Majesty was president of the RWS at Carmarthen in 1947 and was now patron. The show was held on 22–25 July. Apart from Swansea, where it was also four days (with an attendance of 102,101 compared with the average 60,000), this was the only four-day show before 1981. It was held on Pontcanna Fields between Cathedral Road and the river Ely near Cardiff Castle. Mr Robert Templeton JP, who farmed Pontcanna Farm, had been a member of RWAS since 1912, and was a member of council for many years. Welsh pony and cob entries (114 in 18 classes) kept up with previous years. Since 1947 they had been 94, 122, 101, 129 and 108. In 1947 Welsh ponies sections B and C shared the same section, and were separated into three classes each in 1950. While section B entries justified a separate section and increased to four classes in 1951, the situation with section C was very sad, and total entries were one or two tagged on at the end of the cob section. Section C entries continued to be minimal (a maximum of three) until 1960 – a far cry from the 344 entries in 2014.

Mr John Berry judged section A, and What Ho was second and reserve male champion to Madog, who was fifteen years his junior. Sixth in this class, in the ownership of Miss Marguerite de Beaumont, was the 18-y-o Coed Coch Glyndwr. This was the first time I saw Glyndwr, then I saw him again the following month at the Ponies of Britain Show at Ascot, where he was third to Madog and Bolgoed Atomic. Glyndwr will not be remembered as a show stallion, but for being undoubtedly the greatest sire of the second quartile of the twentieth century. Siaradus won the mare class and the championship, with Madog reserve. An interesting entry (eighth) in the mare class was Mrs Cuff's Craven Sprightly Twilight (sold for 16 gns on the 1956 FO Sale), g-dam of the famous Downland Chevalier. Chevalier's grand-sire Star Supreme (gelded) was also placed under saddle. First and second yearling colts were Coed Coch Planed and Fronarth What Ho, who were male champion and reserve male champion the following year, beating Madog and everything else. Fronarth What Ho (sired by Dinarth What Ho) was a mystery – he never grew above 12hh despite his dam, Fronarth Queen Bee, being 13hh 2in, and sired by Brenin Gwalia. Fronarth What Ho won the RW harness class 16 times, the last time at 26 years of age. Dinarth What Ho won in harness, unbeaten for the seventh time, and was reserve to the hackney Hurstwood Lonely Maid for the Tom and Sprightly popular applause cup.

While the going was good, we competed at fourteen shows. What Ho's swan song came in a new show for us – Oswestry – on 30 July, where the judge was Mr Tom Thomas, Madeni Welsh Cob Stud. What Ho was second in the stallion class to Ceulan Serenade (f. 1948, Eryri Gwyndaf x Coed Coch Serliw), but we won the mare / filly class with the three-y-o Ceulan Serenade (Dinarth What Ho x Coed Coch Serliw). At Aberystwyth on 5 August, What Ho was first and Serenade second in a class of five, and Serenade won the mare class of 15 exhibits. What Ho, having won the overall cup twice, was reserve this time to Dewi Rosina. Serenade was also second to What Ho in harness. What Ho and Serenade were also first and second in harness at the United Counties Show on 14 August. The following day, What Ho won in-hand and harness at Radnor County Show, held at Penybont, and Serenade won the filly class from Craven Sprightly Light.

Another new show for us was Llandovery on 20 August, where What Ho won his WPCS medal from the cob stallion Mathrafal (1952 RW ch), and also won in harness. At Llangeitho on 26 August, What Ho won his third outright cup for the best light horse, this time with Meiarth Welsh Maid reserve. What Ho also won in harness. Llandeilo Show personality judge the following day was Mr Geoffrey D. S. Bennett, the leading hackney authority and *Horse and Hound* reporter. Mr Bennett was the 'king' of the hackney world. After the hackney breed shows, he would hold court amongst his friends at the hotel, criticising the events of the day, and his ringing laugh would rise in pitch as the evening progressed! What Ho won the stallion class from Eryri Gwyndaf, and Serenade was second to Lord Kenyon's beautiful bay mare Coed Coch Sidan, daughter of Seirian, daughter of Serliw. What Ho then won the Evan Jones Cup outright for the third year in a row. Because Mr Bennett was judging, some of Britain's best hackneys turned up at Llandeilo. Sir Nigel Colman's Black Magic of Nork won the horse class, and Bossy (now sold to Mrs Kimpton) won the pony class. What Ho won the Welsh harness class, and a miracle occurred for the championship, when What Ho beat Bossy (who had cost his previous owner £4,000) to stand reserve to the magnificent Black Magic of Nork.

Two days later we were off again, this time to the North Breconshire Show at Builth Wells. This show awarded their own bronze medals. What Ho won the male medal, and Serenade was reserve to Coed Coch Sidan for the female medal. What Ho won the new Western Mail Cup at Tal-y-bont Show on 2 September from Geler Bess, who had Geler Daisy (1964 RW ch) at foot and also won in harness. What Ho won the Llidiardau cup outright at Llanilar on 9 September from Sheila (1952 RW ch), also in harness, and Serenade was reserve champion mountain pony. Another new show for us on 11 September was the long-established Merioneth Show, whose catalogue listed all previous presidents back to 1868. The judge was Miss Pauline Taylor of the Llanarth Stud, and What Ho won the Welsh mountain pony open class from an entry of (Sir) Meuric Rees, Towyn.

The two last shows, as always, were Lampeter and Brecon. What Ho, who won the stallion and harness classes at Lampeter, had already won a WPCS medal at Llandovery, and the Lampeter medal was won by Ceulan Serenade (A) with Talley Wendy (C) reserve and Dewi Rosina (D) third. What Ho also won in harness at Brecon, unbeaten in harness in seven years. Ten days later, on 29 September, What Ho died. The idol of Wales was no longer. When the report of his death appeared in the press, dozens of sympathy letters were received at Tal-y-bont from all over Britain and overseas. Crowned bard John Roderick Rees wrote a short-form poem in his memory:

> Pawb ar ei drot yn dotio – egni byw
> Y Gwyn Bach di-ildio;
> Awr ei hydref o'i frwydro
> Yn y tir y rhoed What Ho.

> [His trotting was loved by all – electric
> Was the small white beauty;
> Twilight fell on his plenty,
> In the ground What Ho now lay.]

I began writing show reports for publications in 1952. My report of the Welsh mountain ponies at the RWS was published in the American monthly magazine *Your Pony* in April 1953 alongside an article on 'Our correspondent from Wales'. At that time, sections B and C Welsh ponies, or Welsh cobs, were unknown in the USA. The editor of *Your Pony* was William Simpson of Reedsburg, Wisconsin, who came over to Wales and bought 33 Welsh ponies in October 1955 and again in May 1957, when he bought 56 for himself and clients. I also reported the entire horse section of the 1954 RWS for *Horse and Hound*, for which my payment from Odhams Press was £2. I also reported the Aberystwyth and Lampeter shows for £1 each and Merioneth County for 15s (75p). By 1958 I was being paid £4 for reporting the RW (increased to £10 in 1962), but only £1 for Lampeter, Aberystwyth, Vaynor, North Breconshire and Tal-y-bont. In 1990 I reported 34 shows and sales, for which my payment from IPC Magazines for the RW was £160. I was also paid for supplying photographs at many shows. I was commissioned to write stud articles and historical articles for anniversaries too, as well as monthly articles for *Focus on Wales*.

The editor of *Horse and Hound* in 1952 was Mr Walter Case. A tall, distinguished-looking gentleman with wavy hair, he had been working for the publication since 1931 and took over as editor when Mr Portman (who had been editor since 1890), his wife and household staff were all killed when their house was bombed in 1940. Mr Case, with only one assistant, kept *Horse and Hound* going throughout the war, having to move offices twice due to being bombed and losing all their records, printing equipment etc. Mr Case was a very serious person, and I would be telephoned (even at the university's Chemistry department) if my report was late. Mr Case retired in 1973 (he signed his last cheque to me, £20 for the RW report), and the editorship was taken over by Mr Michael Clayton, a much more easy-going boss, who wrote the most charming letters. He was assisted by Mr Hugh Condry, who was always most helpful. Mr Arnold Garvey then took over from Michael Clayton, and Peter Jeffery was deputy editor.

I was appointed assistant publicity officer of the WPCS to the wonderful Mrs Nell Pennell in 1958, and have been publicity officer since her retirement in 1978. This involves supplying articles to magazines and journals world-wide, and to the UK press. More recently, it has been supplying articles and photographs of show and sale reports for the WPCS website. I was also editor of the WPCS Journal for 12 years from 1992 to 2003.

Because we had lost Dinarth What Ho, our first task of 1954 was to find a replacement for him. We considered the two show stallions Criban Bantam and Vardra Sunstar on the 1952 Criban Sale to be of a rather more 'stuffy' type than the more 'performance' type which we preferred at Ceulan. So, in May 1954 we went back to Criban and bought the five-y-o stallion Clan Marshall from Mr Llewelyn Richards. Mr Howell Richards Senior, at 89 years of age, made a special journey to the Allt to catch up with my father, as they had known each another for forty years. Clan Marshall was the first of the 19 foals of Dinas Moonstone (f. 1945: Coed Coch Glyndwr x Touchstone of Sansaw by Grove Sprightly). Dinas Moonstone was bred by Mrs Armstrong-Jones of Lewes, Sussex, who previously lived in Caernarfon. Before Mrs Mountain (Alison McNaught) was married in 1951, she used the 'Clan' prefix of her father, the next foal to Marshall (1950) being Clan Music (by Coed Coch Glyndwr, who was also her dam's sire), and from then on the other 17 foals were registered as Twyford 'M'.

1954 was the fiftieth anniversary of RWAS and the show, held at Machynlleth, is best remembered for its mountains of mud. Luckily, it was close enough for us to be based at home, but it was very difficult for the exhibitors who stayed on the site. Mr Arthur McNaught judged the section As, and Clan Marshall was second to

Coed Coch Madog in the stallion class, with Bolgoed Atomic third and Coed Coch Samswn fourth. The championships, however, went to youngstock, the male championship to Coed Coch Planed, and Fronarth What Ho reserve, and the overall to the two-y-o filly Ankerwycke Clan Snowdon, with Coed Coch Siaradus reserve. Our other exhibits were Ceulan Carol (f. 1953: Dinarth What Ho x Ceulan Silverleaf), who was fourth and the two-y-o colt Ceulan Shalimar (Dinarth What Ho x Coed Coch Serliw), who won the local class. Despite the mud, every afternoon we were able to stage a display of Welsh ponies and cobs doing varied jobs of work, like trekking, shepherding, in harness and chain harrowing, and on the last afternoon the president, Sir Bryner Jones, donned his wellington boots and came and thanked every participant.

At the Pontarddulais Show on 2 August with judge Mr Tom Thomas, Clan Marshall was second to Bolgoed Atomic, and Ceulan Serenade won the mare class and the WPCS medal since Atomic had already won a medal (only one per year allowed). Two days later at Aberystwyth with judge Mr Alfred Williams, Marshall won the stallion class and the Lion Royal Cup outright, since What Ho had won it in 1951 and 1952, and was reserve to Dewi Rosina in 1953. The two reserves to Marshall were the cob brood mare Tyhen Beauty (dam of 1962 RW ch Tyhen Mattie) and the cob barren mare Teify Welsh Maid (1955 RW ch).

At the Radnorshire Show held at Rhayader with judge Mr Osborne Jones, Marshall beat Atomic and won the championship and Serenade also won a very big mare class. Marshall won another outright cup for the best Welsh pony or cob at Llangeitho Show on 25 August, where the reserve was the cob mare Meiarth Welsh Maid, who was RW champion the previous month. Marshall and Serenade both won at Tal-y-bont Show on 1 September, and Marshall won the Western Mail Cup, the third successive year for us, but the cup was now perpetual. At Llanilar Show on 8 September, the judge was Mr Morgan Williams, a London policeman. Marshall and Serenade both won their classes, with Marshall winning the Llidiardau Cup outright from very stiff opposition from the cob mare class. Finally at Lampeter on 17 September, Marshall was second to Atomic but won the WPCS medal. The reserve this time was the cob mare Dewi Rosina, who won the Morgan Cup outright for the third year in succession.

Owing to the tragic death of Mr Willie Richards of the Cui Stud (the youngest of the three Richards brothers), a sale of 181 ponies was arranged at Tal-y-bont-on-Usk on 1 October. Top of the stallions at 53 gns was Criban Silver Sand (purchased for 32 gns on the 1946 Criban Sale), followed by Gaerstone Beacon at 44 gns and Ceulan Reveller at 36 gns. I bought Ceulan Reveller for the USA at 75 gns the following year. The top-priced mare at 61 gns was Cui Wyth, bought by Mrs Creed of the Wyrhale Stud to join her top mare, Craven Bright Sprite, purchased from Mrs Cuff. Cui Metal was bought by Miss Pam Horton for 50 gns and, after she won at the NPS Show in 1956, I bought her for American Mrs Mohler for 300 gns. When I was collecting ponies for the USA in 1957, I also bought Cui Gavenny, Cui Margo, Cui Moon Flicker, Cui Rally On, Cui Fickle and Cui Moonbeam at prices of double or more what they had been purchased on the October 1954 sale. Five of the mares were bought back on the sale by Cui to keep the stud going for Mrs Betty Richards and her three daughters.

A major reduction sale the following week was of 63 ponies owned by Mr Wilding Davies at his Fayre Oaks Farm, Hereford, due to him selling his Cwmfadog hill farm at Llanafanfawr, Builth Wells. Also included by permission were seven lots from Mrs Cuff and four from Mr Vivian Eckley. The top stallion was Revel Blue Banner, sold for 40 gns, and the top mare was Fayre Black Dawn, also at 40 gns, to Captain Homfray to start the Penllyn Stud near Cowbridge. Seventy-four ponies were sold for a sale total of

£1,669, averaging £21. Mr Wilding-Davies considered the sale to be so successful that he organised a collective sale the following year with auctioneers Russell, Baldwin and Bright (which became Brightwells), and the Brightwells Fayre Oaks Sale has continued for sixty years. At the sixty-first sale in 2014, 303 ponies sold for £210,590 averaging £695. The highest figures came in 2006 when 716 ponies sold for £476,450 averaging £960 – 46 times the 1954 average.

The third autumn sale was of 54 ponies at the Cnewr Stud, a picturesque estate in the Swansea Valley, Cray, near Sennybridge. The Cnewr ponies were registered in the early volumes of the WSB, but they let the registrations lapse during the depression years of the 1930s and consequently, the ponies had to be upgraded from Foundation Stock via FS1 and FS2 to full registration. The 54 Cnewr ponies on the sale were mainly FS with a few FS1. We bought two FS mares, Cnewr Belle (20 gns) and Cnewr Jess (29 gns). Buying them was the easy part – the problem was getting them home! Neither of the ponies had ever been haltered, indeed it was doubtful if they had ever seen humans, but we managed to get them home safely. The cremello Cnewr Belle was sold as soon as possible, but the dark dun Cnewr Jess lived at Ceulan until 1968. We received a good offer for Clan Marshall and Ceulan Serenade at the end of 1954 from Mr Canfield of Merrie Mill, Virginia, and decided to sell them, So to start 1955 we were back on the quest for a stallion. Marshall and Serenade sailed from Liverpool on the S.S. *Media* on 11 February.

My father, who was president of the WPCS that year, judged the section A ponies at the RWS at Haverfordwest on 20–22 July where his champions were Coed Coch Siaradus (female and overall) and Coed Coch Madog (male and reserve overall), and the bay two-y-o filly Twyford Gala was reserve female champion. What I remember about Siaradus was her long, lean 'front' and her long-striding walk – as soon as she started to walk, her tail would rise, her ears would go forward and she looked happy. She was possibly the best Welsh mountain pony mare I have ever seen. For the first time, the RW section A champion was awarded the Captain Howson Memorial Cup, a very large, impressive, silver trophy purchased for £50, donated by RWAS and £50 from the WPCS in memory of Captain T. A. Howson, who had died on 1 February 1954 at the age of 68.

The Brecon Show, usually held at the end of September, was brought forward in 1955 since it was the bicentenary show. Breconshire is the oldest show in the UK, and HM The Queen and HRH The Duke of Edinburgh had agreed to attend. HM presented the section A championship trophy to Mrs Dinah Griffiths showing the two-y-o filly Revel Pinup. Pinup had interesting breeding – her sire Revel Light (later at Ceulan) and dam Revel Playtime were two of only four sired by Pendock Playboy. Light was out of Winestead Larina, daughter of Grove Star of Hope, which Lady Wentworth bought in 1924 for £50 and gave to William Hay of Winestead Hall for 'free' in 1928. Zenia was out of Ness Thistle, bought by Lady Wentworth for £60 in 1927 and also given for 'free' to William Hay in 1930.

The North Breconshire Show on 27 August was the first show at which I was appointed to judge. The owners must have had faith in me, since they turned up in large numbers from far afield. My champion was Coed Coch Madog and reserve the mare Craven Toscanini (which my father had placed champion at Shropshire in 1946), who had a cream colt foal, Pendock Puccini, at foot, sired by Madog, that we met up with at the RWS the following year, and then bought.

On 1 October, a second FO Sale was organised at Hereford by RB&B. There were 117 entries – 23 from Dyrin, 22 from Fayre, 16 from Coed Coch, 10 foals from the Revel, eight each from Criban and Cusop, six from Downland, four from Maen Gwynedd, three from Lan, two each from Pendock, Whitepool and Ceulan, four from A. D. Thomas, and one from Bwlch. Ninety-three of the ponies sold for a sale total of £2,876, an average of £31, up from £21 the previous year. Top-priced stallion at 48 gns to Penllyn Stud was Royal Reveller from Fayre Stud. He was bred at Ceulan (Ceulan Revelry x Coed Coch Serliw) and remained at Penllyn for the rest of his life, won many championships and was one of the few to beat the great Madog. Top of the sale at 112 gns was Cusop Stud's three-y-o filly Hinton Clover by Gaerstone Beacon, and Mrs Mountain bought the two-y-o filly Sundana of Maengwynedd for 90 gns. Top of the Dyrin consignment at 54 gns was the mare Dyrin Peggy – she went to Fayre Stud and was bought ten days later by our American friend Mr Simpson for £120.

Mr Simpson himself flew to Heathrow on 15 October and travelled to see the Clan ponies of Mr McNaught at Lingfield, Sussex, only to find that anything that was for sale had been bought the previous week by Mr Goodrich, who had a ranch of 30,000 acres in central Texas. He then travelled to Gredington, where many had again been bought by Mr Goodrich, including the 1954 RW champion Ankerwycke Clan Snowdon. Lord Kenyon took Mr Simpson to Gretton Stud, where Mr Frank Preece was dispersing his 35 ponies at the Raven Horse Repository, Shrewsbury on 29 October. Mr Simpson picked out five mares and we had instructions to buy them for up to 100 gns each on the sale.

We bought Gretton Sunset (98 gns) and Gretton Suncloud (85 gns), but the other three mares which he had selected sold for over 100 gns: Gretton Sunray (105 gns to Lord Kenyon), and Gretton Sunlight and Gretton Butterfly at 110gns each, bought by Miss Brodrick for American Mrs Mackay-Smith. Mr Simpson then travelled to Fayre Oaks Stud, where he bought Dyrin Peggy, Revel Ringlet, Belvoir Marigold and Fayre Magic for Mr John Tolan of Salisbury, Illinois. I collected Mr Simpson from Hereford and took him first to Cusop, where he bought Fayre Fairy, then on to the Revel, where he bought six, and on to Criban, where he bought Criban Operetta, all for Mr Tolan. A quick trip over the Brecon Beacons took us to Merthyr Tydfil, where he bought the good show mare Criban Marian Sais from David Reynolds, and Bolgoed Princess from Mr Tom Norman Lewis. Next port of call was Blaendyrin, where Mr Gwyn Price was sorry that he had sold 23 ponies two weeks previously on the FO Sale at prices of about half of what Mr Simpson was paying. But at the time of entering for the sale, Mr Simpson had not informed anyone that he was coming, and he produced the magazine *Your Pony* single-handedly, so he had no spare time. Also at Blaendyrin, Mr Simpson bought Dyrin Serenade, Star and Daydream (which I had placed second at North Breconshire) for himself.

I then took Mr Simpson to the nearby Cwmowen Sale (auctioneers: Jones Brothers), and it was a real eye-opener for him to see so many wild, unhandled ponies being sold in one day. At Cwmowen, Mr Simpson bought Ceulan Reveller for £75 (Reg Bowen had bought him for 36 gns on the Cui dispersal sale). Also on the Cwmowen Sale that day was the 17-y-o Ceulan Revolt (sire of Reveller), having served his time at Eppynt Stud, but he was too old for export. Revolt sold to Criban, but the lorry overturned on the way home. Revolt shot out through the roof, miraculously unscathed, and was caught safely. The lorry was righted, and he was delivered to Criban without further incident! I bought Revolt in 1958 and sent him to Reeves Stud to end his days. When we were in the High Wycombe area on our honeymoon in 1961, I bought three of his daughters and named one Ceulan Honeymoon.

From Ceulan, Mr Simpson bought the colt Ceulan Shalimar (Dinarth What Ho x Coed Coch Serliw) for Mr Tolan, and his full-sister Ceulan Sonnet for himself, as well as Revel Just So and the show mare, Merylan (one of the very few sired by Coed Coch Seryddwr before his export to South Africa), from local breeders.

Then we took him to Coed Coch, where he bought only Rhian Heulog – everything else he fancied had already been bought by Mr Goodrich. Miss Brodrick took Mr Simpson to Bryntirion, where he bought Cui Darling and Revel Sweet Briar, and then escorted him to Colwyn Bay railway station to see him on his way back to London. Mr Simpson bought Ceulan Cora unseen from the Duchess of Rutland, but I had given him several photographs of when she was second at the RWS. Mr Simpson then sent me $9,200 (equivalent to about £7,500 today), with instructions to pay for the 33 ponies and arrange their transport to Glasgow to go on the M. V. *Elysia* on 9 December. For a few days before I wrote the cheques, I would have been one of the richest students in Britain!

The ponies from south and mid-Wales and Hereford were assembled at the Revel. Our friend from Tal-y-bont, Jenkyn Morris, was paid £30 by British Livestock Exports to escort the ponies from the Revel to Glasgow, and look after all 33 until their arrival in New York. He was allowed to spend two weeks with his brother-in-law in America and was given free transport back to Tal-y-bont. Mr Joe Edwards, Bryn Garage, Cwmdu (near the Revel), charged £100 for three lorries to transport them to Glasgow. The shipping cost was $220 (about £80) per head so the average price on arrival in the USA was about £190 each. Some of the ponies were sold soon after arrival at considerable profit, with one pony paying the purchase price of eight to ten. The export fees of this consignment, along with those for Mr Goodrich, Mrs Mackay-Smith and others, provided a boost for the finances of the WPCS. The income for 1955 was £878, and expenditure £770, including £175 in secretarial salaries, which increased to a surplus of £2,279 in 1958. My father's last duty as president for 1955 was to organise a Welsh Cob conference at Lampeter on 25 November, where the main speaker was Mr Moses Griffith, MSc, who outlined the development of the Welsh cob since the time of Hywel Dda (c. 940AD).

In 1955 I was elected onto the WPCS Council for the period 1955–1958, and continued to be re-elected every three years for the next 54 years, until the regulation was passed at an EGM in October 2006 that: 'No person who has served a total of six consecutive years as a member of council shall be eligible to be elected for a further term until at least three years have passed.' So my term of office came to an end at the March 2008 AGM. No other member has served for 54 years, and because of the new constitution, it will not be possible for anyone to ever equal this total. As well as some five or six council meetings a year, I was a member of the editorial committee and chairman of the publicity committee for 31 years, and at one point, I calculated that I had spent four years of my life in WPCS committees! Before my retirement in September 1989, it was not always possible for me to have the day off from college to attend the meetings, which were usually at Shrewsbury or Aberystwyth, but I must have done something right, since I topped the council election every three years since 1984, usually collecting over 1,000 votes (1,188 in 1993) – the top vote in 2015 was 365. The situation has changed immensely since 1955, but I like to think that I have contributed something to the WPCS over the years. I wrote the centenary book *One Hundred Glorious Years* in 2011, which generated a profit of £40,970 to the society, and the profit from the colour calendars I produced amounted to £24,853.

Since 1912 the Board of Agriculture and Fisheries had awarded six premiums of £50 each to Welsh cob stallions to travel within Wales. This was considerable money when one considers the annual agricultural wage at that time was £37. Up until 1956 WPCS judges travelled Wales awarding these premiums, but on 6 April 1956, twelve stallions were brought to Lampeter to compete for eight premiums of £80, and spectators were charged a shilling for entry. It was organised as a show class, with results first, Llwynog-y-Garth, second Meiarth King Flyer and third Caradog Llwyd. In

1957 the premiums were increased to £120 each, and a class for section A stallions added, where the results were Criban Bantam first, Fronarth What Ho second, Cenarth Bluebird third and Revel Starlight fourth (which I bought for £80). By 1958 the show classes were increased to five, including section C stallions and colts, and sections A and D youngstock. Llwynog-y-Garth again won his class, and in the section As, Coed Coch Madog was first, Royal Reveller second and Fronarth What Ho third. This show was organised by the WPCS, but in 1962 a local committee took over under the chairmanship of Mr D. O. Morgan, Parc Stud. The show was held on 3 April 1962 when there were 25 entries and admission had increased to five shillings. This show celebrated its fiftieth anniversary on 23 April 2011, when there were 688 entries in 45 classes.

To return to 1956, our next show was Shropshire on 16 May, where my father judged, and his overall champion was Coed Coch Madog with Bolgoed Atomic reserve. It was a long-standing arrangement with the WPCS that two medals were awarded at Shropshire – the only show outside the RW where this happened. The female medal went to Coed Coch Seirian (the foal left behind at Coed Coch when my father bought Serliw in 1937), and reserve to Craven Toscanini, which my father had placed champion at this show in 1946. At the RWS at Rhyl on 25–27 July, the judge was Mrs Pennell, who had also judged section As in 1951, when her champion was Coed Coch Siaradus. This time, her champion was Brierwood Honey, and when I want to illustrate the extremes within section As, I show the elegant, free-moving Siaradus and the heavy-boned Honey, with her huge eyes and small, mouse-like ears. Honey was bought by Mr George Fernley for £400 four months later. Reserve champion was the yearling filly Revel Cascade, another of the progeny of Revel Choice, bought on the Vardra dispersal sale. Two interesting exhibits were the three-y-o filly Tanlan Wennol and her yearling daughter Tanlan Lili, who went on to be noted show winners. This is one of the very rare examples I have seen of a filly producing a foal at two years of age, although it did not seem to harm Wennol, since she lived to be 32 and had 22 foals altogether.

Winner of the yearling colt class and reserve male champion was the palomino Pendock Puccini (sired by Coed Coch Madog out of the Shropshire reserve champion Craven Toscanini), that I had judged as a foal at North Brecon. We bought him that very day, and he was much in demand as a sire the following year for good visiting mares such as Coed Coch Nans, and others sold to the USA on the condition that they had been covered by Puccini. At 23 years of age, Serliw was looking in great shape, and it was decided to let her have a last appearance at Tal-y-bont Show on 5 September. With judge Mr John Edwards, Llwyncolfa, she won her class and was reserve to Bolgoed Atomic for the championship.

There were 160 ponies entered for the FO Sale on 6 October, which required an earlier start of 11.30 a.m. Top pure-bred at 100 gns was the four-y-o palomino section A stallion Llanarth Pimpernel, son of Dyrin Peggy, which we exported to Mr Tolan after the previous sale. Craven Sprightly Twilight, g-dam of the famous Downland Chevalier, sold for 16 gns to Counsellor Campbell Moodie of Canada House. There were 16 Revel colt and filly foals entered, and they sold for 13–21 gns for the colts, and 21–46 gns for the fillies. The following year, prices shot up because I took American Mr Vern Rider to the sale, where he bought ten, and the Revel foals reached 250 gns. The increased demand at the 1956 FO Sale prompted RB&B to conduct an autumn sale at Hay-on-Wye (from 2014, this sale has relocated to Hereford), mainly for hill foals. At its peak, this sale would attract 500 or more hill foals – one vendor alone, Mr W. R. Evans of Coedowen, annually sold 50–80 foals.

In terms of American visitors, 1956 was a quieter year. Miss

Hetty Mackay-Smith (Mrs Abeles) of Farnley Farms, Virginia came to judge at the Vaynor Show and bought the first-prize foal Gurnos Gaylight and stayed on in Wales buying another twelve – three each from Criban, Cui and Dyrin, two from Revel and one from Vaynor. In November, I had a request from Mr Canfield of Heatherstone Stud, Virginia, for 14 mares / fillies, and was sorry that the request had not come in time for the FO Sale. However, I was sure that I could find ones worthy of export. From the Revel, I bought four, Revel Snapshot from Aberystwyth, Cui Moon Flicker (lot 121 on the Cui dispersal sale) from Fayre Stud, Dyrin Brunette from Dyrin, four from Whitehall Stud and Heatherstone Soned (daughter of Gwen Tafarn Jem, who was also dam of Dovey Prima Donna and Ceulan Madam Butterfly). These, together with Cusop Chip and Cusop Bluebell (which we had bought on the FO Sale) made up the fourteen. Mr Joe Edwards transported these for Heatherstone, plus the 13 for Farnley from the Revel to Glasgow for £100, and they left on Christmas afternoon on the S.S. *Tyria*.

1957 was a very eventful year for myself and the WPCS. Exports of section As to the USA and Canada rocketed, which provided encouragement to breeders and extra income for the WPCS. Registrations of 510 in 1956 increased to 1,823 in 1957, 3,024 in 1958 and 6,007 in 1965. Export fees were £5 per animal and registration fees were £1 for males and 50p for females, producing £2,747 for exports and £1,618 for registrations. The £292 surplus for the year 1956 increased to £2,279 in 1957 despite an additional £410 having to be paid in staff overtime. 1957 exports to the USA were 62 males and 405 females, of which 28 males and 164 females were via E. S. Davies and Wynne Davies. Exports to Canada were 27 males and 267 females, plus a trickle of exports to Belgium, Holland, Sweden and South Africa.

Mr Simpson flew over in May on his second trip to Wales, with commissions to buy a stallion and 12 mares for Mr and Mrs Elliott

Bonnie, Ohio, five mares for Mrs Mohler, West Virginia, 15 mares for Vern Rider, Gordonsville, Virginia and 12 mares for Ray Feltner of Indiana. He also bought 12 mares for himself, and I got him a complete set of Welsh Stud Books volumes 1–32 for £15. I collected Mr Simpson from Hereford railway station and took him first to Fayre Stud, where they were all very sad at having had to put down Craven Daylight the previous day due to him having broken a leg. However, they cheered up when Mr Simson bought 11 ponies for £980.

One was Fayre Merrylegs by Royal Reveller, for which Mr Simpson paid £100. She was sold soon after arrival for $4,200 (£1,500), which almost paid for the purchase and shipping of all eleven. Fayre Nightshade was another bought for £100 and sold at auction for $2,000. Then we went on to Cusop, where he bought six for £777, then to the Revel where they were more expensive (average of £180), and he bought seven. At Criban, Mr Simpson bought three at £110 each: Criban Dark Chick, Gretton Monica and Criban Dun Doll. The latter sold by auction in the USA that year for $2,125 (£760). Miss Pam Horton (niece of Mr Richards) was at Criban with Cui Metal (which she had bought on the Cui Sale in 1954 for 50gns), who won several prizes in 1956, and Mr Simpson paid £315 for her – the second most expensive pony of all he bought. Next port of call was Dyrin Stud on the Epynt, where Mr Simpson bought 14 mares / fillies (four of the mares having foals at foot) made up of seven mares, four two-y-o and three yearling fillies for £1,400. One yearling filly, Llaneglwys Beauty Cream (bought for £90), topped the auction at Winchester six months later at $5,000 (£1,765) – more than the cost of all fourteen. The *Daily Express* got wind of our visit to Blaendyrin and sent a reporter and photographer to cover it. The newspaper report the following day read: 'Mighty Fine Day for a Lone Ranger', and referred to Mr Simpson as a 'bearded Buffalo Bill from ole Virginny'.

On our way north, he bought Hogen Cymru (Dinarth What Ho x Gwen Tafarn Jem, who had won a huge class of yearling fillies at the 1952 RW) for £180, and Fron Silver Leaf (£95) from Dr Arwyn Williams, vice-chairman of WPCS Council. Arriving in north Wales, two were bought from Betws (£370) and seven from Coed Coch (£1,010) including the most expensive, the superb Rhydyfelin Serol, for £350. One was Snowdon Walnut X, bought for £75, that was unfortunately killed by a falling tree, but Miss Brodrick claimed off the insurance and she was replaced. And so it was left to me to pay out £9,297 to 23 sellers and arrange collection and shipment. I wonder what that would be worth today. A bungalow which we bought for £2,200 at around the same time sold recently for £250,000, so for a few days in 1957, I was a millionaire! This £9,297 was 250 times my first month's salary (£35) when I started teaching four months later.

On 5 June I judged at the Cheshire County Show, where my champion was Coed Coch Seirian, at 20 years of age looking better than ever. Reserve champion was Coed Coch Madog who was, of course, her grandson, so he could not object to that! My father spent two months in Machynlleth Chest Hospital, and I took him a marked catalogue on my way home. He agreed that, if of equal merit, he would also always favour the female over the male. My father was elected an Honorary Life Vice-President of the WPCS for having been a member for 42 years and member of council for 27 years. The RWS was held at Aberystwyth on 24–26 July, and the local Gogerddan Pony Club members were invited to stage a historical pageant which took place in the Main Ring each day. It was great fun rehearsing this pageant for several weeks. We were very fortunate in being able to borrow five carriages – which had not been used for 40 years – from Mrs Powell, Nanteos mansion, and we drove these carriages through the streets of Aberystwyth a few times to get the horses used to crowds. The 40,615 attendance on the second day was the highest ever recorded to date and a loss of £6,881 in 1956 was turned into a profit of £7,810.

This was the first year of the Sir Bryner Jones Memorial award, the highest accolade of the RWAS, which went to Captain Bennett Evans, who farmed 4,000 acres at Manod, Llangurig. Sir Bryner Jones, the Welsh Secretary to the Ministry of Agriculture, had been closely involved with the RWAS and was president in 1954, the year of the mud at Machynlleth. I was honoured to receive this award in 2002 for my contribution to Welsh ponies and cobs. Mr Theron Wilding-Davies, Fayre Stud, judged the section As and there was a very satisfactory entry of 73 in six classes. Mr Emrys Griffiths was champion and reserve with the mare Revel Springsong (dam of Twyford Sprig that we had at Ceulan for 19 years until his death in 1994 at 29 years), and the yearling filly Revel Joain by Owain Glyndwr, who was exported two months later to Mr Goodrich of Texas. The previous year at Merthyr Show, I bought a roan filly foal Dyrin Jennifer (Ceulan Revolt x Criban Vanity) from Mr Gwyn Price, and another foal (which I registered as Ceulan Calypso) by Tanffynnon Twm Shanco out of Gwen Tafarn Jem, from my father's cousin Evan Davies. Calypso was placed third to Revel Joain and Jennifer was 'also ran'. Miss Mary Brough, Eryl Stud, offered me £100 each in cash for them, which I gladly accepted. I had never had so many pound notes on me, and was relieved when I got them home safely that night. The ponies stayed on at the showground, and you can imagine my horror on arriving on the last day to find half the showground under water, and exhibitors sailing in canoes. My immediate fear was for the two fillies but, despite having water up to their knees, they were none the worse.

MOVING TO SOUTH WALES

In July, I completed my Ph.D. and looked for a post teaching Chemistry. I was called to an interview at Porth County School for Boys in the Rhondda valleys and secured the post to start in September. I had never previously been to the Rhondda, but knew of the school through Ruth, who had been a pupil at the Porth Country School for Girls next door. I found lodgings at £20 a month with Mrs Cryer at 35 Davies Street, Porth who was an excellent cook. The headmaster was Mr W. J. Howells who was himself a chemist. At the end of every month, all the teachers queued outside the headmaster's office for their salaries, which Mr Howells counted out in cash. My first salary was £37, and I was very envious of senior teachers in front of me in the queue who were paid double or more. I was lucky to have Mr Cledwyn Kiff as senior Chemistry master – he had a great sense of humour, and as someone new to the job, he gave me every encouragement and assistance.

The entrants to Porth County (about 100 a year) were siphoned off as the top layer from all the Rhondda 11-year-olds who sat the entrance examinations, and the remaining pupils were sent to Ferndale, Tonypandy, Pentre and Porth secondary schools. It was so easy teaching Chemistry to classes such as Form IIIA – they were brilliant young minds, and many went on to be university professors, consultants and leaders in industry. To get pupils from Form III up to 'O' level took three years, but many would have passed easily at the end of their first year. I have kept in regular contact with a few who, by now, have retired from important positions. I am constantly amazed when some still come up to me at our local supermarket and introduce themselves. I cannot have changed much in 58 years!

I was soon elected onto the Rhondda Urdd Committee, the chairman then being the Rev Alban Davies, minister of Bethesda Congregational Chapel, Ton Pentre. Along with the Welsh teachers

Ifan Dalis Davies and Berian Davies, we formed a concert group, and were in great demand all over the Rhondda and further afield. I have kept press cuttings from the *Rhondda Leader* describing the concerts where I sang 'cerdd dant' to my own harp accompaniment. Until I acquired an estate car, I transported the harp on a roof rack, which was not very satisfactory if it rained. Our concert group represented Glamorganshire in the BBC Wales talent competition 'Sêr y Siroedd', where I was the 'cerdd dant' representative. In 1957 we were paired against Merionethshire, and were knocked out in the first round. The following year we were against Denbighshire, and survived until the third round. For every round, we were paid £2 by the BBC.

The FO Sale took place on 5 October, with 157 entries, of which 135 sold for £7,973, averaging £59. I collected Mr Vern Rider from Cardiff railway station the previous day, and his presence, and the general interest in ponies overseas, sent prices rocketing. The top price was a commission bid of 250 gns for a filly foal, Revel Sugar Bun, from American Mr Montgomery of Warrenton, Virginia. The top price for a Revel filly foal the previous year was 46 gns for Revel Buttercup, sold to Mr Wilding-Davies. Mr Rider bought ten, and the top price he paid was 225 gns for the two-y-o filly Vaynor Jennifer from Mr David Meredith of the Vaynor Stud, Merthyr Tydfil. There were a few section Bs offered. Mrs Binnie of Brockwell Stud bought the yearling filly Fayre Ladybird for 85 gns, and in 1959 Ladybird produced the top sire Brockwell Cobweb, sired by Harford Starlight, which Mrs Binnie found in a pigsty in the Elan Valley. Mrs Binnie also bought Criban Ester (daughter of Criban Marian Sais) for 80 gns, and she sold her for 410 gns on the 1961 sale. For myself, I bought the cream colt foal Revel Neon (Criban Winston x Bolgoed Nymph) for 50 gns. He was a very successful sire for us, and after he served his time at Ceulan I sold him as a premium stallion on the Gower, where he was equally successful.

Mr Rider was still short of another 36, and we spent a frantic three days visiting Fayre (where he bought seven), Vaynor (seven), Revel (two), Rhiw (four), Rhulan (two), Blaen (four), Cefn (two), Bryn (two), Bryniau (two), Gurnos (two), Parc (one), Vardra (one) and Dovey (one). The seven from Vaynor could only be seen in the far distance, and they had never been handled. Since I was in charge of cross-country running at Porth County, the running training was done on the Brecon Beacons for a few weeks, assisting the Vaynor shepherds, Bryn Morgan and Clive Loring, to round up Mr Rider's purchases. My next task was to pay for the 36 additional ponies and arrange the collection and transport of 46 ponies to Gordonsville, Virginia. Jones Brothers, auctioneers in Builth, expanded their Epynt Sale to two days on 15–16 October, the first at Llanafan and the second at Cwmowen, with a top price of 148 gns for the filly foal Cwmnantgwyn Lucy. RB&B had 300 entries at their Hay-on-Wye Sale, mainly foals.

Exports to the USA during 1958 reduced to 344 (from 472 in 1957), but exports overall were up, due to Canada purchasing 322 (up from 73 in 1957). The biggest American purchaser was Mr Rider, who asked me to find 50 for him, and I selected seven males and 43 females, including 14 from Vaynor (£1,726), 10 from Fayre and six from Revel. This large consignment took a lot of organising, and some Porth County pupils assisted with the catching on the Brecon Beacons once again. We got them all assembled and delivered safely to Glasgow. The other American purchases during 1958 included our old rival Bolgoed Atomic, who went to Dr Wilbur Ball of Illinois. The 322 to Canada were a bit of a mystery. Two hundred and ninety-six of them all went to one family, and they were mainly from Carcwm (33), Orgwm (26), Penrhos (24) and Derwen (21). Their export was rather haphazard, as many had arrived in Canada before their export documents were applied for. This family bought only 20 in 1959 and none thereafter.

As a result of the 1908 Commons Act, the Board of Agriculture and Fisheries allocated grants to pony premium stallions to run out on the commons, and in 1913 nine premiums each of £5 were awarded to the Long Mynd (Church Stretton) and Epynt mountains. The judges, a veterinary surgeon and a representative from the board would travel to various centres to inspect the stallions and allocate premiums. These inspections continued throughout the war years at ten areas: Long Mynd, Epynt, Black Mountains (East), Black Mountains (Trecastle), Cefn Bryn (Gower), Fairwood and Pengwern (Gower), Mynydd Illtyd, Vaynor and Pontsarn, Penybont Common (Radnorshire) and Aber Hills (Caernarfonshire). By 1958 the areas had increased to 24, and the judges, Miss Brodrick and Mr Douglas Meredith, with Mrs Alison Mountain as recorder, would travel to each of these areas, starting on the Aber hills and travelling down to the Gower and Ebbw Vale. I went to meet them at Pontlottyn and travelled with them to Trefil and Ebbw Vale, where I took some photographs of the judges with Clan Gille, which the local society had leased from the Revel.

The inspection for four areas – Aberyscir, Hundred House, Llandefalle and Llangorse – was postponed until 2 April to coincide with one of the most important British eventing fixtures, the Glanusk One-Day Horse Trials, which had 120 horses competing over 28 fences in Glanusk Park, Crickhowell. To attract more Welsh pony spectators to the horse trials and premium inspection, open show classes were offered. Lord Kenyon won the championship and reserve with his dun stallion Gredington Hynod (f. 1953, Coed Coch Madog x Coed Coch Sidan), and grey stallion Coed Coch Planed (f.1952, Coed Coch Madog x Coed Coch Pelen). In the catalogue for the fiftieth anniversary show on 3 May 2008, I wrote the history of the 50 years and illustrated it with my photographs of Hynod and Planed at the first show. Hynod was sold to the USA in September, only to return to Lt Col Sir Harry Llewellyn's Foxhunter Stud five years later.

My father judged at Pontypridd on Whit Saturday, and stayed down in south Wales for the Merthyr Show on 26 May, where there were classes of 10 to 20 entries for judge Mr Rowland Harris. With Bolgoed Atomic having left for the USA, Wellfield Stud showed Glascoed Mervyn, who was champion. Gurnos Stud won the yearling class with Gurnos Lucy (Bowdler Blighter x Revel Foam), which I bought and sent to the Vardra Stud, Pontypridd, to join the other ponies that I had 'on tack' with Tom and Barbara Williams and their daughters Diane, Liz and Rosie. On 28 June I judged at the Pengam and Fleur-de-Lys Show. It was customary in those days for the judge to drive the harness exhibits, and Cadle Starlight gave me a good drive and won the class.

Next was the RWS at Bangor on 23–25 July, where HM The Queen was planned to attend and present the Queen's Cup, which would be offered to every livestock breed in rotation. Unfortunately, a last-minute illness prevented Her Majesty from attending, and the Cup went to Wellfield Stud's section A barren mare Shan Cwilt. This was a surprise to all, since Shan Cwilt had never won anything before, and was shown without success afterwards at several other shows before being exported to the USA at the end of the year.

When an animal wins the Captain Howson (A), Coed Coch (B), Chetwynd (C) or George PofW (D) RW trophies, I think it is best to retire them that day, because they only rarely repeat this achievement. Shan Cwilt appeared at Gower Show on 7 August and was seventh out of nine mares, and third out of five at North Breconshire on 23 August. Coed Coch Symwl was second in the mare class, and she was sold to Lord Kenyon the following September on the Coed Coch Sale for the record price of 1,150 gns, with the description that she had won 10 championships, 17 reserve championships and 37 first prizes. Coed Coch Madog won the stallion class from Gredington Hynod, and Coed Coch also won two more classes with Madog progeny, the 2–3-y-o filly class, with the elegant Coed Coch Pelydrog. Coed Coch Salsbri won the yearling colt class, and his greatest claim to fame later was as the sire of the two full-brothers Coed Coch Bari (f. 1971) and Coed Coch Saled (f. 1963), which sold for 21,000 gns and 14,000 gns respectively at the 1978 Coed Coch Dispersal Sale.

My father judged next at Abergavenny Show on 30 July. Royal Reveller was champion, and for reserve he preferred the barren mare winner, the big and rangy Revel Rosette, over the brood mare, the small and 'dumpy' Revel Choice. The four south Wales shows – Pontypridd, Merthyr, Pengam and Abergavenny – were discontinued in the 1980s. Ceulan Valentine had a rather nice colt foal by Pendock Puccini, which we named Ceulan Valentino. He won first prizes at Aberystwyth (6 August), United Counties (15 August) and Tal-y-bont (3 September). Valentino was sold after weaning to Mr John Goronwy Jones MRCVS, of Bronllwyn Stud, for whom he won many championships and WPCS medals. Two Ceulan Revelry progeny, Royal Reveller and Bryn Shaun, were champion and reserve at the United Counties. My father judged at Eglwysbach on 9 August, where three classes were all won by Coed Coch-bred ponies – Coed Coch Planed and Coed Coch Seirian, owned by Lord Kenyon, and the exceptional Coed Coch Pelydrog won the youngstock class.

After the show, we were able to visit Eglwysbach vicarage, where I had spent many of my holidays with my mother's sister Josie and her husband, the Rev Cecil Jones and their daughter Anwen. I judged at Barged on 30 August, where Lyndon and Jean Evans, Tyla Morris, Pentyrch, won the mare class with Ty'r Bryn Fenella. This was the first time they had exhibited Welsh ponies, and they went on to become major breeders. The Lampeter Show was cancelled because of the waterlogged showground. Finally, the Brecon Show was on 20 September, and the judges were the Misses Mary Pennell and Rosemary Philipson-Stow. Mr Emrys Griffiths won the stallion class with the grey Bowdler Brewer (RW ch 1961), the mare class with the grey Revel Rosette (RW ch 1959), the two-y-o class with the palomino Revel South Wind and the yearling class with Revel Caress (RW ch 1963). Having won so many first prizes, Mr Griffiths had a handler problem when it came to the championship. He showed Rosette, who was champion, Mr Griffiths' cousin Mr Phil Morris showed Brewer, Mrs Griffiths showed South Wind and Mrs Alison Mountain, who was there as a spectator, was roped in to show Caress, who was reserve champion. Second to Caress was Mr Llewellyn Richards' bay Criban Fay that I bought in 1966 and I won many championships with her.

The FO Sale planned to be held at the stud on 4 October had to be moved indoors to Hereford Market because the farm was waterlogged. Mr Wilding-Davies himself set up a FO Sale record when he bought the three-y-o filly Criban Bantam Bird for 460 gns. American Mrs Mollie Butler bought the second highest, a two-y-o filly, Hinton Alloy, for 380 gns. Miss Brodrick bought the two-y-o filly Twyford Columbine (Twyford Moonshine x Reeves Coral by Ceulan Revolt) for 300 gns. Twelve Revel colt foals sold for between 10 gns and 85 gns, and eight fillies between 60 gns and 300 gns. There were 240 entries and 159 of them sold for £12,269, an average of £77.

In April 1959 I was appointed Assistant Lecturer in Chemistry at Llandaff Technical College, where I remained for 31 years. In 1959 there were 81 members of staff in four departments, with about 100 full-time and 1,000 part-time students. It is now Cardiff Metropolitan University, with 17,000 students, 19 partner institutions, eight in the UK and eleven overseas. I accompanied my great-nephew Jonathan (his grandmother is my older sister) to the Cardiff Metropolitan University graduation ceremony in July 2014, and 4,200 students graduated at the Cardiff Millennium Centre over two days. In 1959 the principal was Mr Joseph Cotterell, an electrical engineer who was certainly the right man in the right job at the time. He expanded the college by adding all types of new courses, and the expansion meant a greater status for the staff. I was promoted to Lecturer, Senior Lecturer, Principal Lecturer and Deputy Head of Department. The biggest department by a long way was the Department of Engineering (34 staff) with Mr William Norris as head, followed by Science and Mathematics (25 staff) under head Mr Glyn Phillips, who was transferred with some junior courses from the Welsh College of Advanced Technology, Cathays Park, the Department of Building and Construction with 12 staff, and the head was Welsh-speaking Mr Alun Humphreys, and a very small Department of Commerce of four staff. I found really homely accommodation for myself and my two harps at Ruthin Gardens, Cathays with the Rev John Henry Griffiths (from Ystumtuen), Mrs Bessie Griffiths and their children, Dolig and Illtyd. Mr Griffiths' sister was Mrs Polly Hughes of Pencwm Farm, Penrhyncoch, and I knew the family. It was from Ruthin Gardens that I went to our wedding in April 1961.

One of the first incidents I encountered at Llandaff was in October 1960 when the river Taff burst its banks and flooded a large area of Cardiff, including Llandaff Technical College, to a depth of four feet. The underground boiler house was flooded, so there was no heating for four weeks. The bottom two rows of books in the library were covered with a thick slime, and trees, debris and carcasses of dead animals that had been washed downstream were found in various rooms. All the staff were asked to wear wellingtons and waterproofs, and we cleaned out the whole college in one day. Until the boiler was functional again, staff and students wore overcoats and scarves.

When the 1960–61 session started, the Department of

Engineering had been split into separate mechanical and electrical departments, and the Department of Science and Mathematics remained as such, but with Chemistry and Biology taken out to form a new department with Dr Donald Lewis, an organic chemist, as head. Dr Will Hughes was responsible for Chemistry, Mr John Marsden was responsible for Biology, with six members of staff between them – myself, Dr Jim Moody and Mr Roy Vaughan-Williams for Chemistry, and Mrs Margaret Jones, Mr Helig Jones and Mrs Non Powell (mother of Miss Kay Powell, later national president of Aberystwyth OSA) for Biology. I knew Will Hughes from my Aberystwyth days, where he obtained his first degree then went to Cambridge, where he obtained his PhD.

An innovation of Mr Cotterell's in the Department of Science and Mathematics was a course for chiropodists with Mr Derek Ames in charge. Mr Howard Jones was responsible for Mathematics and Mr Bill Mason for Physics. One lecturer in Electrical Engineering was Mr A. D. (Bill) Thomas, an accomplished harpist who played at our wedding. Bill and Buddug retired to Llandre (next village to Tal-y-bont), and Bill lived to 95 years of age.

The college at Llandaff was a two-floor front teaching block on the left of the entrance, three floors on the right and with the Engineering and Building single-story workshops behind. The front section is still there, but the workshops were demolished and numerous enormous structures built, including the College of Art, which relocated from Howard Gardens in 2014. The laboratory for practical chemistry was on the second floor of the front building, from where we could see all the traffic on Western Avenue. One of my earliest students was Elaine Williams from Michaelstone-le-Pit, who was a very successful showjumper on the south Wales circuit riding Grange Popit, and often beating David Broome riding Ballan Lad. A very unpopular class was Chemistry practical on a Friday afternoon until 5p.m. I would watch out for Stan Mellor's very smart sports car arriving about 4.30, and would whisper to Elaine that she could leave as long as the principal didn't see her! After they were married, Stan Mellor was champion National Hunt jockey for three years in a row, and Elaine has been described as the 'best woman rider in racing history'. Other early 'horsey' students were John Pritchard and his sister Mary (Mrs Griffiths), who bred cobs with the Brynawelon suffix. They owned Rhystyd Welsh Maid, who produced the noted harness horse Brenin Brynawelon in 1968 by Hendy Brenin. I sold the section A stallion Pendock Mercury to their neighbour, and in 1971 he got in with the cob mares. Since he was only 11.2 hands, and both mares were over 15 hands, it was thought that all would be well, but in 1972 they both produced section C colt foals, Dafydd Brynawelon and Llewelyn Brynawelon by Mercury, and I felt obliged to buy them both.

Not having any family commitments, I was keen to carry on doing research into reaction kinetics in the evenings, and I was given access to some very sophisticated equipment at the Chemistry department of the Welsh College of Advanced Technology, which became the University of Wales Institute of Science and Technology (UWIST) in 1967. I published my results in the *American Journal of Physical Chemistry* in 1961. As a result of this, the college was awarded a Department of Science and Industry research grant from the government to purchase our own apparatus. Principal Cotterell was very impressed, and insisted that my report and my photograph be published in the *Western Mail* and *South Wales Echo*. The following week, when I bought some gates at a farm sale, Mr Robert Thomas (of Herbert R. Thomas and Son), amidst much amusement, asked, 'Is it you or the government paying for these?'!

Although we had about 60 full-time chemistry students, most of our students were part-time, on day release from companies in the local chemical industry, following the Ordinary National Certificate (ONC) course one day and one evening a week. For the biggest employers, we would visit the site to enrol students, including British Resin Products, Guest Keen Iron and Steel, Guest Keen and Nettlefolds, Midland Silicones at Barry (which later became Dow Corning) and BP. With plenty of full-time students, a college rugby team was formed, and the first captain was David de Lloyd, a grandson of Professor de Lloyd, a former professor of music at Aberystwyth. Ruth's uncle Robert graduated from Cardiff University in 1912 and held a teaching post in Aberystwyth, where he married a member of the de Lloyd family. He was killed in the First World War before his daughter Roberta was born. Roberta lived on at Aberystwyth and married Mr Hywel Watkins, headmaster of Aberystwyth Secondary School.

Another of Principal Cotterell's innovations in 1962 was the setting up of a course for dieticians. We had nine students in the first year and, until a dietician, Miss Gwen Powell, was appointed, I was directed to be in charge of the course. I knew nothing about Dietetics, but the administration was the same as for any other course. My colleague Roy Vaughan-Williams taught Chemistry to the Dietetics students, and ended up marrying one of them, Elaine Watkins. By 1962, our successful ONC students were eligible to proceed onto the Higher National Certificate (HNC) course, and we were given approval to stage these courses. To cope with all these additional courses a third phase was built, and was officially opened by Sir Edward Boyle, Secretary of State for Education and Science, in 1963. The biggest boost to our part-time courses came in 1981 with the transfer of part of Amersham International from Buckinghamshire to north Cardiff, near exit 32 of the M4. Dr John Maynard was transferred from Amersham to be manager of the site. He was extremely helpful to the college, and served on the Science Advisory Committee for many years. Jim Moody took up a post at the College of Advanced Technology in 1965, and Will Hughes moved to be head of department at Liverpool Technical

College, which left me promoted to be in charge of chemistry at Llandaff.

Mr Cotterell was very keen that the staff should socialise and get to know one another. He would hold monthly dances in the main hall, and if a member of staff did not attend, he or she would be summoned to the principal's office to explain their absence. On these occasions, tea and sandwiches were provided, and in 1965 he was persuaded to include a licensed bar, after which the attendance improved dramatically! Mr Cotterell organised an annual Christmas carol service at Llandaff Cathedral in 1955 with a choir made up of staff and students. Len Starr from the Engineering Department was conductor, and my Chemistry colleague Bryan Ashmead was organist, on what must be one of the finest organs in Britain. Retired members of staff were invited to the service in 2005 to mark its fiftieth anniversary. Mr Cotterell also encouraged the staff to put on an annual St David's Day concert in the Main Hall, where I usually accompanied soloists on the harp.

I was president of the 1977 National Cerdd Dant Festival held at the Tal-y-bont Memorial Hall, where the opening address was given by Lady Amy Parry-Williams, who had been the adjudicator when I qualified for the final of the solo competition at the Bangor Inter-college Eisteddfod. The comperes were Mr Geraint Lloyd Owen of Pwllheli, Mr J. R. Jones of Tal-y-bont and the Rev R. Alun Evans, Cardiff, and chairman was Mr Huw Huws, Felingyffin, who was a cousin of my father's. The event was advertised thus: 'They say you will hear harp music in heaven. You need not wait that long – come along to Tal-y-bont on 12 November'! This festival turned out to be the most successful to date, and since then has become one of the major events in the Welsh cultural calendar.

In 1966 another college was opened within the city at Rumney, and our lower level courses were transferred there. In 1970 the college was upgraded to the Llandaff College of Technology. Dr

Donald Lewis left Llandaff to become principal of a college in the north of England, where he died at a young age, and Mr John Marsden took over as head of department. In 1967 the first full-time Higher National Diploma (HND) course was established at Llandaff, in Applied Biology. I had become an associate member of the Royal Institute of Chemistry (later renamed the Royal Society of Chemistry) as soon as I was eligible in 1956. We had a very strong branch of the RIC in south Wales, and I was a member of the committee for many years, along with Professors A. G. Evans and Anthony Jackson of the university, Professor David Williams of UWIST and secretary Mr Ken Thomas. Both Professor Jackson and Mr Thomas were our external examiners, and one lecture every year was held at Llandaff. The visiting lecturer in December 1980 was Professor Orville Thomas (University of Salford), who was a lecturer in my Aberystwyth days, and he stayed with us on the farm at Miskin.

When we began holding HNC and Licentiateship courses at Llandaff, I was promoted to fellowship of the RSC, and elected to be the honorary representative, which involved an annual trip to London where I would meet up with the representatives of the other colleges. By 1976 there were four advanced colleges in Cardiff – the Cardiff Teacher Training College (est. 1945) at Cyncoed, with principal Mr Len Bewsher and 93 staff, the Cardiff College of Food Technology and Commerce (est. 1957) at Colchester Avenue, with principal Mr Leslie Smith and 108 staff, the Cardiff College of Art (developed from the Cardiff School of Science and Art, est. 1865) at Howard Gardens, with principal Mr Derrick Turner and 48 staff, and Llandaff with 180 staff. It was hoped that they, along with the Welsh College of Music and Drama, would merge at some point, but the latter was opposed to any form of federation, and wished to keep its separate identity. So the other four colleges merged in 1976 under the name South Glamorgan Institute of Higher Education.

Dr Ernest Brent was appointed principal, with Mr Cotterell as deputy principal, and Messrs Bewsher, Turner and Smith as assistant principals. In 1973 we had started another new course at Llandaff – Speech Therapy – and again, I was course tutor until a qualified speech therapist, Mrs Auriole Gough, was appointed. Mr John Marsden transferred to Colchester Avenue in 1971, and biologist Dr John Juniper, from a London college, was appointed head of department.

In 1976 the college was asked to put on a full-time HND course in Medical Laboratory Sciences for Libyan students and, as deputy head of department, I accompanied Mr John Clarke to Libya for two weeks to organise a course and enrol 50 students. The enrolling was conducted in the mornings, mainly around Tripoli, and the afternoons were free for us to travel to historic sites such as Leptus Magna, and I persuaded our chauffeur to take us to visit a few Arabian horse studs!

In 1984 I was invited to judge at two shows in Australia, one in Sydney and one in Melbourne. With the co-operation of other members of staff I finished lectures at Llandaff on the Wednesday afternoon, flew to Australia, judged at two shows (which will be described later) and was back for lectures the following Tuesday. This was very demanding, and set me thinking about retirement, but I had thirteen years to go before my official retirement age of 65. Although I thoroughly enjoyed my 33-year career in chemistry and made many friends, whom I still meet monthly, when I was offered early retirement in 1989, I took the opportunity.

Since then, none of my judging commitments in South Africa, Canada and New Zealand have been as hectic as my Australian experience. I had been appointed examiner to the WJEC 'A' level in Chemistry in 1980, and continued with this for another ten years after my retirement. I marked mainly the examination scripts written through the medium of Welsh, and was very impressed with the development made over the years. The problem with this undertaking was that deadlines had to be met, and all the scripts had to be marked by a certain date and then assessed by the other examiners. Invariably, these enormous parcels of scripts would arrive at the same time as mares foaling or dates of shows, so I decided to retire from this commitment after twenty years, and did ten years of lecturing, one afternoon a week, in Equine Studies at Pencoed Agricultural College .

Back to 1959: Mr Rider's Welsh mountain pony needs had been satisfied with the 50 which I bought for him in 1958, and this time, he instructed me to buy six hackney ponies under 12 hands for him at Mr Frank Haydon's sale at Shovelstrode Farm, East Grinstead, on 19 May. I bought five on the sale for £724 and a sixth privately from Mr Jack Havard of Gorseinon for £200. They were shipped in June, and Mr Rider was very pleased with them, but whether they were used for breeding pure-breds or part-breds, I was never told. Our other 1959 American exports were Ceulan Carol, Gurnos Lucy, Revel Whimsical and Revel Willow to Dr Ray Crist of Washington. While I was at Vaynor Stud the previous year buying for Mr Rider, I bought for myself an untouched seven-y-o bay mare, Vaynor Sian by Owain Glyndwr (bred by Lady Wentworth), and with help from David Reynolds, managed to get her to the Vardra Stud, Tonteg, where I had collected a few others, such as Ceulan Strawberry Princess (f. 1957, Ceulan Revolt x Strawberry Queen, daughter of the champion riding pony of the year, Criban Biddy Bronze), and also had there the stallion Ceulan Gondolier (Clan Gylen x Ceulan Valentine). Again with help from David Reynolds, we managed to get Vaynor Sian to Banwen Show on 20 June, and Mr Vivian Eckley placed her second in a large class to Criban Fay.

David was never a keen driver and, with Land Rover and trailer, it was his older brother Cei who was roped in for the driving. Miss Beryl Prior of the Marsh Stud, New Romney, Kent, sent

Marsh Crusader to be produced by David and Cei at Dowlais, and Beryl and Cei were married in 1963. Miss Lorna Gibson of the Springbourne Stud, Newbury, asked David to show her cob stallion Madeni Welsh Comet, and Lorna and David were married in 1965. When I bought Vaynor Sian, she left behind at Vaynor Stud her yearling daughter Vaynor Serenity, who was sold to Lord Kenyon, who sold her on the 1958 FO Sale to Sinton Stud for 230 gns.

In 1960 Serenity produced Sinton Solomon, sire of two of the top sires of the breed Bengad Nepeta (f. 1967) and Cui Mi'Lord (f. 1970). Serenity was lot 105 on the FO Sale, and lot 106 was an un-named colt foal sold to Mr Jack Lloyd, Meiarth for 30 gns, and later registered as Gredington Oswallt, sire in 1963 of Menai Fury, who sired the great Synod William in 1969. I sold Vaynor Sian to Foxhunter Stud in June 1963, and one month later she was second at the RWS to Crossways Dimple. The show was held at Margam Park on 22–25 July, with the RWAS taking advantage of the large population of Glamorgan. It turned a handsome profit of £6,855 after the heavy losses of the north Wales shows at Caernarfon, Machynlleth and Rhyl (loss of £6,881). The section A judge was Mr Alfred Williams, and his champion was Mr Emrys Griffiths' good-bodied Revel Rosette, who had won the mare class from Miss Brodrick's Coed Coch Siwan, and the winning stallion, Coed Coch Madog, was reserve champion.

My father's cousin Evan Davies had a little bay FS1 mare, Gwen Tafarn Jem (f. 1947) born on the Gower, out of Kilvrough Fairy FS by Caerberis Imaway. It would have been beneficial to have had the dam of Kilvrough Fairy registered as FS, then Gwen's male and female offspring would be eligible for full registration, but it was never done. Nevertheless, Gwen produced such exceptional progeny that her ancestors were doubtless the result of half a century of implementing the stallion premium scheme on the Gower. At Margam, the section A youngstock champion was Mr

Douglas Evans' two-y-o filly (Tanffynon Twm Shanco x Gwen Tafarn Jem), and we were third in the yearling filly class with Ceulan Madam Butterfly (Pendock Puccini x Gwen Tafarn Jem), to Coed Coch Swyn (RW ch 1969), dam of Coed Coch Bari and Coed Coch Saled. Prima Donna was sold for the top price at Hay-on-Wye in May 1961 to Rowfant Stud, where she produced the 1970 RW female champion Rowfant Prima Ballerina (f. 1962) and the popular sire Rowfant Peacock (f. 1968). We sold Madam Butterfly (palomino) to Lord Kenyon in 1961, where she produced the top sire Gredington Serydd (Foxhunter Stud, f. 1961), Gredington Aron (f. 1963) and Gredington Bugail (f. 1964), who was sold with his dam to Denmark. Madam Butterfly was a champion mare for Egetofte Stud in Denmark and later started Mrs Inger Becker's Welsh pony stud in Sweden.

There were 15 section B entries in three classes (champion was Criban Victor) at Margam for judge Mrs Pennell, and 24 Welsh cob entries (champion was Parc Lady) in five classes for judge Mr John Berry. The section C situation was still dire – only four exhibits, won by Pride of the Prairie out of Piercefield Lady Lilian, second was Gerynant Rosina out of Dyffryn Rosina dam of Piercefield Lady Lilian, third was the stallion Teify Brightlight (RW ch eight times 1953–1964), and fourth was Llanarth Flying Saucer, dam of Llanarth Flying Comet (RW ch five times 1972–1978). Gerynant Rosina (dam of Synod William, f. 1969) was bought by Mr Cerdin Jones of Synod in April 1960 at Llanybyther market for £72, an event that changed the course of section C for ever.

A new show for us was the Monmouthshire on Thursday 27 August, where my father judged. His champion was Revel Rosette, and youngstock champion the three-y-o filly Weston Fair Lady by Coed Coch Planed. Her dam was Revel Fair Maid by Ceulan Revolt, a mare which made a big contribution to the formation of Weston Stud. The senior horse authority, Mr Fred Unwin, judged the palominos, and this was the first time we saw Bwlch Zephyr, who would become one of the greatest riding pony sires. Since buying the farm at Miskin, I have competed nearly every year, and commentated at, Monmouth Show. Almost sixty years later, it is still held on a Thursday. Monmouth has developed into the biggest one-day show in Wales, while the longer established Abergavenny and United Counties have ceased to exist. I judged at Brecon on 19 September, where Revel Rosette won another championship, this time with Coed Coch Planed reserve, and my youngstock champion was the yearling colt Vaynor Revolt, another sired by Ceulan Revolt. My co-judge for the riding ponies was Mrs Greta Phillips, author of *Horses in our Blood*, which was made into the film starring Robert Hardy. The next time I judged at Brecon was 55 years later in 2014, though I was commentator for many years, and won championships there several times.

The 1959 WPCS President was His Grace The Duke of Beaufort, who allowed a display of Welsh ponies and cobs within the Badminton Horse Trials. Despite the awful weather, the display was well received and persuaded some spectators, such as Mrs Doris Gadsden of the Bengad Stud, to become a leading breeder. 1959 can be regarded as the turning point in the fortunes of the Welsh pony section B. Up until then, section B sires were produced in various haphazard ways, but in 1959 four sires were born out of FS2 section B mares, which provided much-needed stabilisation. They were Solway Master Bronze, Downland Dauphin, Brockwell Cobweb and Chirk Crogan. Crogan's full-brother Chirk Caradoc (f. 1958) was also a much-needed sire. There was great excitement when Miss Brodrick conducted a sale of 89 section As and all her section Bs (31), with the exception of Coed Coch Berwynfa, and three mares at her stud on 26 September. There were also 21 riding ponies and 37 ponies from neighbour breeders. This event attracted an enormous attendance, including many from overseas, and was

Ceulan Venus with my brother-in-law John Richards

Ruth's father, Mr Walter Williams, in the snow near Ceulan in winter 1962–63

Our children David and Jane driving Ceulan Nipper, 1970

My father receiving the Brodrick Memorial Trophy, 1971

The tradition continued – David with Monkham Snow Bunting and Jane with Ceulan
Sapphire

WPCS parade handlers and participants, Benson & Hedges Show, 1974

With John Clarke in Libya enrolling students, 1976

Judging at Egetoftegaard, including Clan Jennifer and Ceulan Madam Butterfly, 1965

With HM The Queen and HRH The Duke of Edinburgh, Cardiganshire RWS, 1983

With Ruth in a carriage at the 1984 International Show in Ermelo, Holland

Sitting on one of the bronze statues made by Arthur Spronken, 1984

Before my talk in Sydney, Australia, 1984

David and Trefaes Taran at HOYS, Wembley, 1997

Reserve for the Gwyn Price Progeny Cup, RWS 1989 (from left): Ceulan Cariad, Catrin and Cantores

In South Africa with Ruth and Miss Sue Cook, vice-chairman WPCS SA, 1992

The screen says it all, RWS 1992

One of my proudest moments. With Jane, Ruth and David receiving my MBE at Buckingham Palace, 1995

With Mrs Alison Mountain, WPCS President Mrs Mary Edwards and our special birthday cakes, 1997

Glynmawr Petunia, winner of the supreme in-hand championship, New Zealand North Island Show, 1999

Ceulan Mariah winning the Edgar Herbert Trophy at Lampeter, 1997, with our grand-daughter Leah

(Photo: Arvid Parry Jones)

Ceulan Ceryl with David and his children (from left, Rachel, Joseph, Leah and Miriam), 2000

With HRH The Prince of Wales at the launch of my WPCS Centenary book, 2001

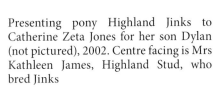

Presenting pony Highland Jinks to Catherine Zeta Jones for her son Dylan (not pictured), 2002. Centre facing is Mrs Kathleen James, Highland Stud, who bred Jinks

Jane and Simon's wedding, 2005

Rachel, Leah, Miriam and Joseph at Jane and Simon's wedding (clockwise from top)

the first time a Welsh pony had ever been sold at auction for four figures. This was the well-known winner Coed Coch Symwl, for which Lord Kenyon paid 1,150 gns. Next at 925 gns was Coed Coch Pwysi, that went to Canadian Governor Ross, and Mrs Alison Mountain of Twyford paid 900 gns for the bay Coed Coch Sws, whose son, the two-y-o Coed Coch Siglen Las, sold for 700 gns to Lord Swansea. The two daughters of the Vardra-bred Coed Coch Nans went to the USA – two-y-o Nerys, the foal she had when she visited Puccini at Ceulan, for 500 gns, and the Puccini daughter Neli for 300 gns. We bought three: Coed Coch Telor and the Madog daughter Melai Madlyn, which we sold in 1960 to the USA, and a top-class mare, Glascoed Tryfan, that we sold to Lady Muir of the Stoatley Stud, and regretted it when we saw her exceptional progeny in later years.

The 1959 FO Sale was an anti-climax, possibly because everyone was spent out after Coed Coch! One hundred and fifty-nine ponies were sold for £10,609, averaging £67. With exports to Canada reduced from 322 in 1958 to 23, and to the USA from 334 in 1958 to 224 in 1959 (and to 16 in 1960), it was encouraging to see the start of exporting to Holland with 17 (including some from the FO Sale), a figure which would increase to 1,500 in 1967 and 1,900 in 1972.

1960–1969

We attended 12 shows in 1960 and were the judges for half of them – my father and I judged three apiece. Starting with Aberystwyth on 25 May, Mr Ted Evans, Pitchford Stud, judged the cobs and Mr Llewellyn Richards, Criban, the section As. Overall champion was Coed Coch Symwl, with Teifi Welsh Maid reserve. There was a class of 19 section A yearlings won by Lord Kenyon's exceptional Whitepool Skylark sired by Coed Coch Planed out of Penarth Violet, which we had seen at the Radnor Show in 1950. In 1973 Skylark had a filly by Twyford Sprig registered as Taliaris Calypso, that was a very successful brood and show mare for Ceulan. When I judged at Cothi Bridge on 2 June, Teifi Welsh Maid was again champion, and champion section A was Kilvrough Delight II, that also spent some years at Ceulan. There were good cob entries at the RWS on 20–22 July, judged by Mrs I. M. Yeomans, and the champion was Parc Lady with Llwynog-y-Garth reserve. Section C entries were down to three of the regulars, and were placed in the order Teifi Brightlight II, Llanarth Flying Saucer and Pride of the Prairie. Criban Victor was section B champion with judge Mr Alfred Williams, and Downland Lavender reserve. Mr Gwyn Price judged section As, and Lord Kenyon must have thought he had made the correct decision at the Coed Coch Sale when his purchase, Coed Coch Symwl, was champion, and Coed Coch Madog reserve. Newcomers to Welsh ponies, Ivor and Pam Ridgeway of Banbury, having bought the bay Penmor Lovely Lady and the grey Betws Mai on the FO Sale, had great encouragement in a class of 19 two and three-y-o fillies when they were first and second. All three winning foals were sired by Coed Coch Proffwyd, who had been sold to Australia. We bought the winner, Eryl Alis, at Hay-on-Wye Sale, and she is another who was very successful for Ceulan.

At the Breconshire Show on 17 September, it was a clash of the titans. The judge was Swansea auctioneer Mr Rowland Jenkins of Kilvrough, whose father Mr T. E. Jenkins judged at the RW in 1930, and was WPCS President in 1939. Coed Coch Symwl was there after an almost unbeaten season, but Revel Rosette was entered at her only show that year. Mr Jenkins placed Symwl first and Rosette second in a class of 18, and Symwl went on to capture the championship. Gredington also won the stallion class with Coed Coch Planed, and the 29-strong yearling class with Whitepool Skylark. In 1963 the 1957 and 1959 RW champions, Revel Springsong and Revel Rosette, were sent to the warmer climate of Twyford Stud in Sussex to end their days, with alternate foals going to Twyford and the Revel. Springsong's 1965 foal Twyford Sprig was one that went to the Revel, fortunately for Ceulan, where he spent his last 19 years, and was undoubtedly the greatest sire we ever had at Ceulan.

Because there were 492 entries for the FO Sale, RB&B decided to extend it two days from 30 September to 1 October. It was not possible to have the Langford Sale Ring on the Friday because there was a long-standing agreement to hold a cattle sale there, and the Friday FO Sale was held outside. Unfortunately, it rained, which did not give much encouragement to purchasers. Equal top of the sale at 340 gns was the nine-y-o section A mare Downland Blythe Spirit and the two-y-o cream filly Betws Ebrill, that was sold after the death of her breeder Mr John Berry. Blythe Spirit, daughter of the beautiful Craven Bright Sprite, was one of the very few (16) exported to the USA in 1960. She went to Mr George North of Oregon. Betws Ebrill was bought by leading horsebox manufacturer

Mr G. C. Smith of Loughborough, who bought Dovey Dynamite the following May at Hay-on-Wye, and amassed a very large stud of top ponies over the next twenty years. We bought a bay yearling filly, Betws Nans, by Revel Crusader, with which we won the Velvet Cup for ridden ponies at the 1962 RWS.

Ruth and I were married on Easter Monday 1961 at Hebron Baptist Chapel, Ton Pentre, Rhondda, where her grandfather was minister for 40 years from 1888 until his death in 1928. Ruth was teaching at Bronllwyn Secondary School in nearby Ystrad, and amongst the guests were staff of Bronllwyn, Porth County and Llandaff schools, former Aberystwyth colleagues of mine and Ruth's and many members of the WPCS. Ruth's pupils also turned up at the chapel in droves! Ruth's bridesmaids were her university friend, Miss Pauline Rowe, and Miss Diane Williams, Vardra Stud, and my niece Janet Richards was flower girl. Dr Terry Williams was best man. The service was conducted by the Rev Griff Sorton Davies (Ruth's uncle) and the Rev D. O. Williams (my uncle). We went to the Compleat Angler Hotel at Marlow for our honeymoon, to be near enough to visit our friends, Gordon and Dorothy Gilbert, of the Reeves Stud, Penn, and to catch up with the Ceulan ponies they had. We had bought a new bungalow, No 2 Merthyr Street, Pontyclun, which was on the Cardiff to the Rhondda bus route, and about half way between Llandaff and Bronllwyn, where we worked. Mr and Mrs Albert Martin lived at Hillside Farm on the Hensol Road, Miskin, which he had worked as a market garden, but turned to grass when the work became too much for him. We were able to graze the ponies there as well as make use of the buildings, and we got to know them very well.

In May, we were asked by Mrs Alison Mountain of the Twyford Stud to look out for a cob mare of riding type for her to breed from and hunt in the winter to replace Collen Queen, who was now getting on a bit for hunting. My father was always a fan of the big Garibaldi cobs to be found in south Cardiganshire, and on 2 May we went to see a five-y-o daughter of Garibaldi Welsh Flyer, Madeni Duchess, with Mr Tom Thomas, Pantyrodyn, Newcastle Emlyn. After giving Mrs Mountain a favourable report, the price was agreed and transport to Sussex organised. What Mr Thomas had never told us was that Duchess had never been touched, but she was transported safely to Horsted Keynes. The following March, Duchess unexpectedly produced a very nice filly foal which Mr Thomas insisted on having back, saying we had only paid for one! Unfortunately, that was the only foal that Duchess produced, despite many attempts and expert veterinary attention. However, she won the RW ridden class twice and carried Mrs Mountain hunting for many years.

The RWS was held at Gelli Aur, Llandeilo on 25–27 July, the first time it had been held on a Tuesday, Wednesday and Thursday. The glorious weather brought out enormous crowds, which resulted in a fantastic profit of £15,142, which increased the reserves sufficiently to enable the RWAS to purchase the permanent Llanelwedd site for £38,497. Welsh pony and cob entries also exceeded 200 for the first time ever, led by the section As with 24 yearling fillies and 22 brood mares. With judge Captain Brierley, the Revel swept the board, winning the championship with the stallion Bowdler Brewer and the reserve with the mare Revel Choice. This was one of the very rare occasions when the great Coed Coch Madog suffered a defeat, standing third to Brewer and Coed Coch Socyn. Treharne Tomboy (RW ch 1967, 1968 and 1970) made his first RW appearance and, although he had plenty of admirers amongst the spectators, he did not find favour with Captain Brierley.

My father judged section Bs, and three of the four 'milestone' two-year-olds appeared. He placed them: first (and ch) Solway Master Bronze, second Brockwell Cobweb and third Downland Dauphin. Mr Dafydd Edwardes judged the cobs and reversed the customary form, placing Llanarth Braint male champion, but reserve overall to the indefatigable Parc Lady. Section Cs were the same four again in the order: Queenie, Pride of the Prairie, Gerynant Rosina and Llanarth Flying Saucer. A significant increase of interest in section C was beginning to become apparent, and their figures reached 10 by 1965, 100 by 1980, 200 by 1992 and 300 by 1995. There were many varied judging commitments, among them Bishop's Castle, a new show for me, and exhibitors whom I did not normally encounter – Miss Russell Allen, Miss Kay, Mrs Michael, Mrs Hambleton, Mr Dick Swain and Mr George Preece. We found a south Wales rider for Betws Nans – Sue Rowland of Bedwas – who rode her at Margam and Pyle Show on 12 August and was third to Greetings, ridden by Serena Morgan (now Mrs Pincus of dressage fame), and Fayre Knowhow, ridden by Jill Day, currently the biggest owner of ridden hunters in Britain. At the Tal-y-bont Show on 6 September, we won the mare class with Ceulan Valentine and also the foal class with her daughter, Ceulan Venus, who stayed with us for the rest of her life.

Apart from a few selective and expensive ponies, there were no sales to the USA and Canada. Instead, there were six mares sold to Denmark, 27 to Holland and eight to Sweden, an indication of greater things to come, to 38 mares to Holland in 1962 and 654 mares in 1964. The week before the FO Sale on 23 September, Lord Kenyon organised a collective sale of 126 ponies at Gredington, where the average price was £70, but with the top show fillies Coed Coch Sucr and Gredington Pefren selling for 800gns and 760gns to the USA. The two days of the FO Sale were arranged for a Saturday (30 September) and Monday (2 October), so that both sales could be conducted under cover. There were 445 lots, but nothing to cause much excitement. The Revel colt foals sold for between 12 and 32 gns and the fillies from 30 to 62 gns. The five-y-o palomino stallion Revel Solo topped the section As at 240 gns to Fayre Stud, from where he was exported to Japan in September 1964.

Mr Arthur McNaught of the Clan Stud, Lindfield, Sussex, had died in the summer, and his daughter Mrs Alison Mountain had married and moved to Twyford Farm, Horsted Keynes. Mr McNaught left nine stallions / colts and 12 mares / fillies to Mrs Mountain, and Mr J. J. Borthwick, Chairman of WPCS Council went to value them for probate on 9 October. Included amongst those valued were the two-y-o colt Clan Pip (RW ch 1963, 1964) valued at £35 and his full-sister the yearling filly Clan Peggy (RW ch 1966, 1967) valued at £40. Their dam Clan Prue was valued at £105, and her filly foal Clan Pin at £25. Mrs Mountain offered seven stallions / colts (Clan Cub, Dash, Dave, Dirk, Huc, Jug and Pip) and five mares / fillies (Doll, Heather, Jill, Peggy and Pin) to Mr Emrys Griffiths at valuation, on the condition that he bought them all. My father was invited to the Revel the day after they arrived (8 December), and remarked on returning home that he had seen the best two-y-o (Clan Pip) that he had ever seen, and he had seen many over half a century. Despite so many breeders (including myself) taking advantage of the services of Clan Pip, Mrs Mountain would never use him because he had King Cyrus (Arab), Sahara (Barb) and Cairo (Arab) in his pedigree within four generations. With this oriental blood, it is amazing that he had so much bone and substance and looked so 'Welsh Mountain'.

THE CEULAN STUD RELOCATES TO MISKIN

1962 was a year of change. For the WPCS, this was the first appearance of the now world-renowned Annual Journal, a 90-page publication (800 pages in the fiftieth journal in 2011), edited at short notice by Mrs Alison Mountain. We bought Hillside Farm, Miskin, in January, where we had use of the land and kept our ponies and those owned by David Reynolds. We moved into the house in July, when David was one month old, and changed its name to Ceulan, since there was another Hillside in nearby Mwyndy, and our mail was frequently delivered to the wrong one. Until we got some stabling sorted out, we decided not to show that year, but my father and I had several judging commitments and attended 26 shows altogether. The first show where my father judged was the Ponies of Britain Show at Ascot on 17 March, and I had arranged to collect a two-y-o colt, Shergolds Cinzano, and a 10-y-o mare, Dyrin Larina, which I had bought unseen. My father was not impressed, and advised me to offer the lady a profit to keep them, but they were only £90 for the two and they came back to Ceulan. He persuaded me to sell Cinzano at Hay-on-Wye in two months (at a loss!) to Mr Ivor Greenow of the Blaenau Stud, where he turned out to be a very valuable foundation sire. We still have the blood of Larina here, including Ceulan Lodes, whose pedigree goes back 55 years to Larina in only three generations, and Lodes' colt foal Ceulan Louis was sold to Nova Scotia on the 2014 FO Sale.

Lampeter Show was the next event experiencing change. A small local committee comprising of Mr D. O. Morgan (Chairman), Mr A. L. Williams (secretary) with Messrs Watt Davies, W. J. Thomas, Daff Davies, Sam Morgan, John Edwards and William Thomas, volunteered to organise the show previously done by WPCS staff, and attracted 25 entries in seven section A, B, C and D classes on 3 April, compared with 493 entries in 51 classes in 2015. I see that the best I achieved personally was in 1997, when our stallion Trefaes Taran was section A champion and reserve supreme to Blaengwen Brenin. Also in 1969 our two-y-o section C filly, Nantfechan Seren, was youngstock champion, a success repeated with a section A Ceulan Mariah in 1977. The John Evans Trophy for supreme was first awarded in 1989 and was won by the section B Cottrell Pendragon. This is the only time a section B has been supreme. In the 20 shows from 1989 to 2010, a section D has been supreme 12 times, section C four times and a section A and ridden twice each.

Glanusk Show followed on 5 May with 77 entries in six section A and B classes. The strongest class was for section A stallions, and the first three were greys Criban Bantam, Coed Coch Salsbri and Coed Coch Brenin Arthur. I fancied the bay stallion Criban Pep, standing fourth, and bought him jointly with David Reynolds for £70. We were also able to lease for the rest of the year a big section B grey colt, Sinton Gyration, which had won first prize. This was the first time I saw Brierwood Blue Boy, a stallion that was to produce pronounced dished heads with huge eyes and minute ears generally known as 'frog heads', a fashion which was to become all the rage for the next twenty years (although not with me!), but gradually became less popular when the emphasis became more performance-oriented.

On our way home at Pontsticill, I bought Tylerybont Queenie (which I sold to Denmark in Nov 1963), and a three-y-o filly Cwmgarn Bonnie, and David Reynolds bought her two-y-o sister Cwmgarn Heidi – never have two sisters been so different. I sold Bonnie commercially at Abergavenny, Heidi was overall supreme at Northleach in 1976, RW champion in 1977 and her daughter, Springbourne Hyfryd, was RW champion in 1975. On the FO Sale, amongst others, I bought the bay mare Bryn Celia by Ceulan Revelry, and the bay yearling filly Revel Siesta sired by Revel Light, my favourite when I stayed at the Revel. These were two of my luckiest purchases ever. I won the RW progeny competition in 1973 with Ceulan Celina, Celandine and Cygnet, three daughters of Celia, and the same competition in 1972, 1982, 1983 and 1984 with progeny of Ceulan Sprite, daughter of Siesta. We do not normally cover fillies at two years old, but Siesta was covered by Criban Pep and produced Ceulan Sprite in 1964.

There were 207 in-hand entries at the RWS held in Wrexham, where the champion section A was Revel Jewel, and she was also the winner of the new progeny competition introduced that year. The ridden Welsh cobs, with 12 entries, were judged by the hunter judge Mr Edward Farmer, who was full of praise for the winner, Madeni

Duchess. On the whole, the ridden Welsh cobs were a rather motley lot, including one mare which had her foal held outside the ring! At the 2014 RWS there were 145 ridden Welsh cob entries divided into three classes – stallions, mares and geldings – and a further 74 entries in the HOYS ridden qualifier class.

The next show for my father to judge was Royal Windsor on 12 May, where I took a photograph of HM The Queen and HRH Princess Anne inspecting the Welsh ponies. Then he judged at Pontarddulais, NPS Malvern, where his section A champion Twyford Gala was overall M&M Supreme, palominos at Abergavenny and section A at Anglesey County, where Coed Coch Anwyled was champion and the reserve was Tan Lan Wennol, the subject of many Charles Tunnicliffe watercolours. This was our first visit to the Vale of Glamorgan Show (where we have competed 52 times since), which was held on Penllyn Castle Park, the home of Mrs Serena Homfray where we were later frequent visitors. With the move still on, we were not organised for exhibiting ourselves, but certainly made up for it in the next 50 years by exhibiting at 1,177 shows!

The winter of 1962/63 is remembered for four weeks of deep snow and no running water – not the ideal situation to be introduced to living on a farm with a six-month-old baby. Ruth's parents were living in our bungalow, where luckily the water was still running, so we collected water from there and Ruth's mother kindly did our washing. I bought four Penllyn yearling colts at £25 each for a circus in Switzerland but, with the snow up to the top of the hedges, they had wandered away and there was no sign of them anywhere. When I was driving to college one morning, I met the ponies coming towards me on the main road. I managed to get them into a field owned by our friends Lyndon and Jean Evans of Pentyrch Stud, and phoned Ruth to arrange for Dilly Jenkins (uncle of the famous rugby player Neil Jenkins) to collect them and return them to Ceulan. They were none the worse for their adventure, and the *Western Mail* featured a photograph of them in the snow just before they left. By all accounts, they developed into a very popular circus act.

The WPCS AGM had to be postponed twice owing to the weather conditions, and was eventually held in March 1963. Another change during 1963 was the resignation of the Chairman of WPCS Council Mr J. J. Borthwick, a post he had held for thirty years. Then on 20 December, Miss Margaret Brodrick MBE, of Coed Coch, died suddenly at the age of 65. She had written a note to my father that day which he received the following day at the same time as learning of her death. I suppose over my life connected with the WPCS, my idols have been Miss Brodrick, Emrys and Dinah Griffiths of the Revel, Mrs Alison Mountain of Twyford and Mrs Nell Pennell, who had been my boss when I was elected assistant publicity officer in 1958.

We attended 30 shows in 1963 and, with new stabling, were able to exhibit Criban Pep and Revel Siesta, but Pep's main duty was covering the mares. We transported David Reynolds to the Ponies of Britain Show on 20 April to show Marsh Madcap for his brother and sister-in-law Cei and Beryl Reynolds. Next we went to Royal Windsor, where he showed Solway Master Bronze for Miss Miriam Reader and was first, and Madeni Welsh Comet for Miss Lorna Gibson, and was last! The Shropshire and West Midland Show had been a stronghold for Welsh ponies for half a century, it was the only show outside the RW to be allocated separate WPCS medals for males and females. In 1963 this show attracted 104 entries in eight classes. They also catered for novice stallions and novice mares, and we won the former with Criban Pep and were reserve male champion to Coed Coch Planed.

A new show for me to judge, which I had never attended previously, was Liverpool on 20 July, where I placed Whitepool

Skylark first in the mare class above the famous Coed Coch Symwl (who was barren that year and not showing herself as well as when she had a foal at foot), both owned by Lord Kenyon. Little did I suspect that in 1980 I would have Skylark's daughter Taliaris Calypso (f. 1973 by Twyford Sprig) at Ceulan, and she won the RW progeny competition with Ceulan Caredig, Ceulan Caryl and Ceulan Campus in 1993. My champion section B at Liverpool was Solway Master Bronze. His owner, Miss Miriam Reader, knew that he was a favourite of mine, and when she passed away in 2010 she left me a painting of Master Bronze by Alison Guest (1973) in her will, which now has pride of place at Ceulan.

The RWS on 23–25 July was the first to be held on the permanent site at Llanelwedd. Mr Emrys Griffiths was both section A champion and reserve with the six-y-o mare Revel Caress and the four-y-o stallion Clan Pip. Solway Master Bronze was champion section B for the third consecutive year, section C mustered 15 entries which warranted separate classes for males and females, with Gwynau Puss champion, and the George PofW Cup for champion section D left Wales for the first time ever in 55 years, won by Tyngwndwn Cream Boy, owned by Mr Eddie Price of Marlow.

On 1 August, I judged at the North Wales Show at Caernarfon, where my champion section A Tan Lan Wennol (we had several of her descendants at Ceulan from 1985) went on to win the Lord Penrhyn Cup for the best horse or pony in the show. My father then judged at the National Pony Show at Kempton Park on 3 August, where Madeni Welsh Comet was section D champion.

Then followed Bank Holiday week, when we attended five shows on consecutive days: Pontarddulais on the Monday, Aberdare on Tuesday (judge WD), Barry on Wednesday, Gower on Thursday (judge ESD) and the United Counties on Friday. The three-y-o Betws Nia, owned by Miss Rosie Russell-Allen, was champion at the last four. Siesta, although only two years old, was second in the any-age open class at St Mellons Show on 14 August, and first in the youngstock class on 17 August at Bedwellty, a show which was established in 1876.

Clan Pip then came to the Vale of Glamorgan on 21 August, where my father judged (they then catered only for section As), and was champion from Betws Nia. The following day we were reserve champion with Criban Pep at Llandeilo, and Siesta was second at Wenvoe on 28 and Bargoed on 31 August. The final show for us was Tal-y-bont on 4 September, where Ceulan Venus won the championship and WPCS medal.

In order to publicise the Welsh breeds outside Wales, a Midlands committee of Mrs Pennell, Miss Anne Wheatcroft, Mrs Joan Crotty (owner of Turkdean Cerdin), Mrs Ivor Reeves (breeder of large Welsh cob x thoroughbred part-breds), Mr Theron Wilding-Davies and Lt Col S. R. M. Jenkins organised a Welsh breeds show, named the Northleach Show, at Hempnett Farm, Northleach (home of Lt Col Jenkins), on 24 August. This show was a great success, attracting 368 entries in 38 classes, including 47 part-bred entries, which was an unexpected number considering that there were only 240 part-breds registered in the WSB. It was in fact a part-bred, the colt Criban Dash, who won the supreme championship. Over the 52 years of this show up to 2014 (50 shows, no show in 1965 or 2001), the supreme championship has been awarded to section A 15 times plus two ridden, section B seven times, section C five times plus two ridden and section D 17 times plus one ridden. Looking at the records which I compiled for their fiftieth show, I see Ceulan did best in 1979, winning with Ceulan Sidan (out of 32 yearling fillies), Ceulan Lindy Loo (novice brood mare), Ceulan Lady May (foal), and the Lord Vestey Cup for the exhibitor winning most points. The show outgrew the facilities at Hempnett, so it was then staged at Lord Vestey's picturesque Stowell Park, and more recently on the superb facilities at Cirencester Park. Entries for the in-hand classes have decreased over 50 years to 192 – 63 section As in 11 classes in 2014; 42 Bs, nine classes; 32 Cs, nine classes; 43 Ds, nine classes and 12 WPB in three classes but entries were boosted by 55 in the HOYS qualifying ridden classes.

On 30 July at RB&B's Hereford Market sale, Mr Dunn of Aylesbury dispersed his Tuckers Welsh Cob Stud. The stallions were Parc Express II (Mathrafal x Parc Lady, both RW ch) and Churchill II (Brenin-y-Bryniau x RW ch Sheila) and there were well-known names amongst the mares – Werndriw Peggy, Creuddyn Mair, Arthen Black Beauty, Meiarth Modern Maid, Meiarth Royal Maid, Rhystyd Welsh Maid, Cathedine Gwlith, Heather Polly and Chancerie Ray, and their progeny by Parc Express II and Llangybi Seldom Seen. This was possibly the best collection of Welsh cobs in the UK at that time. We bought Meiarth Modern Maid for £130, and later also bought the yearling cob filly Teilo Chocolate privately to keep her company. Teilo Chocolate was sired by Verwig Mathrafal out of the good show mare Wyre Star, who was also dam of Cathedine Gwlith and Cathedine Welsh Maid, g-dam of Ebbw Victor, RW male champion five times and overall in 1998.

There was encouraging trade on section As, mainly due to exports to Holland, which were 57 in 1963, increasing to 671 in 1964 and 1,276 in 1966, with a corresponding increase in membership to exceed 2,000 (up from 370 in 1954). The Gredington Collective May sale had outgrown its premises and was moved to Bangor-on-Dee Racecourse. The RB&B Hay-on-Wye Sale became more frequent, with sales on 25 April, 16 May, 13 June and 18 July, while the October sale was expanded to three days, and wooden stables were constructed at Hay-on-Wye to cope with exports. Auctioneers Eric Thomas and Harpur held a sale at Gurnos Farm, Merthyr Tydfil, on 21 September, and Foxhunter Stud on 3 October, and Jones Brothers had their sales at Cwmowen and Llanafan. There had been a trickle of exports to Denmark since Brierwood Honeyway, Derwen Lilly and Twyford Ribbon to Mr Holger Hvenegaard Lassen of Selleberg in 1961, followed by eight mares and six FS mares in 1962 and 12 mares in 1963, including Ceulan Cascade, Ceulan Honeymoon, Tylerybont Queenie and Highfields Highlight from Ceulan. The Dansk Welsh Mountain Pony Selskab was formed in 1963 with Mr Lassen as secretary and they produced their first Stud Book in March 1965.

We had offered two mares on the first RB&B FO Sale in 1955, where there were 114 ponies entered. The sale total was £2,876 and the average was £31. The next time we were in a position to sell at the FO Sale was in 1963 but we bought two, three or four in the seven intervening sales and have sold on every one of the 52 sales since 1963, sometimes two or three, seven in 1980 and 1982, six in six sales, five in ten sales etc. Our 1963 entry was the filly foal Ceulan Largo (Sinton Gyration x Dyrin Larina), who was the top foal, and when she returned to the FO Sale in 1973, was sold to New Zealand to join the RW champions Treharne Tomboy (A) and Kirby Cane Scholar (B) which had gone there the previous year.

We competed at 17 shows in 1964, starting with Aberystwyth on 23 May, where we took the cob mare Meiarth Modern Maid and her colt foal Ceulan Mandarin. It was asking for trouble to venture into the heartland of the Welsh cob, but she was placed third in a class of eight. Looking back, it seemed a lot of effort to transport a big cob mare and her foal 115 miles from Miskin to Aberystwyth to win £1! We took Celia and her foal Cygnet, and Siesta and her foal Sprite, to the Vale of Glamorgan Show on 19 August – the two foals sired by Criban Pep. Celia and Siesta both won their classes, and in the foal class, Cygnet was first and Sprite was third.

An exciting event on 9 December was a visit in her Rolls Royce of Mrs Jennifer Williams, wife of the TV broadcaster Mr Dorian Williams, who was looking for a young section A mare for South

African author Mrs Mackie Niven, and a filly foal for herself. I sold her Siesta for export on condition that I would keep her foal, Sprite, and I also sold her Cygnet for herself. One of Cygnet's progeny at Pendley / Fontley Stud was the 1976 HOYS Riding Pony of the Year Fontley Arabesque. Mrs Williams then sold Cygnet to Mrs Dorothy Cope to start her Beckside Stud in Harrogate and, amongst her many wins for Beckside Stud, she was overall supreme champion at the Ponies of Britain Show in 1972. Cygnet died at Beckside aged 34. Ceulan Sprite was then the sole representative of Revel Siesta in the UK, and was originator of the Ceulan 'S' dynasty which has representatives all over the world, including son and daughter Ceulan Sovereign (f. 1977) and Ceulan Sapphire (f. 1970) in Australia, and g-daughter Ceulan Shoned (f. 1984) in the USA. The most recent star of this family is Ceulan Shem, who was third Ridden Pony Of The Year at HOYS 2014.

We had several visitors from Denmark during 1964 and sold Ceulan Cascade to Mrs Gerda Fredbo Larsen, who had Lauritsminde Farm on Jutland, and Tylerybont Queenie to Mr Hvenegaard Lassen, who owned the Selleberg estate on Funen. Mr Lassen was so impressed with Wales that he returned to spend his honeymoon here later that year. Other Danish visitors included Dr Richter Jorgensen, who had a weekend residence and land near Kolding, and the brothers Michaelsen of Hedensted, who were surprised to discover that they had manufactured the central heating boiler which we had at Ceulan! We also sold Ceulan Honeymoon and Highfields Highlight to Lady Gerda Thornton and Mr Mogens Falk-Jensen who owned Egetoftegaard Farm near Helsinge on Zealand. Sir Gerard Thornton was a famous British scientist who was principal of Rothamsted Agricultural College and lived in St Albans. They had also bought the colt Gredington Aneirin by Coed Coch Madog and the mare Ceulan Madam Butterfly, and her colt foal Gredington Bugail by Coed Coch Planed, from Lord Kenyon, and the mares, the dun Alsa Rambling Rose and the palomino Shergolds Chiante from their breeders.

Miss Pauline Taylor of the Llanarth Stud had realised for some time that, while section A and B had the FO Sale at Hereford, there was no sale specifically for sections C and D. At the Llanarth Stud in 1948, Miss Taylor and Miss Barbara Saunders-Davies had bred the dark palomino section D stallion Llanarth Braint, the produce of a Breconshire riding-type stallion and a Cardiganshire harness-type mare, and they were about the only stud in Wales which took their cobs to compete at the major English shows, thereby advertising the breed over the border.

In another attempt to get the Welsh cob known further afield, they organised a sale of 62 section Cs and Ds (of which 23 were from Llanarth) on their Blaenwern Farm on 17 October 1964 (St Luke's Day, hoping for fine weather for an outdoor sale on a boggy field). Twenty-seven of the lots sold for £3,197, averaging £118. The top figure of 300 gns was paid by Mrs Betty Sowerby of the Arth Stud, Yorkshire (who bought Meiarth Modern Maid from us in June 1966 on condition that her colt foal Gwynfil Comet came back for Mr Tristan Jones), for the palomino yearling filly Llanarth Sissel, daughter of Llanarth Flying Saucer, whose other progeny include the multi-champion Llanarth Flying Comet, Llanarth Meteor and the Australian champion Llanarth Jack Flash. Next highest price of 210 gns was paid for the yearling colt Teify King, who had won his class at the RW. The section C stallion Gwynau Boy (RW ch 1963) sold for 200 gns and the two-y-o filly Faelog Frolic (RW ch 1979) sold for 100 gns. We sold the colt foal Ceulan Matador (Parc Express II x Meiarth Modern Maid) for 35 gns. Mrs Sowerby was top purchaser also on the 1965 sale, this time at 160 gns for the two-y-o filly Llanarth Winllan. The colt foal Tyhen Comet (RW ch 1966, 1969*) was bought by Mr John Hughes (owner of his sire Pentre Eiddwen Comet) for 60 gns, and the chestnut colt Parc Dafydd (first prize winner at Lampeter) was not sold at 150 gns, but was sold privately the following year to Twyford Stud, where he became a well-known sire.

To return to Ceulan in 1965, we sold Criban Pep to Mr van de Berg of Holland at the Hay-on-Wye spring sale to dissolve the partnership of Davies and Reynolds because of David's marriage and move to Newbury. I was very sorry to see Pep go and, as joint vendor, I could not bid on him, but I should have had someone else buy my half-share for me. RB&B used Pep's head photo on the cover of all their FO catalogues up to 1973. To replace Pep to have a stallion to cover our dozen or so section A mares in the interim, I bought the grey Twyford Matador (f. 1958: Coed Coch Glyndwr x Dinas Moonstone) from Mrs Mathews, Ivybridge, Devon in May. We had enormous success with Moonstone's first foal, Clan Marshall, which we had bought in 1954, and I thought very highly of Matador's full-sister Clan Music (f. 1950) and full-brother Twyford Moonshine (f. 1953). I had seen Matador at a month old when I visited Twyford – he was almost black – and Clan Music, Twyford Moonshine, Dinas Moonstone and Matador at foot are the main feature of the painting by Barbara Waller.

We competed at 20 shows, taking the cob mare Meiarth Modern Maid to Llantwit Fardre and Llandeilo (we sold her in June 1966), and the section A mare Dove Xanthe (which we had bought on the 1964 FO Sale) to Aberystwyth and another eight shows. At Aberystwyth and Tal-y-bont, Xanthe won in-hand and was also placed ridden by three-year-old David in lead-rein classes. Sprite was placed sixth out of 31 yearling fillies at the RW in the most atrocious weather under judge Lord Kenyon, and was also first and champion at Rumney and first and reserve champion to Dyrin Silver Spray, beating the winning stallion Coed Coch Planed at Devynock.

We had sold several ponies to members of the Danish WMP

Selskab (started in 1962 and had 31 members, many of whom had visited us at Ceulan), and sold some more recently to other members, who were not happy with the rules and regulations of the Selskab, so in March 1965 they had started a Welsh section within the Danish Ponyavls Forbund (a society of over 300 members covering all breeds of ponies). The committee of the Selskab were insisting that mares be put to stallions of their choice rather than left to the discretion of the owners, and that some of the best Welsh mares be placed on a remote island with the Exmoor stallion Clayford Horner and left to breed undisturbed for five years. An article written by the Danish Selskab in *Welsh News* (USA, July 1965) claimed that: 'The WMP breed in Britain is crumbling away', and that the Danish Selskab was formed to save the WMP breed from extinction. This was nonsense. Anyone watching the magnificent ponies at the 1965 RWS would realise that the standard had never been higher, and evidence of its popularity (and that the breed was far from extinction) is obtained from the export figures to Holland at that time.

In an attempt to ease the situation, members of the Forbund invited me (as I had friends in both groups) to Denmark for three weeks in August to try to resolve the situation. So in the first week of August, Ruth and I sailed from Harwich with David, one-year-old Jane and Diane Williams (Vardra Stud) to help with the children. First, we stayed with Gerda Fredo Larsen for two days and visited other breeders on Jutland, including Dr Richter Jorgensen and the brothers Michaelsen, and saw many ponies that I had known in Wales. Then we took a ferry to Funen where we saw Bowdler Bliss, Twyford Megan, Revel Shrimp, Mari Llwyd II (former big winner for Lisvane Stud), and the stallion Brierwood Honeyway, who was siring foals with excessive white on their faces. One male which had been gelded was the colt Clan Pip x Revel Rosette – with such illustrious parentage, he was worthy of keeping entire. Then we took a ferry from Funen to Zealand, and made a long car journey to Helsinge, where Mr Mogens Falk-Jensen and Lady Thornton put a superbly-fitted farm cottage at our disposal for the next three weeks.

On the first day, over 30 members of the Forbund assembled at Egetoftegaard when I gave them a talk and film show, ably translated by Mrs Anna Wodschov, a well-known international Swedish rider. The next day, 15 mares and two stallions had to be graded i.e. placed into classes I, IIA, IIB and reject. A full description of each had to be written and read out (which later appeared printed in their stud book). With the former RW winners Clan Jennifer and Ceulan Madam Butterfly present, it was easy to find animals worthy of class I. The following day, 16 mares appeared at Asnaes, and it seemed as if the entire population of the village attended as well, including the vicar, who showed a very nice filly (Belvoir Tarragon x Tan Lan Susan), and again some were given class I. Next, back to Jutland, where 18 ponies assembled at Fredericia, and again, three mares were worthy of class I. Some mares were rejected at Asnaes and Fredericia for either being of inferior quality, or suspected of having the incorrect registration documentation.

While we were at Egetoftegaard, I persuaded Mr Falk-Jensen to accompany me to Selleberg to try to sort out the unsatisfactory situation of having two societies aspiring towards the same goal. Mr Falk-Jensen and Mr Hvenegaard Lassen were two of the finest gentlemen that I have ever met, and I was optimistic that a solution could be found without involvement of other members of the Selskab. One compromise which was agreed was that Selskab entries could attend the Forbund gradings and vice versa. I attended the Forbund gradings another five times with Mr Fred Reynolds (1966), Mr David Garrett (1968), Lt Col Rosser-John (1969), Mrs Teresa Smalley (1970) and Mrs Alison Mountain (1971), by which time the Selskab had almost petered out and the Forbund had 176 members.

Some excellent Welsh ponies were bred on the Danish island of Bornholm in the Baltic Sea with the stallion Coed Coch Helgi, and rather than bring the ponies to the mainland to be graded, in 1970 the judges were flown to Bornholm, where we were treated royally and taken sightseeing. Mrs Smalley and I also went to Bornholm in 1977 after three gradings on the mainland. The chairman of the Forbund in succession to Mr Falk-Jensen was Mr Holger Winding, whose uncle Mr Ole Haslunds (the largest antiques dealer in Copenhagen) had bought a large property, Raeveskiftet, near the glorious beaches of Hornbaek, mainly forest, containing several small residences which he had bequeathed to the Danish nation where artists / musicians could spend free holidays. In 1978 I was labelled 'Welsh harpist', and Ruth, David, Jane and I were allocated one of these forest cottages for three weeks after I had completed the gradings with Mrs Hambleton of the Llanerch Stud. Raeveskiftet was ideally situated to shopping centres and some wonderful beaches nearby, and we visited many studs too. Secretary Mr Carl Trock wrote in the WPCS Journal that 'the Ceulan quartet could be heard singing until long after the sun had gone down.' Danish breeder Mr Preben Russell, writing in the 1999 WPCS Journal, described a visit to Ceulan to 'catch up with Dr Wynne, who single-handedly in the 1960s saved the Welsh breeds here in Denmark.' I cannot claim to have been solely responsible, but am happy if my contribution helped in some small way.

By 1978 there was a substantial number of section Bs and cobs to be graded. The standard had improved immensely, as reflected by the fact that the Dutch-bred section B stallion Mollegaard Spartacus was RW champion in three successive years 1992–94. I returned with Mr Len Bigley in 1985 and Mr Emrys Bowen in 1996, by which time the Welsh cobs bred by Carl Trock at his Valhallas Stud were as good as one would find anywhere in the world. After the 1996 grading, I was glad that I visited the Hornbaek beaches with Holger, where we had been 31 years previously. Holger died in 1997, and Inga remained at Raeveskiftet until her death in 2013. The Danish Society celebrated its fiftieth year in 2015 and a 15-page report with 20 photographs which I wrote about my Danish visits was published in their anniversary journal.

I also travelled to Roskilde in 1990 as commentator at the International Show, where the judges were Mrs Doreen Jones (UK) and Mrs Theuissen (Holland) (A, C and D) and Miss I. de Moerkerke (Belgium) and Mr Len Bigley (B and WPB). The overall champion was Revel Hibiscuss (A, Holland) and the reserve Mollegaard Spartacus (B, Denmark). Mrs Marianne Seidenfaden and Carl Trock had done a fantastic job organising this international event, which included a most wonderful party on the Saturday night and a display of a Welsh wedding in traditional Welsh dresses with Carl as a vicar! My most recent visit to Denmark was to judge their autumn show in 2001. The report in the WPCS Journal states that they had a good supply of *One Hundred Glorious Years*, and because I had signed them, they were all sold in a few minutes!

Mrs Alison Mountain was the retiring president in 1966 and HM The Queen graciously gave permission for the AGM to be held in the Royal Mews. This was the first time that the AGM had been held outside Wales, and some members had gone to the press objecting to this fact. However, it turned out to be an extremely successful event, with many members present from Sweden, Holland and France. Mrs Mackie Niven came from South Africa, which gave me an opportunity to catch up with news of Revel Siesta.

We competed at our usual 20 shows again. We bought the top-priced mare Eryl Alis from Friars Stud on the RB&B Spring Sale and she won at Ebbw Vale and Machen, and Sprite won at five shows including Devynock, where she was champion and won the WPCS medal. Sprite at two-y-o was fourth to 3-y-o Twyford Diamond,

Foxhunter Coegen (g-daughter of Ceulan Madam Butterfly) and Brierwood Rosebud (1971 RW ch) in a class of 24 at the Royal Welsh, which was a good indicator of a successful career ahead. David won some prizes riding the bay gelding Ceulan Nipper (f. 1961: Coed Coch Socyn x Nant y Mynydd) on the lead-rein. We kept Nipper until 1970 and won some private driving classes with him, after which we sold him to Lady Reiss.

In 1966 the 788 exports of 1965 exploded to 1,599, of which 1,276 were to Holland. The WSB increased from 742 pages to a massive volume of 1,430 pages. To cope with this increased demand, RB&B held monthly sales at Hay-on-Wye and put on additional sales at Llandeilo and Newcastle Emlyn. The first day of the October sale at Hay-on-Wye contained 631 foals, with some vendors selling as many as 50 foals. Around this time we were breeding 10 to 15 foals a year and would have ten or so local mares at stud to Twyford Matador, who had a reputation for siring mainly fillies. To get established with section Bs, at the FO Sale we bought the colts Weston Pom Pom, Dove Beaumaris and Kirby Cane Joker, and the wonderfully-bred filly Kirby Cane Swift (Kirby Cane Plunder x Coed Coch Seron, daughter of Serog, sister to Siaradus).

Two days before the 1967 RWS, a breeders conference was organised at Twyford for overseas breeders, and 65 people attended from Denmark, Sweden, Holland and Belgium. Talks were given by Mrs Pennell, Mr Dick Richards and myself before the delegates judged some of the Twyford section As and Bs and gave their reasons. On their way on to Builth Wells, the overseas visitors called in at Springbourne Stud, where they were given a stunning display of true WMP action by Treharne Tomboy, who ended up reserve champion to Clan Peggy at the Royal Welsh, and Sprite was second to the chestnut Cui Maria out of 32 entries. There were not many adult section Bs competing, and the championship went to the palomino three-y-o filly Lydstep Rosetta. Section C entries with

Lyn Cwmcoed champion had increased to 19 which warranted an additional youngstock class. The palomino stallion Honyton Michael ap Braint won the Kilvrough cup for the best Welsh cob, but could not receive the George PofW Cup which was restricted to animals bred in Wales because his breeder, Mrs Dorothy Mathias, had moved his dam Verwig Rosina from her Cardiganshire farm to her property in Shipston-on-Stour, Warwickshire, a few days before Michael was born. All restrictions on the PofW Cup were removed before the 1968 show. In 1967, the cup went to the reserve champion Derwen Rosina. Michael ap Braint qualified for the HOYS Fredericks supreme in-Hand championship and beat all the other qualifiers at Wembley.

Sprite was champion at Merthyr, Bargoed, Tal-y-bont and youngstock champion at Brecon, receiving the Rosser Prosser trophy. The 1966 exports of 1,599 decreased drastically to 741, with the Dutch buyers paying higher prices but being much more discerning in what they bought. At the FO Sale, this was the first time a male (Revel Springbok) had reached 1,000 gns on auction. At the Hay-on-Wye Autumn Sale I bought two top 10-y-o mares, Criban Fay (which I had admired ever since she won the yearling class at Brecon) from Lady Glanusk, and Eryl Marog, sister to Eryl Alis, which I had bought in 1965. Marog was in foal to Cui Maestro and produced Ceulan Minuet, which I sold to Whalton Stud, where she bred Whalton Drummer Boy, the top riding pony sire for many years and g-sire of the 2014 HOYS Cuddy champion Rendene Royal Charm.

The 1968 Glanusk Show was held in atrocious weather all day, and this was the last to be held on that site. The champion section A at Glanusk was Treharne Tomboy, who went on to be RW champion from the winning mare Ready Token Glen Bride, which had been purchased on the 1961 Hay-on-Wye Sale for only 80 gns. Glen Bride was certainly a bargain, and her daughter Crossways

Merle was RW overall champion in 1980. Treharne Tomboy was produced by Springbourne Stud, who also won the RW section B championship with their two-y-o colt Springbourne Golden Flute, a son of Reeves Golden Lustre. Lyn Cwmcoed was again section C champion and, because Treharne Tomboy had already qualified for the HOYS Fredericks supreme at the Three Counties, Lyn Cwmcoed represented the RW at Wembley, where Treharne Tomboy was the second successive Welsh to be supreme. Derwen Rosina won the George PofW cup for the third and last time – she died in 1970. A reduction sale of 74 ponies was held at the Weston Stud just prior to the FO Sale, and trade was buoyant, with the three-y-o filly Weston Airbell selling for 1,200 gns. At the FO Sale, 331 sold to home purchasers and 178 overseas, with top prices section As Coed Coch Pert (950 gns) and Twyford Matador (925 gns), and section Bs Rotherwood Crocus (900 gns) and Downland Demure (900 gns).

We competed at our usual 20 shows, Criban Fay doing best at Margam and Gower, where she was first barren mare and reserve champion, and Gowerton, where she was champion section A and ended up as the best horse or pony in the show. Sprite was first at Monmouth and reserve for the WPCS medal at Vaynor, and her foal Spice (by Clan Pip) also won. We had an enquiry in July from top American hackney breeder John Cuneo of Chicago for a team of four bay Welsh cob stallions which he could drive in a coach. After much travelling and photographing, we offered him Parc Welsh Flyer, Hafrena Brenin, Regency Brigadier and Gwenfo Dafydd, but he turned the offer down because the white markings on their legs did not match. Mr Sam Morgan was asking £250 for Parc Welsh Flyer. How fortunate for the Welsh cob breed that Parc Welsh Flyer did not go to the USA in 1968 – he turned out to be one of the most successful sires of that era, including 14 out of Cathedine Welsh Maid and the top sires Craignant Flyer, Nebo Brenin, Tireinon Shooting Star, Ty'rcapel Morgan among others.

Exports for 1969 were at their lowest (556) before starting to shoot up again to 741 in 1971 and 1,933 in 1972. The Lampeter Show moved to a Saturday and included cob premium classes for outside Wales. The cob youngstock classes saw the first appearance of the famous Llanarth Flying Comet. Lyn Cwmcoed was champion section C, and we won the youngstock championship with the cream two-y-o filly Nantfechan Seren. With the Glanusk Show moved to Llanelwedd, premiums were allocated to 11 Pony Improvement Societies. Pentyrch Prince Llewellyn won the section A championship, and a section C stallion class was introduced, which was won by Llanarth Cerdin. Welsh in-hand entries at the RW reached 420, and Coed Coch were champion and reserve section A, with the 11-y-o mare Coed Coch Swyn and the five-y-o stallion Coed Coch Pryd.

At the Coed Coch dispersal sale in 1978, Swyn achieved great fame by being the dam of the stallions Bari (21,000 gns) and Saled (14,000 gns). Weston Stud won the section B championship with Revel Glimpse, who went on to produce Weston Glimpse (f. 1972 by Chirk Crogan), RW overall champion in 1980 and female champion in 1982. Reserve section B champion was the stallion Kirby Cane Scholar, who was sold for 750 gns on FO 1970 to New Zealand, and was the last pony to travel by boat to that country, a journey which took five weeks via South Africa. Criban Fay was the 'full-back' of our 1969 showing team, and won at four shows, and was a very creditable fifth out of 25 entries at the Royal Welsh. Sprite also did her bit and won at four shows and was eighth at the RW, where her foal Seraph (by Clan Pip) was fifth out of 38 entries. We also showed our new acquisition Twyford Chick (f. 1965: Twyford Grenadier x Twyford Cuckoo, daughter of Reeves Crystal, bred at Ceulan in 1946), and she won at Machen and the Vale of Glamorgan. Eryl Marog was barren, and she was shown in lead-rein classes ridden by Jane, often competing against David riding Ceulan Nipper.

Mrs Pricilla Neill (mother of actor Sam Neill) wrote in the 1969 WPCS Journal that the section A old indigenous colours, bay, black, brown, dun, dark chestnut in New Zealand and the UK were in danger of being lost, with three-quarters world-wide being grey (up from 12 per cent in 1911). I found myself sharing this fear with her, and since 1962 we have had 26 bay stallions / colts at Ceulan. We still had plenty of the progeny of Criban Pep and Revel Light here, and since then have had five chestnut stallions, including Twyford Sprig (at Ceulan 1972–1994, and sired three RW progeny group winners) and Wernderris Caramel, which we bought as a foal in 2003. He returned to Wernderris in 2014 since we have six of his daughters here. We have also had three black stallions. Notable amongst the bays are Criban Pep, Revel Light, Bengad Rustling Grass, Synod Captain, Synod Birthday Boy, Trefaes Taran (reserve HOYS in-hand champion 1997), Joiners Kilkenny, Frongoch Cardi, Powys (NL) Shon, Sunvillow Irving (we won second prize with him in harness at the 2008 RWS), Weston Distinction (winner of first, second and third prizes at the RW, WPCS silver medal 2014), Ysselvliedts Highwood (bronze medal 2014) and Ysselvliedts Irresistible.

1970–1979

The 1970 shows started with Lampeter, which experienced the worst weather I can remember, including arctic hailstorms, but the judges Lord Kenyon (A and B) and Mrs Alison Mountain (C and D) battled on valiantly. I judged sections A, C and the ridden classes at Glanusk, where the weather was glorious by contrast, and my champion section A was the two-y-o colt Coed Coch Norman, who I thought was a grand little model and a spectacular mover. At the RB&B Hay-on-Wye July sale I bought the 10-y-o FS1 section B mare Monkham Snow Bunting for 350 gns (top of the sale). She reminded me very much of Ceulan Silver Lustre, and we showed her a few times successfully at the later shows. She was sired by Harford Starlight (sire also of champion Brockwell Cobweb) and her dam was by the TB stallion Potato, who was also sire of the champion palomino stallion Bubbly. Snow Bunting's daughter Cusop Sunshade had sold on the 1969 FO Sale for 500 gns, and her 3-y-o daughter Cusop Sunset and yearling son Cusop Steward (sire of 1989 RW ch Linksbury Celebration) sold for 1,250 gns and 850 gns on the 1983 FO Sale. After a filly in 1971, Snow Bunting had five colt foals for me, and in 1976 I gave her to Scottish breeder Mrs Joyce Colthard, in foal to Twylands Firecracker, and she immediately had a filly, Tricula Jenny Wren, that was ridden champion at the Royal International and Royal Welsh, and reserve champion at the Ponies of Britain Show in 1981.

Sprite was third out of 28 mares at the RW, and her filly foal

Sapphire was first out of 33 entries. Sapphire, with her yearling full-sister Seraph, joined by the third prize mare Pendock Pansy then won the progeny sire group for Clan Pip. Sapphire also won seven first prizes, including Brecon and Abergavenny. Treharne Tomboy won his third championship at the RW and his owner, Lt Col Rosser-John announced his retirement at the show, and he was sold to New Zealand in 1972. Reserve champion was the mare Rowfant Prima Ballerina, who was then owned by Foxhunter Stud. Coed Coch Norman was youngstock champion. The two-y-o filly Rotherwood Honeysuckle was section B champion from the mare Gredington Blodyn – they were related since Gredington Tiwlip (dam of Honeysuckle) was a sister to Gredington Saffrwm (dam of Blodyn).

Up until 1970, there was only one WPCS Area Association, which was the Scottish and Northern, formed in 1962 owing to the large distances which its members would have to travel to attend any of the events of the WPCS main body. Mr Ken Runcie was chairman for ten years, Mrs Teresa Smalley was secretary and Mrs Winifred Morrison treasurer, and they immediately set about organising annual trips to Wales. In 1966 they visited Coed Coch, Ceulan (Tal-y-bont), Llanarth, Synod, Menai and Downland Studs and Llanybyther Market. Two areas to follow suit in 1970 were the South-western (Cornwall, Devon, Dorset and Somerset) under the chairmanship of Miss Margaret Gethin and South-eastern (Surrey, Sussex and Kent), with chairman Mr John Mountain. Then followed the Southern Counties (Hampshire, East Dorset, Berkshire and Wiltshire) and East Midlands in 1972, Gwynedd (Caernarfonshire, Anglesey and Merioneth) in 1975 with veterinarian Mr Henshaw as chairman, Eastern with chairman Mrs Crisp (Kirby Cane) in 1976, Midland with secretaries Mr and Mrs Harry Parsons in 1977, North-western with chairman Mrs Francis (Gwyndrig) in 1982, the Isle of Wight with president the

Hon Mrs Monck, also in 1982. A further four were established in 1983: Clwyd, with secretary Mrs Audrey Weaver, who remained in post for 31 years, Gwent with chairman Mr Brian Foster (Gerrig), Home Counties with chairman Mr N. Butler and Glamorgan with president Mrs Serena Homfray (Penllyn), vice-president Mrs Pat Johns-Powell (Cottrell), chairman Mr David Prichard (Castellau), treasurer Mrs Pat Leadbitter (Thornberry) and secretaries Mr and Mrs Tegwyn Price. These thirteen Associations have now increased in number to 29.

As publicity officer, I gave a talk and slide show to launch the Gwent and Isle of Wight Associations in 1982, having been previously to the South-western (1972), Midland (1979 and 1980) and Southern (1981). During my first visit to the South-eastern (1974), it took three days to carry out the stud judging competition of groups of three animals of any section: (i) by the same sire or out of the same mare, (ii) mare with two progeny, (iii) three direct generations, (iv) any group of three Welsh cobs/section Cs and (v) ditto for part-breds. In all I visited 27 studs and judged 88 groups. I was driven around at breakneck speed by Miss Anne Muir, and at one stud I was nearly eaten alive by two of the largest St Bernard dogs I have ever seen. I am also notorious for losing my belongings. Mrs Alison Mountain once wrote in her report in the WPCS Journal that my hat was found in Surrey, my raincoat in Sussex, but that my umbrella was still somewhere in Kent!

A typical twelve months for the publicity officer would include ten or more talk and film shows, at home and abroad. My first visit to Scotland was to Glenrothes in 1972 when, with my co-speaker Mrs Joanna MacInnes, we gave a demonstration on 'Show production and good and bad points', with a variety of animals present. I organised a 1972 stud visit for the Scottish Association in Gwent, and their coach got stuck in a narrow lane going up Foxhunter mountain. I also did a breed demonstration at Kilwinning, Ayrshire, on 17 April 1977 and judged the Welsh cob premiums at Greenloaning Show on 6 April 1985. Also in 1985 the Scottish Association paid us a visit at Ceulan. At the South-western Association's Welsh pony and cob discussion at Milverton School, many animals had been assembled for me to comment on, including Ebbw Victor (D) all the way from Blackwood, the local Aston Loveknot (B), who looked superb despite his 18 years, and Millcroft Sunstar (B), ridden by Anthony Carter. The talk and film show at the Irish Association in June 1986 was followed by a show at Newcastle, County Wicklow, where the handler of the winner of the lead-rein class was Mrs Avril Doyle, Minister of Finance in the Irish Government. Nowadays, the major role of publicity officer is answering queries passed on to me from the WPCS office, and supplying show and sale results and photographs for the WPCS website and UK and overseas press and magazines. During 2014 I reported on 26 events covering 73 pages and 329 photographs on the WPCS website.

On the 1970 FO Sale, I sold the yearling filly Ceulan Seraph for 420 gns (section A youngstock record) to the Wharley Stud. I had previously bought privately the red roan section B two-y-o colt Wharley Caruso (by Coed Coch Pedestr), and on the FO bought the two-y-o section B filly Weston Ribbon for myself, and the yearling filly Mynd Neillia and the two-y-o Mynd Pollyanna (both by Coed Coch Pedstr) for Swedish breeders Bertil and Anne Marie Bengtsson. Bertil was a director of Volvo cars, and he and Anne Marie retired to Lyndhurst in the New Forest in 2000, where we went to visit them. Caruso would not have been a suitable stallion for these two mares (half-siblings), and I bought Bertil the up-to-height Kirby Cane Guardsman (g-sire of the famous Orielton Aristocrat) on the 1964 FO Sale. Bertil came to collect the ponies from Ceulan, and the documentation had to be signed by our local policeman, who refused to sign until he had donned his helmet.

After having three mares in foal to Caruso and showing him a few times under saddle in 1971, I sold him to Gerda Fredbo Larsen (Denmark), where he became a very popular sire. Mr Emrys Bowen bought the section B colt foal Downland Kestrel for 100 gns on this sale, and sold him to Australia, also on FO Sale in 1977, for 1,800 gns!

I judged the section As at the 1971 RWS where there were 217 entries. My champion was the bay mare Brierwood Rosebud (Bowdler Brewer x Brierwood Rosemary), and the reserve the bay two-y-o filly Twyford Napkin out of Revel Nannie E P. Mrs Mountain had named the dam after her nanny Evelyn Powell, who left her money under her bed to buy a pony to remember her by. The three-y-o colt Coed Coch Norman was male champion, with the stallion Gredington Simwnt reserve. Brierwood Rosebud was g-dam of the 1985 and 1988 RW champion Brierwood Rocket, and it is interesting that when David judged at the RWS in 1997, his champion Fronbach Crystal, and reserve Yaverland Delight, were g-daughters of Brierwood Rocket, while his male champion and reserve, Synod The Colonel and Betws Fflach, were both Brierwood Rocket sons. Every day at the RWS I did the commentary on a display of 52 Welsh cobs in harness, ridden, shepherding, carrying disabled riders, dressage, side-saddle etc., and leading the display was WPCS President Miss Pauline Taylor, riding 30-y-o Llanarth Fortress.

We exhibited at 24 shows in 1971, with Sapphire champion (WPCS medal) at Barry, and Snow Bunting champion section B at Gower. We sold Snow Bunting's filly foal Ceulan Bluebird to Holland, where she was a good producer, among others, of Twickels Joy, champion at Apeldoorn in 1979 and 1980. My father was awarded the WPCS Brodrick Memorial trophy for 1971, an award that pleased him immensely, since he and Miss Brodrick had been good friends since 1924. He attended the AGM at Aberystwyth to collect the award but was in failing health, and he passed away on 29 March 1972.

1972 showed a marked increase in interest in the Welsh breeds, the average price on the FO Sale rose from £120 to £177, and on the Llanarth Sale almost doubled to £260 with 19 mares averaging £577. Exports of 741 in 1971 increased to 1,933 in 1972 and did not decrease as rapidly as they did in 1965–1967. Gredington Simwnt, having been RW reserve male champion in 1971, went two stages further and was overall champion, an achievement which he repeated in 1973. Dyfrdwy Midnight Moon (daughter of Coed Coch Planed) was female champion, with the novice mare winner Weston Mink Muff reserve – she was sold to Australia for 2,300 gns on the 1974 Weston Sale. Ceulan won the Gwyn Price Progeny Cup with the three-y-o Ceulan Seraph, two-y-o Sapphire and the yearling colt Senator, all progeny of Ceulan Sprite. Llanarth Stud won four of the six cob classes, including the stallion class with Llanarth Flying Comet, but the championship eluded them and went to Parc Rachel for the second successive year. Having sold Wharley Caruso to Denmark, I replaced him with the chestnut Glansevin Goshawk (f. 1970: Kirby Cane Pilgrim x Kirby Cane Gopher), a good sire and a three-quarter brother to Vardra Stud's Kirby Cane Golden Rod, who had been champion at Lampeter three times and 1971 champion at Glanusk.

The most successful exhibit for Ceulan was Sapphire, who won six championships, including a WPCS medal at Barry and the Roger Prosser Cup (youngstock) and the Gwynne Holford Cup (overall) at Brecon. I was contacted in the spring by Mr Douglas Tovey of Highmoor Park, Nettlebed, who wanted to sell his entire stud of Welsh ponies, consisting of the stallion Ceulan Gondolier and the mares Downland Grasshopper (g-dam of Goshawk, Golden Rod and others), Revel Ella, Sally of Highmoor and Antonette of Highmoor (sister to Abercrychan Antonella, dam of the HOYS champion riding pony Harmony Bubbling Champagne). I bought the four mares (I bought Gondolier later) and the whole family went there to collect them, the children having been invited to take along their swimming gear. Highmoor Park was a very impressive property with a huge indoor swimming pool, which David and Jane were very loath to leave, and there was also the largest collection of ornamental caged birds we had ever seen. The four mares travelled back to Miskin in our trailer, something we would not be allowed to do these days. I see Highmoor Park now has 34 properties on it, each with an average value of £1.37m.

When I went to Glenrothes in Fife in April to give a demonstration on the Welsh breeds and show production, I met a pair of schoolboys, David Blair and Tom Best, who had a nice enough, but not top-class, section A two-y-o filly Lowfields Andrene, which they had shown locally but not had much success with. I offered to lend them a section B two-y-o filly, Sparkler of High Tor (by Weston Glow Worm), which I had bought with her dam Springbourne Jewel (f. 1966 by Chirk Crogan) and they had immediate success, including champion at the Royal Lancashire Show, and they bought 'Sparky' in 1974. In 1979 I sold them Cantref Glory (f. 1977), sired by Cui Mi'Lord (which I also bought), out of the lovely bay Criban Glory Be by Criban Pep, and gave them Revel Hetty (f. 1968: Revel Chip x Revel Hipip, daughter of Rhydyfelin Seren Heulyn), because I could never catch her. This pair produced a legendary string of champions, including the RASE HOYS qualifier and Australian top sire Waxwing Herrod. From these beginnings, the Waxwing Stud has developed into one of the major Welsh Pony studs in the world and holds an impressive number of HOYS ridden qualifiers in sections A, B and C.

Under the umbrella of the publicity committee, the WPCS supported the running of a performance competition, with varying numbers of points awarded to winners in harness, ridden, working hunter and showjumping. In the first year (1972), 36 ponies and cobs entered, and all their points cards were checked by Mrs Jill Rogers of the Willesley Stud. Trophies were awarded for each section: Treharne Cup (A), Gredington (B), Turkdean (C), Blaenwern (D) and Criban R (WPB). Overall champion with 2,485 points was the section B mare Marston Mirage, who was awarded the magnificent Riding Cup at the presentation held at the Five Ashes Village Hall, Sussex, organised by Miss Anne Muir of Haslemere. Miss Muir then took over the running of the competition until her death in 1988, when Mrs Rogers re-took it over and the presentation was moved to the Hare and Hounds Hotel, Tetbury, where the Duke of Beaufort often attended. When the competition outgrew this venue, it was moved to the Thistle Hotel, Cheltenham, where it has been organised for the last 25 years by Mrs Kathleen James of the Highland Stud, assisted by Mrs Jane Weller of the Stoatleytwo Stud. By 2014 entries had increased to 149, the number of trophies increased to 48 and the Riding Cup was won by the section D stallion Dycott Welsh King, who had collected 5,375 points. I read out the names and described the recipients at Five Ashes in 1972, and have done likewise another 42 times since then. One little winner in 2014 informed me that I had awarded the same trophy to her grandmother in 1972!

1973 was one of the happiest and most successful years ever for the WPCS. The financial situation had improved out of all proportion (due to increased exports, membership and registrations) and the society bought its own new premises at 6 Chalybeate Street, Aberystwyth, for £13,500 (sold for £400,000 in 2010), a not ultra-convenient building on four floors, but one that served the society admirably for almost forty years. The building was officially opened by the president Lady Margaret Myddelton, and chairman Lord Kenyon. At 1,387, exports were down from the 1972 figure of 1,933 (and were to reduce to 231 in 1977), but exports to Australia, which had been between one and seven annually from 1959–1972, rose to 19 (up to 60 in 1974 and 102 in 1976, but have not been in double figures since 1981). For the first time ever, the in-hand Welsh entries at the RWS exceeded 400, including 23 WPBs (their registrations for 1973 were 953, up from 534 in 1971). Gredington Simwnt was champion section A although Coed Coch had won four first prizes. Reeves Fairy Lustre (daughter of Ceulan Silver Lustre, the untouched mare which we sold to Reeves Stud along with her son and two daughters for £100 in 1947) was champion section B, Lili Cwmcoed was champion section C and Nebo Black Magic won the PofW cup and qualified for the HOYS in-hand championship.

We have only ever had a trailer for transport to shows (never a horsebox after 1960), with room for only two adults at one time, so it was quite an achievement (on two different days) to transport four animals of three sections (A, B and C) and end up with every one in the top four in very large classes. Sapphire (A) was third to Gredington Judith (dam of 1993 and 1994 RW ch Gredington Calon Lân) and Twyford Napkin (res ch RW 1971), Goshawk (B) was fourth to Llandecwyn Ffefryn, Nantfechan Seren (C) was fourth to Lili Cwmcoed and her foal Ceulan Nesta by Synod Dafydd, third to Liliddu Cwmcoed. Nesta was dam of Sackville Nicky (f. 1987 by Synod Roy Rogers), overall champion of the WPCS performance competition in 1997, 1998 and 1999.

The number entered for the FO Sale (982) was the highest ever, and the average increased from £177 to £233, with many section B records broken. One stud fee to Downland Chevalier sold for 740 gns to Whatton Stud, an unbelievable figure equivalent to £11,000 today. The five-y-o mare Downland Justina and the yearling filly Tetworth Tinkerbell (g-daughter of Reeves Golden Lustre) each sold for 1,300 gns, the yearling colt Shimpling Pioneer sold for 1,250 gns to France, and the yearling filly Sunbridge Bet made 1,200 gns. Sunbridge Bet was a daughter of Hollytree Bettryn, whose son Orielton Aristocrat is the most successful current riding pony sire. Bettryn was sired by Kirby Cane Guardsman (which I bought for Bertil Bengttson in 1964) out of Blossom Bach by Ceulan Revelry. Bengad Stud, having decided to keep only home-bred stock, sold Ceulan Largo (f. 1963: Sinton Gyration x Dyrin Larina) to New Zealand for 650 gns. Her son Bengad Laburnum was later a big winner in south Wales. We sold Larina's three-y-o daughter Ceulan Ladybird (by Revel Light) for 250 gns, and Mr Emrys Bowen sold Larina's six-y-o daughter Ceulan Lyric (by Twyford Matador) to Holland for 200 gns. I bought the big section B palomino yearling colt Glanymor Golden Gareth jointly with my friend Mr Ken Thomas of the Llandaff Stud, Lord Kenyon having bought his sister Glanymor Lorelei for 960 gns. Golden Gareth died in 2005 aged 32 years. I bought Lorelei's sister Glanymor Nirvana on the 1975 FO Sale, and showed her very successfully, selling her to Mme Christine Bocquillon of Senlis, France in 1978, and her daughter Ceulan Nicola (by Twylands Firecracker) to Millcroft Stud, for whom she was reserve overall champion section B at Lampeter in 1979.

The Llanarth Sale was held on 20 October – certainly the wettest day ever for this sale. David had won first prize riding our cob mare Creuddyn Seren Eleanor at Barry Show in 1972, and we sold her 1973 filly Ceulan Enfys (by Madeni Wonder) for 250 gns, and a friendly cream section C riding gelding, Ceulan Rupert by Andos Rupert, for 150 gns. Ceulan Elsa (f. 1975: Madeni Wonder x Seren Eleanor) was the foundation mare of the Ffald Stud, which has produced many RW winning cobs. The colt foal Parc Brigadier sold for 400 gns to Scole Stud, and when he returned to this sale in 1980 he made 3,000 gns! We left Llanarth soaked to the skin and covered in mud, with two young children, the WPCS calendars which I had to sell there ruined by the rain. We vowed never to go there again, but were back selling again in 1974. We competed at 24 shows in 1973. Sprite was champion (WPCS medal) at Caerphilly, and Sapphire (three-y-o) was champion at Llandeilo (WPCS medal) and Barry and reserve champion at another ten shows, and was put in foal to Rowfant Pathan (Twyford Gurkha x Rowfant Primdora, daughter of Dovey Prima Donna), which I had bought on the 1968 FO Sale.

Although exports kept up well at 1,251, trade did not seem as buoyant due to the poor state of the British national economy and the bad summer harvest. There were 960 ponies entered on the FO Sale. Of the 338 section As present, 180 were not sold and 153 sold for an average of £162. Section Bs fared better – 251 sold for an average of £242. Half of all lots sold went for export. The eight Downland section Bs sold for £7,644 with two fillies, Downland Rosewood and Downland Dresden, selling for 1,700 gns each. We sold two yearling fillies – Ceulan Leading Lady by Glansevin Goshawk, and Ceulan Lucy Glitters by Wharley Caruso to Baron de Lamberterie, Les Noniers, France. Better prices for section As were experienced at the Weston Stud Sale (Weston Mink Muff, who had won at the RW that year, sold to Australia for 2,300 gns) and Foxhunter Stud Sale, when Rowfant Prima Ballerina sold to Australia for 900 gns. Welsh in-hand entries at the RW exceeded 500 for the first time. Section A champion was the three-y-o colt Coed Coch Bari (who sold for 21,000 gns to Australia in 1978), and reserve champion was the winning novice mare Bengad Love in the Mist, g-daughter of Penarth Music. I was delighted to be second to Love in the Mist with Ceulan Sprite out of 31 of the top mares in Britain. I had entered Ceulan Sapphire and her colt foal Ceulan Sceptre, but had sold them along with Ceulan Chiff Chaff (Revel Light x Twyford Chick) and her filly foal Ceulan Chick to Mrs Diana McDonald (now Lawrence) of Victoria, Australia. A yearling colt, Cusop Banknote, was section B male champion (he went on to be champion three times) and reserve overall to the mare Coed Coch Dawn. The five-y-o palomino mare Cefn Moonlight beat Lili Cwmcoed and Lyn Cwmcoed for the section C championship. She was sired by Maylord Starlight and her dam was Cefn Princess by Ceulan Revelry. The cob mare Cathedine Welsh Maid was barren in 1974 (she had 15 foals, all by Parc Welsh Flyer), and was female champion and reserve to Llanarth Flying Comet, who had his first notch out of four on the George PofW Cup. Gondolier was second under saddle at Glanusk and second in-hand at two shows. Jewel won the section B mare class at six shows, and was third at the Bath and West.

Mrs Pennell and I were asked by Benson & Hedges to stage a display of six Welsh section A and six D stallions within the grounds of Cardiff Castle during the International BSJA Showjumping Show on 1–3 August organised by Mr John Stevens MBE, who was also organiser of the HOYS Show at Wembley. This took place every afternoon, with a repeat floodlit evening performance, and proved immensely popular. We were booked for another display the following year and, after the last night, all owners and handlers were invited to a civic reception by the Lord Mayor of Cardiff. The Ceulan caravan served as publicity stand, and WPCS items did a roaring trade. After being with a very happy and enthusiastic Tom Williams at the WPCS AGM at Chirk Castle in April, it came as a great shock a few weeks later to learn that he had undergone a major operation, and he passed away in July aged only 56 years.

I bought Twyford Sprig, and three Vardra mares came here to live with him. Forty years later, there are still Vardra ponies at Ceulan to keep the 101-year-old Vardra prefix going. A sale of 37 Vardra ponies was organised at Hampton Bishop the following July. Ponies shown from Ceulan included Vardra Serenity, reserve champion foal at the 1998 RWS, Vardra Cherie, second highest-priced yearling on the 1999 FO Sale, and Vardra Sirius, first at the

1999 RWS and second in 2000 in-hand, and then M&M overall ridden champion at the BSPS winter championships in 2003.

In 1975 the Ministry increased the minimum value of ponies which could be exported to £120 (A) and £160 (B) in order to protect the welfare of cheap animals. Consequently, WPCS exports fell to 610 (from 1,251 in 1974), the main reduction being to Holland, which decreased to 281 from 745. The top prices on the FO Sale (which was reduced to two days) held up well, with a top price of 1,450 gns for the WPB yearling colt Small-Land Orsino, and 1,300 gns for a section B yearling colt Colbeach Bonaparte. The section A yearling colt, Carnalw Hyderus sold for 880 gns to Weston Stud, where he was used extensively at stud, and went with them to Australia in 1979. He had huge eyes and minute ears – he was not a Ceulan 'type'. Yorkshire TV filmed this sale, and for three days on the Brecon Beacons, to produce a spectacular film with Robert Hardy based on Mrs Greta Phillips' book, *Horses In Our Blood*. Because the Llanarth Sale was bursting at the seams, the auctioneers RB&B organised a cob sale at Llanelwedd two weeks before it. This was quite a success, and became more established when the Llanarth site was no longer available after 1982.

Because Glamorgan was the sponsor county for the 1975 RWS, and I had been a member of the Glamorgan RWAS Advisory Committee since 1960, I was asked to put on a display of Welsh ponies at the 'Country Comes To Town' event in Sophia Gardens, Cardiff, two weeks before the show. Again, the Ceulan caravan served as headquarters, and a place to supply literature and merchandise. The ponies were supplied by Mrs Homfray of the Penllyn Stud, Mrs Jean Evans of the Pentyrch Stud – whose Pentyrch Pablo was one of the winning RW female progeny group – and Mr and Mrs David Prichard of the Castellau Stud, with Springbourne Jewel and her foal Ceulan Jasper by Glansevin Goshawk from Ceulan. For participating in this event, Ruth and I were invited to a luncheon at the show hosted by the County Council Chairman Mrs Joy Davies JP and the RWAS President Sir Julian Hodge LL.D.

On the first day of the show, I organised a display of Welsh ponies and cobs at the behest of HRH Prince Philip, and did the commentary. Starting with all four sections in-hand and under saddle, it was then a free-for-all of in-hand exhibits, a sight not seen outside Wales. After the show, I received a letter from the RWAS secretary Mr John Wigley, stating that HRH had enjoyed my commentary, and inviting me to be part of the commentating team for the three days (and four days from 1981) and now, having done so for forty years, I think it is time to reduce my commitment. Lloyds Bank's representative in Wales, Sir Hugo Boothby of Fonmon Castle (brother of Mrs Serena Homfray, Penllyn Stud), judged the Lloyds Bank HOYS in-hand qualifier and selected the section D champion Parc Rachel. I organised the second Benson & Hedges display in Cardiff Castle along the lines of a historic pageant with Penclawdd cockle pickers, Welsh preachers riding cobs to chapel, tradesmen's turnouts, tinkers and shepherds.

There was an increased interest for section Cs and Ds from Australia, with Redwood Derw (D) and Tyssul Cardi (C) exported. Notable among the other exports were Gredington Gamelyn (A), Revel Chelsea Fan (A), Pendock Miracle (A), Sinton Whirligig (B), Brierwood Fumble (A), Fayre Zany (A) and Llanerch Soprano (A). I sold Springbourne Jewel to Mrs Barrett-Lennard of Beverley, Western Australia. An S4C crew had filmed her in the mud and cold at Miskin, and went with her to Australia. What was amusing in the film was seeing her reaction to the Australian heat – the runway was so hot that she didn't want to walk on it. I was informed that, when she foaled in May, the foal was born with a winter coat since it was then winter in Australia.

1976 saw the collapse of the European market for the smaller ponies, and there was a noticeable drop in sales to Holland, Germany,

Denmark and France. The £118 average on the FO Sale was the lowest for ten years. A few sold well, but the rest were nowhere. Top of the sale (1,600 gns) was the yearling colt Rosedale Falcon (B), sold to Germany, and top A (1,400 gns to Holland) was the seven-y-o stallion Rowfant Seal, which had been bought on this sale as a foal for 70 gns. The Llanarth Sale experienced its best trade ever, with many records broken. The yearling colt Derwen Arwr sold to Canada for 1,600 gns. I sold the top section C, the two-y-o filly Synod Glenda (400 gns), which had won for us at Taf Fechan and Llandeilo, to Mr and Mrs Wynn Colville, Persire Stud, to be a member of their four-in-hand driving team of chestnut section C ponies.

Our most successful show pony was the chestnut filly foal Ceulan Sienna (Revel Sirocco x Ceulan Sprite), who was second out of 39 at the RWS, and first at ten more south Wales shows. At the RWS, I had also fourth with Glanymor Nirvana (B) and third with Ceulan Nia Ben Aur (C). Having been to Denmark to judge and / or grade six times, it was interesting to be invited to judge in Belgium on 27 August. Ruth and I stayed with M and Mme d'Ogimont at their enormous château in Houtain-le-Val, which was so big that by the time M d'Ogimont had opened all the shutters in the morning, it was almost time to start shutting them again for the evening. Supreme champion was the tremendous moving section A stallion Revel Playsome (1968: Twyford Sprig x Revel Playtime), who had spent 1970 at Eppynt Stud then was sold to Belgium, only to return to Sunwillow Stud in 1978 on his way to Australia in 1980, where I placed him champion again in 1984. While at Sunwillow, Playsome sired Sunwillow Mutters (f. 1979) dam of Dukeshill Magnum (f. 1993), who was second in the 2014 WPCS sire ratings. Reserve supreme in Belgium was the section B mare Langford Butterscotch by Solway Master Bronze. The first three section B mares were all owned by the Comtesse de Moerkerke and her daughter Babelle, who was secretary of the Belgian Society for thirty years.

Champion cob was Rhystyd Sunrise, very well shown by young Ducatelle, who handled a winning cob filly at the RWS a few years previously. For the 1976 Benson & Hedges international showjumping event in Cardiff Castle (18–20 June), they asked for a WPCS display along the lines of the 1974 display of champions rather than the 1975 historical pageant, so Mrs Pennell and I selected 12 stallions. The wonderful Mrs Pennell, who had devoted so many years of her life to WPCS publicity, decided that her health would not allow her to continue, and I was asked to take over from the end of 1976. Mrs Pennell passed away in 1978. The selected stallions for Cardiff were: section A, Coed Coch Bari, Coed Coch Norman, Revel Cassino, Whatton Spritely; section B: Kirby Cane Golden Rod and Milncroft Spun Gold; section C: Lyn Cwmcoed and Isamman Dafydd, and section D: Brynymor Welsh Magic, Llanarth Meredith ap Braint, Hewid Cardi and Honyton Michael ap Braint. The London organisers, Messrs Raymond Brooks-Ward, Tom Hudson and John Stevens, were so delighted with the display that they were going to organise a similar 'Welsh' one to end their Olympia show. Benson & Hedges looked after the animals and their stables superbly, with handlers and owners staying in the Angel Hotel, where the Welsh singing (assisted by showjumper Harvey Smith) went on until the small hours.

Two owners who were particularly happy with my arrangements and the five-star treatment they received were Lt Col Edward Williams-Wynn and the Dowager Viscountess Chetwynd. I regard the visionary Lady Chetwynd as the 'saviour' of section C. A former world-class racing driver, she was given a police summons at Cardiff for her trailer not being roadworthy, but when she asked for her case to be heard at Tywyn Magistrates Court (where she was Chairman of the Bench), the summons was changed to a warning. Lady Chetwynd passed away in 1979. The weather on the Sunday was glorious, and all the WPCS merchandise sold out.

Here at home at Ceulan, we were disrupted for most of the year by the construction of the M4 motorway. Our boundary fences were taken down without warning, and some ponies went east towards Cardiff, some west towards Swansea, but all were rescued safely.

Welsh pony and cob exports were down to 231 in 1977 (from 1,251 in 1974), and at the sales, the best sold well, but there was no demand for the rest, with only 303 of the 578 lots selling on the FO Sale. Downland Kestrel (B stallion) sold for 1,800 gns to Australia, and we sold the bay colt foal Ceulan Sovereign (Twyford Sprig x Ceulan Sprite), also to Australia, to Diana Lawrence, who had bought his maternal half-sister Ceulan Sapphire in 1974. During the year, Sovereign had won first prizes at six shows. Also sold to Australia in 1977 was Brierwood Victoria (2,000 gns), from the Brierwood Sale on 10 September, when Captain Brierley decided to give up at the age of 87 years. The bargain of this sale was the yearling colt Brierwood Rocket II (320 gns to Cerdin Jones), who went on to be RWS champion in 1985 and 1988. There was much better trade at the cob sales. The yearling colt Derwen Trysor sold for 1,500 gns, and the filly foal Derwen Last's Request for 1,400 gns. I bought an up-to-height chestnut four-y-o mare Saltmarsh Shani by Turkdean Gaffer, in foal to Synod Dafydd, for 280 gns.

The Builth Wells Cob Sale was now well-established, and the average of £187 increased to £311 the following year. Twyford Sprig proved a popular stallion at stud, and we had 26 visiting mares in addition to eight of our own, mainly from south Wales studs, but also from leading English studs such as Pendock and Sunwillow, and four visiting mares to Twylands Firecracker. We were all shocked to learn of the death of Lt Col Edward Williams-Wynn of Coed Coch, and arrangements were put in motion for a dispersal sale of over 200 ponies to be held at the stud the following September.

1978 got off to a good start when HM The Queen's Master of

the Horse, the Earl of Westmorland presented the performance competition awards at the Hare and Hounds Hotel, Tetbury on 8 January. In those days, I had to make 14 photocopies of all the reports of these events, shows and sales, print off extra photographs and post them to our 14 overseas associations – nowadays, emailing makes life much easier. On 8 July, first-day issues of the 11p stamp depicting Criban Victor were posted in Aberystwyth, with Mr Eric Davies riding Madeni Welsh Comet delivering the letters to the postmaster. S4C had made a film at Lampeter Show about the production of the stamp, in which I appeared, since I did not approve of Patrick Oxenham's first production (a grey mare!) but was very happy with the final version. This film was broadcast as a filler by S4C for many years afterwards.

Llanarth Flying Comet was Mr John Cory's choice to carry the RWAS flag at the HOYS, Wembley. This was the last appearance at the RW of Fronarth What Ho, who won an enormous harness class of sections A, B and C. Had I not held the sire Dinarth What Ho at Llanilar Show at the time of service in 1951, I would not have believed that he was 26 years old. The events of 1978 were dominated by the Coed Coch Dispersal Sale on Thursday 7 September, when 219 ponies sold for £184,453, with a top price of 21,000 gns for Coed Coch Bari to go to Lady Creswick's stud in Australia. Two days after the Coed Coch sale, Weston Stud held a sale of 68 ponies which sold for £52,116, with a top price of 4,000 gns for Weston Choice, who also went to Australia.

The section A colt foal Weston Bestman (full-brother to the yearling Weston Unique, which I had placed overall champion at the RASE that year) sold for 1,200 gns and proved over the years to be a good investment as a sire. Having failed to buy the cream mare Weston Rebecca (she was retained and went with the stud to Australia), I bought her three-y-o daughter Weston Rana, who was never an easy mare to handle, although her progeny by Twyford

Sprig had superb temperaments. I sold Rana's 1980 daughter Rebecca to Israel, and her 1981 daughter Romance was our show mare for many years. I sold two of her daughters – Rhamant (f. 1997) and Roma (f. 2000) – to the USA, and Rana's 1983 daughter Rowena was youngstock champion at Glanusk in 1985. At the FO Sale, 202 out of the 556 lots present were not sold, but the section B yearling filly Downland Dabchick sold for 1,800 gns, and the yearling colt Orielton Aristocrat, who later had such an influence as a sire of riding ponies, sold for 1,600 gns.

The first International Show was held at Baden-Baden, Germany on 10 September, where the judge was Mrs Alison Mountain. The supreme champion was Epona Candy (B) from France and the reserve was Hewid Lyn (D) from Germany. Hewid Lyn was overall champion in 1979, with Ripton Sophia (A) from Holland reserve, but after 1980 in Belgium, where the champion was Menai Catrina (C) and the reserve Chirk Starling (B), it was decided to stage the International every other year. I have already written about my 1978 (eighth) visit to Denmark with Mrs Hambleton. That year, I also travelled to Belgium and France, first to Belgium in February for their stallion grading, which was held as part of the Semaine Internationale de l'Agriculture (International Agriculture Week), which included horses, cattle, sheep, pigs, goats and poultry, and had an attendance in excess of 200,000 over the week. All stallions were given a mark, with 85–100 per cent gaining excellence, 70–85 per cent good, 50–70 per cent medium and under 50 per cent rejected. My co-judges were the Comte Le Grelle, with whom I had judged previously in 1976, and Arnold Jacques, whose stallion Revel Playsome (now back at Sunwillow) I had placed champion. We marked every stallion independently, but it was amazing how consistent the marks were from each judge. The eight young section A stallions were disappointing and seven were rejected. Best of the adults was Ovington Sir Galahad, but even he did not receive the excellent grade. Young section B stallions were also disappointing, with three out of six rejected. Senior section B stallions were better, with Shalbourne Prince of March, Dyle King Berwyn and Wickenden Platignum gaining excellence. Valiant Flying King (D) was good, as were three WPB stallions. The WPB stallion Rose Masquerade, that I knew well when owned by Neville Budgen in Raglan, already had his licence, and was only paraded.

Two weeks before I was to judge at Poitiers, France, I received the sad news of the death of the President of the French Society, M Jacques Richard, a very kindly gentleman who had visited Wales several times and stayed with us at Ceulan. The standard at the show was excellent throughout, which was a fitting tribute to the contribution put in by M Richard. Coed Coch Tirion and Foxhunter Shanty won the section A adult classes. Mme Christine Bocquillon, who bought many Welsh ponies from 1969 onwards, was champion section B with Mynach Priceless over the stallion Epona Candy, the first Welsh pony to be bred by Mme Johnson, who was the first Welsh pony breeder in France. I was surprised to find such large classes of sections C and D, and suggested to the committee that they should be split in future. The French-bred Julie Cherauds was champion over Llanarth Marc ap Braint, and reserve supreme went to Mynach Priceless. Mme Bocquillon attended the FO Sale and bought Laithehill Cameo, Nefyn Innocence, Tynycae Tiptoes and Tanygroes Twilight. I bought Twilight from her and sold her Glanymor Nirvana and Ceulan Limelight privately from home, both of which proved very successful at her du Logis Stud. Our star foal of 1978 was Ceulan Sidan, one of nine full-brothers and sisters (Twyford Sprig x Ceulan Sprite). The four males were all sold for export and of the five females, four were kept and one, Ceulan Siwan (f. 1981), was sold to Lechlade Stud, where she produced Lechlade Melissa, the HOYS Riding Pony of the Year. Sidan won 28 championships and seven WPCS medals during her lifetime (1978–2003), and was a member of the Ceulan Sprite RW winning progeny team four times between 1982 and 1985. Her own progeny won it in 1998 with Sulpasc (f. 1986), Salome (f. 1996) and Sali (f. 1997).

WPCS publicity in 1979 started with a film show which I gave to the Midland Association at the Crown Hotel, Wychbold, on 18 April. After a lapse of two years when only the Ceulan publicity caravan attended, and there was no Welsh pony display, we were invited back to the Benson & Hedges Show in Cardiff Castle on 15–17 June. I suggested a combined in-hand / performance theme, which John Stevens agreed to. It started with Aston Superstar (A), Rosedale Mohican (B), Manmoel Mostyn (C) and Honyton Michael ap Braint (D) in-hand followed by Highland Drummer Boy (A), Burstye Kythnos (B), Bolgoed Fusilier (C) and Llanarth Black Magic (D) under saddle, and Whatton Gadfly (A), Wharley Taliesin (B), Gwelfro Tywysog (C) and Tewgoed Trysor (D) in harness. After the in-hand display, Mr Stevens designed a musical ride / drive which was spectacular, especially under floodlights. I produced the first colour calendar for the WPCS with tear-off postcards and, although it was only June, they proved very popular with the spectators who packed the grandstand for all performances.

After some local shows, Sidan was third out of 33 entries at the Bath and West on 1 June, followed by first out of 32 entries at Northleach on 8 July. Also at Northleach, the 10-y-o bay mare Ceulan Lindy Lou was first out of 16 entries, and her foal Ceulan Lady May first out of eight filly foals. Lindy Lou was sired by Revel Light out of Ceulan Looby Loo, who was sired by Criban Pep out of Dyrin Larina, the first mare we bought when we came to Miskin. For winning three first prizes, we were awarded the Lord Vestey Cup for the highest number of points in section A. Then Sidan was first and champion at six south Wales shows. At the RWS, Sidan was third out of 56 entries to Rookery Rhythm and Synod Marvel, beating many which later made a name for themselves. We also showed Ceulan Nesta in the section C mare class of 18 entries and she was also third, this time to Faelog Frolic and the 1974 and 1975 champion Cefn Moonlight, beating such as Nebo Dainty, Cathedine Aggie Gwyn, the 1980 champion Paddock Dawn and the 1981 RW ridden champion Kingdown Rebekah.

I was invited to judge section As at the Dutch Stamboek Show at Flevohof on 18 August, and to stay over for the Apeldoorn Championships on 25 and 26 August. Ruth, Jane and I flew into Schiphol Airport and experienced very warm hospitality, which lasted the whole week. At Flevohof, the animals were shown in-hand in the morning and had to compete either under saddle or in harness in the afternoon, and prizes were awarded after combining their morning and afternoon points. The section A stallions were not particularly impressive, but the ten brood mares (winner Rondeels Peninnah) and the seven barren mares (winner Petrouschka) would have been a force to be reckoned with at any show in Wales. Petrouschka performed spectacularly in harness and therefore won on total points from the ridden Rondeels Peninnah, Rondeels Careless and Cascob Water Baby.

After a very happy party, we spent three days with Mr Willem Brugsma (who was a Dutch TV presenter) at his Craig Bach Stud, where I caught up with some old friends, Twyford Mark (formerly owned by Mr Steve Jones at Aberystwyth), Twyford Merrythought and Hendre Pwsi. Then we stayed with Mr and Mrs Peletier at the Rondeels Stud, Hoenderloo. They have a large forest where deer and wild pigs live, and we saw groups of the animals on our evening drives through the forest. Mrs Peletier had become a household name in Wales in 1975 when the stallion Rondeels Pengwyn (f. 1966: Twyford Thunder x Coed Coch Pwffiad) was RW male champion. A mare which was of particular interest to me was the 19-y-o Twyford Cobweb, since her dam Reeves Crystal was bred at

Ceulan, Tal-y-bont, in 1946. I was also very impressed by her 15-y-o grey daughter, Rondeels Careless by Revel Tobias, and her 10-y-o chestnut son Rondeels Carino by Rondeels Pengwyn.

At Apeldoorn, Messrs Laemers and Teunissen judged 110 section A females, ending up with the grey mare Dyrin Tina as champion. Messrs Boonstoppel and Wiersema judged 103 section Bs, which included 17 bred in the UK, and their champion was the five-y-o dark chestnut mare Twickels Joy, daughter of Ceulan Bluebird (daughter of Monkham Snow Bunting), which I had sold as a foal on the 1971 FO Sale. Hirfryn Lynwen was champion cob, and Cairolyne champion Welsh part-bred. Then followed some spectacular harness and scurry driving classes, ending with a very impressive display of 42 ridden and ten driven animals. Our visit ended with two days spent with Dr van Riessen (whom I had known for twenty years) and his family at Lunteren. One had only to study the breeding of the ponies at Flevohof and Apeldoorn to realise what a big influence the 'Roman' ponies bred by Dr van Riessen have had on Welsh ponies in Holland.

The first sale of 1979 was the reduction sale of 63 ponies of the Weston Stud held on 28 July, when the 30 section As averaged £485, the 24 Bs £583 and the nine riding ponies £294, a sale total of £31,122. The two top prices of 2,000 gns and 1,700 gns were for section B yearlings, and the top section A price of 1,300 gns was for the mare Brierwood Snowfinch, who came to nearby Castellau Stud. The stud retained 17 section As and nine section Bs, which they took with them when they emigrated to Australia that October. Mrs Hambleton of the Llanerch Stud had a reduction sale of 32 section As on 8 September, where the top price was 1,000 gns for the grey mare Llanerch Merrymaid. An additional 35 lots were included from other vendors, and I bought the 7-y-o dun mare Rondeels Cavalla from Mrs Teresa Smalley, Mynd Stud (niece of Mrs Hambleton). Cavalla had been champion at the Ponies of Britain,

NPS and Royal Highland Shows and was a daughter of Twyford Cobweb which I had seen at Rondeels the previous month. I went to the sale determined to buy Cavalla (g-g-g-g-daughter of Seren Ceulan f. 1910), and didn't bid on anything else to make certain that I got her. And what a goldmine she turned out to be. Half of our stud are now her descendants. We entered three filly foals and three colt foals for the FO Sale on 14–15 September, and every one found a good new home. The section Bs sold for an average of £253 (almost the same as for 1978), but the section A average was down from £217 to £169. For the third successive year it was a Downland section B which topped the sale – this time, it was the two-y-o colt Downland Goldleaf (RW ch in 1981), which sold for 2,000 gns.

We had the equal top section A foal price (500 gns, only beaten by one section A mare at 650 gns) for Ceulan Lady May equal with Synod Nutmeg, that we would meet again at Ceulan in 1992. Glorious weather encouraged good prices at the Llanarth Sale on 20 October when the black yearling colt Llanarth Blackjack sold for 2,000 gns, and a filly foal, Derwen Romana, sold for 1,350 gns. Two days later at the RW sale, Parc Chess sold for 1,300 gns, closely followed at 1,200 gns for the dun stallion Rhosymeirch Flyaway, who went on to be a big winner in harness. When we decided to stop breeding section Bs in 1979 and concentrate on the section As because we had our own stallions running out, we sold Twylands Firecracker, Hillbarn Butterfly and her foal Ceulan Brahms, Antonette and her foal and Tanygroes Twilight to Paul and Elspeth Allen of the Cliffe (formerly Bleachgreen) Stud. In the 1983 WPCS Journal, Mrs Allen wrote in an article about Twilight that it took her two years to catch her!

1980–1989

We started off the 1980s with a bang by competing at 27 shows! We had won one WPCS medal each year between 1975 and 1979, and we went a stage further in 1980 by winning two medals with Sprig daughters, with the yearling Ceulan Whim at Barry (daughter of Fayre Whitelight which I had bought at Hay-on-Wye in 1975 and a g-daughter of the RASE ch Craven Sprightly Light), and another with Sidan at the Vale of Glamorgan. Whim won four first prizes and Sidan won eight, and both were placed several times in different shows. We also showed Revel Phillipa (f. 1970: Revel Chip x Revel Playtime), a mare with a big, square head, which I bought unseen in 1977. I probably would not have bought her if I had seen her, but you could not have better breeding – her dam Revel Playtime was also dam of the Australian champion Revel Playsome and Revel Pinup, dam of the Dutch champion Vardra Julius, and the Weston Stud top sire Revel Pye. Phillipa didn't win anything, but she had a stunning colt foal, Ceulan Proffwyd (f. 1980 by Sprig), who was in the top three at the seven shows in which he competed. Phillipa produced eleven foals by Twyford Sprig including Proffwyd, Perl (f. 1986) and Pablo (f. 1988). I sold Perl as a foal to Dargale Stud, where she was a good winner, and she was sold on the 1989 FO Sale to Joiners Stud (she is the dam of the champion Joiners Kilkenny [f. 1996], who was at Ceulan from 2001–03), and I bought Perl back in 2001. Ceulan Pablo was a super-premium stallion running out on Dowlais, where he produced very good stock and was sold on the 1999 FO Sale to the Orpons / Nynwood Studs, where he died in 2006.

We entered five filly foals and the colt foal Proffwyd on the FO Sale. Proffwyd was sold to Australian Mr Mark Bullen, and a bay filly, Ceulan Wit, full-sister to Whim, sold very well to Cusop Stud. Wit is another which I bought back (in 1988). At the FO Sale, 300 of the 535 ponies offered sold for an average of £207, topped by two yearlings at 1,900 gns each – the section A filly Weston Anniversary and the section B colt Sunbridge Tiger Tamer, who was a g-son of Tanygroes Twilight. A black section A filly foal, Derwen Eclipse, sold for 900 gns, which was the highest foal price to date. On the sale, I bought a chestnut yearling filly, Roseisle Ringtime from the Roseisle Stud, Kelso. She was sired by Sprig, and I greatly admired her dam Roseisle Wedding Ring when she was a visiting mare here in 1978. Wedding Ring was a good winner in the Scottish showrings, and she was sired by Mistral Celebration, son of Bryn Celia, which I bought on the 1962 FO Sale. The top prices at the Llanarth Sale were again higher, with the seven-y-o stallion Parc Brigadier selling for 3,000 gns – a figure not beaten until Mabnesscliffe Survivor (10,400 gns) in 1988. Two days later at the RW cob sale, there was a good, solid trade, and 241 sold for a good average figure of £274, with the top male and female section Ds fetching 1,200 gns.

The Area Associations were very active, and a coachload from the southern counties of England visited Penllyn, Cottrell and Ceulan in June, and the Midlands Association held a judging competition and discussion at Hillhampton Farm in October, where the 'master' judges were the Misses Rosemary Philipson-Stow and Anne Wheatcroft, Mr Llewellyn Richards and me. 1980 saw the publication of my book, *Welsh Ponies and Cobs*, chronicling the 30 families which I thought had had the most influence on the Welsh breeds. The book was very well received, and was reprinted in

1990, 1994 and 1997. Then followed three booklets (also published by J. A. Allen). One was 25 years of RW champions 1947–1982, with pedigrees and photographs, the next, in 1993, was one of the Allen breed series, *The Welsh Mountain Pony*, which sold 1,900 copies. The remaining 600 copies were bought by the WPCS and a few are still available. The third was also in 1993, when I wrote *An Introduction to Welsh Ponies and Cobs* for Whittet Books. It was reprinted in 1997 and 3,600 copies were sold. *The Welsh Cob* (J. A. Allen, 1998) was in great demand. All 5,500 copies were sold and it is now out of print. One copy which I donated to the Thorneyside Open Day sold for £380 and one to the Danaway Stud Open Day made £400. The sister volume, *The Welsh Pony*, sold 2,000 copies and is now also out of print. I wrote *One Hundred Glorious Years* for the WPCS to celebrate its anniversary in 2001. The Royal Welsh Champions publications were updated in 2009 by expanding them to cover sixty years, and the coffee-table book *Sixty Years of Royal Welsh Champions 1947–2007* was published by J. A. Allen in 2009. It was reprinted in 2011 and 2,500 copies are nearly all sold – one copy auctioned at the AGM at Llandudno sold for £760. Finally, I wrote *Welsh Ponies and Cobs, Ceredigion Champions* for the Ceredigion Feature County RWAS 2010, and it was published by Gwasg Gomer Press, Llandysul.

1981 started with a record 414 entries at Lampeter on 14 April. Llanarth Black Henry won a class of 26 section D yearling colts, which must have given great pleasure to Miss Pauline Taylor, who passed away in June. The fortunes of the Welsh cob breed as we know it today would have been very different were it not for the dedication and foresight of this great lady. I was president of the Glanusk Show on 2 May and, because the president has the honour of judging the supreme, I selected the section A champion, the stallion Coed Coch Llwynog, which his owner Mrs Pat Akehurst had bought on the Coed Coch Dispersal Sale.

With sale prices having improved markedly, RB&B held their first ever RW Spring Sale on 9 May and it was a success from the word go. The sale average was £314, with a top price of 820 gns for a section D three-y-o filly. 1981 coincided with the golden jubilee of the Australian Pony Stud Book Society and, as part of their celebrations, driving expert Diana Lawrence (who had bought Ceulan Sapphire and Sovereign from me in 1973 and 1976) made the journey to the UK with her two daughters, Esther, aged seven and Elizabeth, aged four, and their six-y-o Australian-bred pony Allambi Carlyle, who was a descendant of Ceulan Comet.

Initially they stayed in England and competed at English shows where, amongst their many winnings, they were champion at the BDS Show at Smiths Lawn, Windsor. Then they spent July at Ceulan and competed at Welsh shows, when they won the championship at Swansea Valley and took third prize in a class of 26 (beaten by hackneys) at the RWS, where the judge drove the top six. Esther and Elizabeth won many prizes driving Sapphire in Australia, and are now competing internationally. Esther won the Florida State Driving Championship in the USA in 2005, and Elizabeth was a member of the Australian team competing in Italy in 2010. Elizabeth has a daughter, Ruby, who, aged eight in 2013, won the driving class at the Victorian All-Welsh Show driving Carlyle Shakespeare, who is a grandson of both Ceulan Sovereign and Sapphire. In 2013 Diana, John, Ruby and Ned spent a week in the UK on their way to the World Driving Championships in Portugal (where Elizabeth was competing), and spent a day here with us at Ceulan.

We had a busy time ourselves at the 1981 RW, where we had three daughters of Ceulan Sprite, Ceulan Seirian (yearling), Ceulan Sidan (three-y-o), Ceulan Sequin (eight-y-o) and her filly foal, Ceulan Spangle, who won a class of 37 colt or filly foals. The three Sprite daughters were then reserve to the three progeny of

Friars Golden Sunset for the Gwyn Price Female Progeny Cup. We showed a variety during 1981, including Roseisle Ringtime, who was reserve champion at the City of Swansea show, Sidan, who was twice champion, and the palomino mare Tirmynydd Cream Puff and her foal Ceulan Pandora, which won four times. Cream Puff was a daughter of Revel Piquante (daughter of the champion Revel Pinup), which I had sold to Tirmynydd Stud on the Vardra Sale in 1975 and Puff (f. 1977) was by Sprig. I bought Cream Puff in 1980 in foal to Revel Janus, along with Piquante, who spent her remaining years at Ceulan. Having bred eight filly foals and five colts, we had a nice lot of five foals which had been shown to offer on the FO Sale and still retain Siwan (out of Sprite), Penlas (Phillipa) and Cadi (Cavalla).

Spangle and Pandora were both bought by Annette Cosgrove, secretary of the South-western WPCA. Romance (out of Rana) went to Twylands Stud from where I bought her back in 1985, and she was our show mare for a few years. The colt foal Ceulan Will O'The Wisp (full-brother to Ceulan Willow, Whim and Wit) became a good ridden pony, and was placed at Northleach and the Bath and West. There were 543 lots present at the FO Sale, including 17 section As from Bowdler and the major portion of the Gredington Stud of 10 section Bs and 20 As (the remaining 12 Gredington ponies were completely dispersed on the 1985 FO Sale). 347 were sold for £67,360 to an average of £194. Top section B at 1,300 gns was the chestnut yearling colt Rotherwood Cavalier (full-brother to the RW ch R Honeysuckle and Lilactime), and top section A at 900 gns was the grey Bowdler Bowstring who had always lived on the Long Mynd hills, and was only caught the day before the sale!

The 1978 Coed Coch Sale can be regarded as the Sections A and B 'sale of the century', and the Derwen Sale on 26 September was the cob equivalent, where 32 cobs (including 20 foals) sold for £25,632 averaging £801. Two hundred and forty-two lots were offered on the Llanarth Sale, but only 155 sold, averaging £360, with equal top prices of 2,000 gns for the stallion Llanarth Valiant's Image, and the mare Ystrad-Dewi Meg. The average at the RW Sale was £311, but there were many more sold so, for the first time, the sale total exceeded that of Llanarth. Top of the RW Sale was a grey section C, something very rare amongst sections C and D. This was the stallion Aston Breakaway, and his 1,600 gns was the highest figure to date for a section C at auction. Breakaway had been 1981 in-hand champion at Glanusk, and was regularly ridden and driven in traffic.

The highlight of 1982 for Ceulan was the progeny competition at the RWS with the three full-sisters from Twyford Sprig x Ceulan Sprite, namely Ceulan Siwan (f. 1981), Ceulan Seirian (f. 1980) and Ceulan Sidan (f. 1978). All three were placed individually and together, and they won the Gwyn Price Mare Progeny Cup from the group out of Friars Golden Sunset (which had won in 1979 and 1981), and the Ceulan group were reserve for the Pennell Stallion Progeny Cup to the group sired by Bengad Nepeta. The open mare winner Crossways Merle won the section A championship, having won it previously in 1980 and her dam, Ready Token Glen Bride, was female champion in 1968. Prices on the sales were rather depressing – at the FO Sale, one section A mare, Weston Pearly Necklace, sold for 1,500 gns, otherwise the top male was only 280 gns, and 277 of the 430 lots present sold for an average of £189. We offered four filly foals, one colt foal and the five-y-o stallion Knighton Jac-y-Do (who had sired nice foals for us). I bought a palomino two-y-o filly, Crepping Skylark, sired by Twyford Gamecock out of the palomino mare Revel Sorrento, who was top-priced mare when bought on the 1978 FO Sale. The last Llanarth Sale to be held on the farm was beleaguered with the worst weather of all nineteen sales. Only 81 of the 154 lots sold, and the average price was down from £382 to £270. There was much more encouraging trade at the RW Sale, where 261 of the 336 lots sold for an average of £300, with a top price of 1,400 gns for the stallion Kilgour Welsh Monarch, sire of the 1993 RW champion Horeb Euros. Mr Llewellyn Richards, the last remaining link with 200 years of the Criban Stud, died aged 88 years. Mrs Doris Gadsden of the Bengad Stud was elected WPCS President, and I was elected President-Elect.

My mother became ill in August, and her health got progressively worse. We travelled to Tal-y-bont to visit most weekends, and she passed away on 11 August 1983. My mother was a very wonderful lady – she was the only person I have ever known who could add up grocery bills line by line without having to separately add up the pounds, shillings and pence, and she had had to hold the fort single-handedly at Central Stores so many times when my father and I went gallivanting to shows and sales. She always had a smile, and overcame adversity bravely. Central Stores was an open house to a perpetual stream of my father's pony friends in my childhood days.

In his report as chairman of WPCS Council, Lord Kenyon described 1983 as 'a year when trade is in the doldrums, with very little demand from at home or abroad'. Showing started on a very wet 23 April at Lampeter where I was show president, and presented the championship trophies to Galchog Amlyn (A), Paddock Gemini (B), Synod Roger (C) and Ebbw Victor (D). This was the first showring appearance for Ebbw Victor, and it took him another fifteen years to win the RW George PofW cup after being male champion four times. The largest class of the day, which was section A yearling fillies of 39 entries, was won by Ceulan Pheasant, who we took home after she failed to reach the reserve of 100 gns on the FO Sale. Mrs Pat Lewis had taken over the secretaryship of Glanusk Show (and is still at the helm 32 years later), and filly classes were included for the first time. Ceredigion was host county for the RWAS with Mr Geraint Howells MP as president, and had collected funds to build the international building with its downstairs press room. WPCS members had collected £34,000 from donations and built a pavilion on the site for £59,000.

HM The Queen and HRH Prince Philip had consented to attend the show on the fourth day, and on the royal itinerary were the official opening of the WPCS Pavilion and an introduction to the members of council. As WPCS publicity officer and RWAS commentator, I was asked to organise a display of Welsh pony and cob stallions for the royal visitors. The Queen and Prince Philip arrived at the WPCS Pavilion in the Balmoral carriage with outriders brought down specially by train to Builth Road station from the Royal Mews, Buckingham Palace. I had expected to be doing a five-minute commentary on the display, but was instructed to start immediately HM arrived in the grandstand and not to stop until she stood up to make her way into the Main Ring to meet the handlers. I think the handlers got carried away by the occasion, and the display went on for 20 minutes, so HM and everyone else had to put up with my favourite stories: Julius Caesar taking Welsh ponies back with him to Rome, King Henry VIII in 1535 ordering the slaughter of all 'nags of small stature' including Welsh ponies, the presentation from Wales of Vardra Greylight to HM on her thirteenth birthday in 1939 and so on. Then I had to dash into the ring to answer any questions about the animals, and was very impressed when HM, out of the 16 stallions on the display, said, 'this one is a very good mover'! She also told me that Vardra Greylight had been passed on to Princess Margaret, and when he died, he was buried in Windsor Great Park. The following week two letters were received from Buckingham Palace, one to thank Mrs Gadsden for the gift received at the pavilion, and one to thank me for organising the Welsh pony and cob display.

Ceulan exhibits were successful again in the progeny competition, with three of the progeny of Ceulan Sprite namely

Ceulan Scamp (yearling colt), Ceulan Sidan and Ceulan Seirian. I had leased Scamp for the year to Lynton Webb of Langdon Hills, Essex and, from my vantage point in the commentary tower, had seen a chestnut pony galloping loose on caravan park hill. Recognising his bald, white face, I announced (without admitting that he was mine!) that his owner should go and retrieve him. Luckily, he was none the worse for his experience, and I sold him to Holland in September. The progeny of Coed Coch Norman won the Pennell Cup with three by Coed Coch Saled reserve. We competed at 17 shows during the year, and Sidan was champion four times, including Gower (WPCS medal). Her foal Ceulan Serydd (sired by Cui Mi'Lord which I bought in March 1982) was fourth of 38 at the RW, and took another three first prizes.

My 1983 overseas judging took me to the Dutch Vereniging Show on 20 August, where my section A champion was the senior mare Belvoir Windflower (Revel Chip x Revel Southwind) from the junior mare Rondeels Caprice and the stallion Knodishall Tornado. Section Bs were not so numerous, mainly from the Home 'T' Stud. The following day I was taken to a driving rally where there were 68 turnouts, a very impressive sight. With the poor trade experienced during the year, the Friday of the FO Sale was cancelled and, owing to the sale by the University College of Wales of the Llanarth Farms, the Llanarth Collective Sale was also cancelled. Instead, only a sale of 25 Llanarth cobs was held on the premises, where the top price was 1,700 gns for Llanarth Sue Ellen. At the FO Sale, the total was only £46,268 compared with £135,873 ten years previously, the top prices of 1,250 gns and 850 gns being for a daughter and son of Cusop Sunshade, the daughter of Monkham Snow Bunting. We offered four filly foals and two colt foals by Twyford Sprig and Cui Mi'Lord and four were sold. Ceulan Rowena (Twyford Sprig x Weston Rana) did not reach her reserve of 100 gns, so we brought her home and she was youngstock champion at the 1985 Glanusk Show.

One of the top section A mares was the 13-y-o Ceulan Melody (Revel Light x Melai Moonlight), which I bought back. The RW Sale on 17 October was much more upbeat. Two hundred and seventy-six of the 377 lots sold for an average of £313, with ridden and driven animals finding a good trade. Amongst section C, the three-y-o Synod Rachelian sold for 650 gns, and the yearling colt Rookery Fullflight (later a good sire in Denmark) for 600 gns. With very little demand for colt foals, we decided to keep two Sprig sons which were a matched pair and have them gelded – Ceulan Logo (out of Lindy Loo) and Ceulan Caption (out of Cavalla). We sold them in 1985 to driving expert Mrs Caroline Keevil of Shepton Mallet, who broke them to harness and sold them to Mr Jeff Osborne, who drove them in the HOYS scurry driving competition for fifteen years. Mr Osborne has sponsored this exciting competition throughout the UK for thirty years, is an honorary vice-president of the HOYS, and replaced Logo and Caption with more successful Ceulan ponies including Serchog, Siabod, Sion, Lloyd and Libretto.

As president of the WPCS in 1984, I was busy with nine visits to Area Associations, and was also was invited over to be president of the International Show at Ermelo, Holland on 31 August and 1 September. The Netherlands Stamboek decided to stage the 1984 International Show since it coincided with their twenty-fifth anniversary, and they organised three special displays. The first was 22 Welsh cob stallions brought over from the UK, parading to the accompaniment of the Dowlais Male Voice choir; the second, a parade of some of the original ponies from 1959 along with their progeny and the third, a parade of Welsh ponies of various colours assembled by Mr J. K. Wiersema (who had visited Ceulan many times and bought several ponies), an authority on horse colours and a 1959 founder member of the Stamboek.

The night before the show, the choir, handlers, owners and their families were given a civic reception by the Burgomeister of Ermelo.

On the Friday evening, we were guests at a reception and dinner for over 700 international breeders and guests, with the choir giving a concert. I gave a vote of thanks from the WPCS UK and presented a gift of a statuette of a Welsh miner to Mr Bruinsma, President of the Stamboek. One of the cob stallions, Mitcheltroy Survivor, walked onto the stage and stood there unperturbed, without a handler, while the choir sang.

Five hundred entries were received for the 80 in-hand classes, including a record 287 from outside the host country. Every champion was presented in the main ring on the second day, their country's flag was hoisted and the national anthem of that country played. The harness classes were well supported for singles, pairs, teams of four and finally a display of eight mares driven together. Along with Ruth, as WPCS President I was driven around the showground in a carriage drawn by five grey ponies following a carriage conveying Mr Bruinsma and the Dutch Minister of Agriculture, Mr I. G. Braks. Finally, there were chariot races, with four ponies abreast and charioteers in Roman dress. This display was invited to the RWS the following year, and proved a very exciting Main Ring attraction. After the final display of the cob stallions, a crowd of some 10,000 joined the choir in singing 'Men of Harlech' and the Welsh national anthem, and a lap of honour of members of the choir at a somewhat slower speed than the cobs! An S4C film crew was present, and we had several screenings of this wonderful show on television. Before leaving Holland, Ruth and I spent a few days visiting and sightseeing. One visit was to the foundry of Mr Arthur Spronken (owner of Vardra Julius by Twyford Sprig), who has enormous bronze statues in many Dutch cities. They are valued at tens of thousands of euros, and I was allowed to sit on one to be photographed.

Still in term-time, I was invited to judge in Australia at Sydney and give a film show there and at Melbourne and, with the co-operation of the rest of the lecturers at Llandaff, I left Cardiff on Wednesday 24 October and passed the national rugby stadium just as the result of the Wales vs Australia match was declared 16–14 in Wales' favour, which I thought was a good omen for my trip. There were 126 section As at Sydney, of which I had only previously seen two. There were some super youngsters competing, and most of my winners were bays or chestnuts, and it was rather embarrassing to hear, when the results were announced, that Ceulan Sovereign was their sire. So when it came to youngstock champion, I thought I had better give it to a grey. This was the two-y-o colt Carlyle Pocket, a grand type and spectacular mover. When the result was announced, Pocket turned out to be another Sovereign son! The male champion was Revel Playsome (which I had placed champion in Belgium in 1976), a son of Twyford Sprig, and the reserve male champion was a g-son of Ceulan Comet, but I cannot be accused of remembering Comet, since I was only one year old when he left Wales. Both female champion and reserve were by Revel Pye, and I owned Pye's sister Revel Phillipa, and 'aunt' Revel Piquante. Cobs were rather thin on the ground, but Llanarth Jack Flash was an easy champion from Neika Hawfinch (Sydenham Goldfinch x Saltmarsh Amanda, which I had sold to Tasmania). A nice load of cobs, which had travelled for four days from Western Australia to get there, arrived after the classes were finished, believing the classes to be the following day, were allowed to give a special parade.

After a quick change, it was back to the showground, where there were over 200 members assembled. We had a good party, after which I showed about 150 slides. Sunday was section B, riding and driving day, and my champion section B was a stunning chestnut yearling filly, Imperial Lady Anne (Weston Chilo x Rookery Grand Duchess), with reserve the stallion Weston Chippendale, who was bought on the 1978 Weston Sale for 1,700 gns. After a quick tour of Sydney and a visit to Sydney University to catch up with a former Cardiff

University chemistry professor, we visited Mark Bullen's Imperial Stud, where there were plenty of ponies in addition to the ones which he still had on the showground. The section A stallions at the stud were Kidwell Pipson, Brierwood Fusilier, Ceulan Proffwyd and the recently arrived Waxwing Herod, plus the section B Weston Chilo. Then I travelled with my friend who had previously lived in Wales, veterinarian Dr Dick Evans (who was glad to practise his Welsh), for 12 hours with ponies behind in a trailer, through odd-sounding towns like Woommargama, Tumbarumba and Wagga Wagga, to the new home of the Weston Stud, where it was good to catch up with Jack and Dilys Edwards. They were pleased to have news of home, and I showed recent videos which brought tears to their eyes. Then came a lift with Stephen Wiltshire to see Ceulan Sapphire and Sovereign and the biggest collection of carriages in Australia, and on to stay with Lady Creswick at Nattai Stud, to see Coed Coch Bari and plenty of Ceulan Comet grand-daughters. The estate is about half the size of Wales in area, and separate, huge pastures contained about 100 yearlings, 100 two-year-olds and 100 three-year-olds.

Then it was on to Cefn Onn Park, where the ponies were all Criban and Bowdler-bred. Here, I planted a tree, which I am told is now taller than their house. On the Friday night, I gave another talk at the Princes Motor Inn, Beaconsfield, where I was told to expect 30 members, but there turned out to be 94, including many with whom I had corresponded but had never met. I felt very important when Mrs Joan Frost of the Parattah Stud told me she had travelled 4,000 miles from Western Australia to meet me. About ten years ago, a member of the Australian team competing in the Commonwealth Games came up into the commentary tower at the RWS and asked me if I remembered him. When I admitted that I didn't, he said I had taken a photo of the group at Sydney when he was five. He had changed more than a little in twenty years, so I could be forgiven for not recognising him.

Taking part in the pageant at the RWS in Aberystwyth, 1957

My father (right) collecting the ponies for the USA at Revel Farm, Talgarth in 1955 with Mr Jenkyn Morris, who went with them

Section A stallions at the 1954 RWS, Machynlleth (from right): Coed Coch Madog (first, Shem Jones), Bolgoed Atomic (third, Tom Thomas), Clan Marshall (second, E. S. Davies), Coed Coch Samswn (fourth, Gordon Jones) with judge Mr A. R. McNaught

David with Glanymor Nirvana and Jane with Ceulan Sovereign (f. 1977), who was exported to Australia

Judging at the Royal Welsh Winter Fair 2008. Above: Catryn Bigley and Llanarth Delilah (B, supreme); Mrs Siân Morris and Friars True Love (A, reserve supreme)

Geoffrey Carter riding the legendary Ceulan Silver Lustre (f. 1938), 1950

A painting of Ceulan Sprite (f. 1964: Criban Pep x Revel Siesta) by Marjorie Turner

With Ceulan Lwcus, 1994

Twyford Sprig (1965–1994) the greatest sire we ever had at Ceulan

The winning progeny group at the RWS 1982 (from left) Ceulan Siwan, Sidan and Seirian

(Photo: Carol Gilson)

Mrs Ann Jones of Frongoch Stud with Frongoch Cardi, male champion RWS 2007

Ceulan Logo and Ceulan Caption driven by Mr Jeff Osborne   *(Photo: Anthony Reynolds)*

The presentation of Llanerch Topaz to HRH Prince William at Highgrove House, 1986

Caris Love Story, the first Section A foal born in the USA by AI (frozen semen from Trefaes Taran, dam Pontllys Tasmin), 1995

Severn Valley WPCA visit Ceulan, 1995

A rather amusing cartoon featuring the author by Lesley Bruce 2000 *(Courtesy of Lesley Bruce)*

At Lampeter Welsh Breeds Show 2011, being presented with an anniversary clock by the show chairman, Mr Daniel Morgan

(Photo: Ryan Wilson)

Judging in Denmark with Brierdene Napoleon, 2001

Royal Welsh Winter Fair: HRH Prince Charles awarding the foal supreme championship to John James' section B filly Sianwood Bayleaf, 2001

Being presented with the Sir Bryner Jones Memorial Award by HRH The Princess Royal, RWS 2002

(Photo: Tom Best)

Judging in Finland with (from left) Cathael Lisa (D), Polaris Jonquil (B) and Waitwith Delight (A, supreme), 2003

Wernderris Caramel, who was at Ceulan 2003–14

(Photo: Maud Farghen)

Dragon Show Holland, 2010 with Ysselvliedts Navarino, ridden champion, and fellow-judge Mr Edwin Prosser

(Photo: Aniek Rolf)

A group visiting from Sweden with Ceulan Ceirrios and Bethan Hooper, 2013. David and I are in the group behind

The very special palomino Ceulan Calon Lân as a foal, and in action as an adult

Visit of the Carmarthenshire WPCA with Weston Distinction (above) and Ceulan Caryn, 2014

In 1983 Sprite had another filly, Ceulan Serog, by Twyford Sprig, so we set off for the RWS with three full-sisters Serog, Seirian (barren mare) and Sidan (brood mare) with her filly foal Ceulan Shoned by Cui Mi'Lord. All four were placed in the top six in classes of up to 56 entries. Sidan's class was full of famous champions led by Llanerch Decima (female champion), Sunwillow Bernina and Bengad Lavender, three of the best mares in the UK. The three sisters then won the Gwyn Price Progeny Cup with Sunwillow Bernina's group reserve, and they were also reserve for Twyford Sprig to Revel Janus's group for the Pennell Cup. During the year, Sidan was champion at Gower (WPCS medal) and Melody was champion at Cothi Bridge (WPCS medal), Taf Fechan and the Vale of Glamorgan.

I travelled to the Northleach Show as president, but the appointed section C judge did not appear, so I ended up as section judge! After the marathon one-day FO Sale in 1983, it reverted to a more leisurely two-day event, when 242 of the 374 lots sold for £48,830, an average of £202. Lady Margaret Myddleton was dispersing her Chirk Stud, and Chirk Cornbunting topped the sale at 1,250 gns. Cwmsyfiog Trisca, who was in Sidan's class at the RW, topped the section As at 980 gns and went on to produce many famous Colne ponies. We found better demand – the three Sprig filly foals out of Sienna, Piquante and Phillipa sold to breeders, and the palomino yearling filly C Springsong (Cui Mi'Lord x Ceulan Sparkle) was the second-highest yearling selling to Whatehall Stud. The Whatehall Stud was short-lived, and held a dispersal sale in July 1988, where Springsong sold for 1,200 gns to Fairstoke Stud, for whom she won and was reserve champion at the RASE in 1993, and her head shot was on the front cover of the breed series book, *The Welsh Mountain Pony*. The most encouraging 1984 sale was the RW, when 297 lots sold for £118,800 an average of £400, up 28 per cent on the 1983 figure, with a top price of 2,200 gns for the three-y-o colt Tireinon Triple Crown. I presided at the AGM at Cardiff University where the Brodrick Memorial trophy was presented to Gordon Jones, who had been stud groom at Coed Coch with his nephew Shem Jones, then at Gredington for many years.

The resemblance between 1985 statistics and those for the previous year was uncanny: 1985 exports of 127 (122 in 1984), RW in-hand entries of 861 (859 in 1984), the FO Sale average of £207 (£202 in 1984) and the RW Sale of £410 (£400 in 1984). In March, Don and Nan Jenks Handford, who had the Lisvane Stud near Cardiff, contacted me to say that they were emigrating, and they wanted me to buy all their ponies with the exception of the stallion Coed Coch Cariadog, which they had bought on the Coed Coch dispersal sale, and the mares Lisvane Llewela and Lisvane Teleri, which Michael Dovey was keeping to continue as the Brynvane stud. It was rather a daunting undertaking, but the stud's Tanlan Lili Lon had always been a favourite of mine, and her daughter Lisvane Lotus Blossom (by Revel Springbok, same dam as Sprig), produced 14 foals at Ceulan, and died in 2004 aged 25. Lotus Blossom's son Ceulan Lwcus (by Sprig) has been the top sire in USA for four years, and her daughter Ceulan Lucy (by Trefaes Taran) won first of 42 entries at the 1992 RWS. Lisvane Lifris (sixth generation of Lisvane back to 1960) was another good producer at Ceulan. I sold Lisvane Sidan to Pentyrch Stud, and Coed Coch Nelma back to the Bryndansi / Coed Coch Stud. Rather than have the cob stallions travel to Lampeter for their premiums, it was easier for me to travel to Greenloaning, Scotland, on 6 April, where I awarded the WPCS premium to Llanarth Rhun, a stallion who had excelled under saddle.

Then in May, the Scottish WPCA came to south Wales and visited Castellau, Ceulan, Pentyrch, Penllyn, Cottrell and Thornberry. After a talk and film show at a Cardiff hotel to Mary Alice Williams' group from Texas on 14 July, it was another stud visit at Ceulan for them. At the RWS, Sunwillow Bernina's group of three, which included the winning two-y-o filly Sunwillow Quest (record price when sold on the 1994 FO Sale), won the Gwyn Price Progeny Cup with the three Ceulan (Twyford Sprig x Ceulan Sprite) reserve. Because the Bernina group all had different sires, Sprig won the Pennell stallion Cup.

Sidan had her best showing year ever, starting with the championship at Cothi Bridge (WPCS medal) followed by another eight championships, including Pembroke County and Monmouth, and her palomino colt foal Ceulan Seren Aur (by Cui Mi' Lord) won five first prizes. On the Monday after the RWS, we had a surprise visit from a very smart horse-box whose driver proceeded to unload a chestnut filly which had a sales lot number stuck on her. On enquiring what it was all about, the driver said he had instructions to deliver her to Ceulan from the Rotherwood Sale, and off he went. After I had stabled her safely, I contacted the auctioneers RB&B to find out about Lot 5, and was told that they had instructions from American Mrs Hope Ingersoll (whom I had never met, but she had written that she wanted to buy Ceulan Shoned, who went to her later that year), to buy Rothwood Hollyhock and send her to Ceulan! In due time, a letter arrived from Mrs Ingersoll suggesting that I would keep Hollyhock at Ceulan, put her in foal to stallions (named for the next ten years) and arrange for the foals to be forwarded to her farm in Massachusetts. It was not very convenient, since we had sold off all our section Bs, but the wonderful octogenarian Mrs Ingersoll was the 'mother' of the WPCS of America, who had personally started a Welsh cob section of the American Stud Book (she imported Turkdean Sword Dance and Llanarth Phillida in 1968), and ran it alone for many years, so we took it on.

Furthermore, Hollyhock was a very lovely mare (maternal sister to the RW champions R Honeysuckle and Lilactime), one that I liked looking at on the field, and absolutely no problem to cope with. Following a succession of six colts, most of which went to Massachusetts, Mrs Ingersoll's son contacted me in 1992 to buy her, so that foal was named Ceulan Hercules, and the mare and foal sold to Ylva Lindh of Sweden and sent to Llanarth Stud to produce for the Peterborough International Show. Hollyhock had another colt, Simberg Hobnob, by Twyford Signal in 1993. He was something special, and came to the 1995 Glanusk Show, where he was overall champion. Then Hollyhock had a run of fillies in Sweden!

After the Rotherwood Sale came the Bengad Sale on 7 September, which began with a parade of stallions led by the 22-y-o Coed Coch Saled and the 21-y-o Revel Cello. Top of the sale at 1,150 gns was the six-y-o stallion Bengad Montique, who was male champion at the RASE. Highlight of the FO Sale on 13–14 September was the sad final dispersal of the Gredington Stud, which had been at the forefront of sections A and B for forty years. Top of the sale at 2,500 gns was the eight-y-o stallion Coed Coch Bleddyn, and two mares, Gredington Arian and Gredington Thetis – both made 2,000 gns. Top of the Bs was the beautiful Gredington Lily, who sold for 1,200 gns, and I bought the two-y-o colt Paddock Orion for Denmark at 700 gns. Sunwillow Mutters by Revel Playsome sold for 900 gns. I sold the second-highest filly foal Ceulan Simone (T Sprig x Ceulan Sienna) at 400 gns, and the top colt foal C Seren Aur (Cui Mi'Lord x Ceulan Sidan) at 350 gns. For myself, I bought the bay mare Carnalw Heledd (who had been champion at the United Counties), and the bay colt foal Fronbach Carlo by Synod Captain.

Top of the RW Cob Sale on 19 and 21 October was Menai Stud's three-y-o colt Menai Welsh Sparkler, who went to Germany for 2,000 gns, where his brother Menai Modern Comet was doing so well. The show mare Ystrad-Dewi Margarita sold for 1,700 gns. Geldings reached a new high for the Llanarth or RW sales when Ffald Baron sold for 1,350 gns. He was a son of Ceulan Elsa, which I sold as a foal in 1975. I sold the section C colt foal Ceulan

Nobleman (Cui Mi' Lord x Ceulan Nesta) on this sale. His maternal brother Ceulan Nero (f. 1981, Twyford Sprig x Ceulan Nesta) was the overall supreme champion of the 1985 south-eastern WPCA stud judging, and his owners, Mr Friskey Fieldwick and his son Jason, of the Sackville Stud, came to Ceulan two weeks later and bought Nesta. It was they who bred her son Sackville Nicky, overall supreme of the WPCS performance competition in 1997 and 1998. In December, I sold Ceulan Nans (f. 1982, Twyford Sprig x Ceulan Nesta) to Holger and Inga Winding of Raeveskiftet, Denmark, so temporarily, until the next RW Sale, we did not have any section Cs at Ceulan.

The highlight of 1986 was the presentation at Highgrove House, Tetbury, on 3 August, of the section A mare Llanerch Topaz as a riding pony for HRH Prince William. It had been agreed in 1982, the year that Mrs Hambleton (breeder of Topaz) was president of the WPCS, and the year that Prince William was born, but the presentation was delayed until the prince was old enough to ride her. Prior to the occasion, Topaz had spent two months with Mrs Anne Williams of the Crawel Stud, Sennybridge, and her daughter Victoria, and had been taken out with a young rider most days onto the Epynt shooting range to make certain that Topaz was 'bomb-proof'. At the presentation, Prince William rode Topaz, who behaved impeccably. After William outgrew Topaz, she was ridden by Prince Harry and then passed on to other members of the royal family.

I judged at the Irish WPCA Show at Newcastle, County Wicklow on 28 June, where the supreme was the section B Stradbally Allyssum. Winner of the lead-rein class was Nefyn Blue Boy led by his owner Mrs Avril Doyle. After the show I gave a talk and film show at the Cullenmore Hotel, Ashford, where there was excellent attendance and a very happy crowd. Revel Japhet was RW section A champion and qualified for the Lloyds Bank championship at

HOYS, where the winner was the WPB Chirk Windflower. Three progeny of Revel Janus won the progeny competition. They were Baledon Jubilation, her full-brother Baledon Johnathon, and the barren mare Baledon Venus. The Twyford Sprig group consisted of Ceulan Sidan (brood mare), Ceulan Romance (barren mare) and Taliaris Calypso (brood mare) who came to live at Ceulan in 1987, where she spent the rest of her life.

Weston Stud had the top consignment at the FO Sale with the section B stallion Pennwood Eldorado, who went back to his breeder at 2,100 gns, and two filly foals, Weston Bouquet and Prelude at 750 and 520 gns. Ceulan Lilian (Sprig x Lisvane Lotus Blossom) was fourth-highest foal. Having sold Cui Mi'Lord to Denmark, I leased the bay stallion Twyford Noggin for the 1986 season, but although he was a grand little sort, we did not have one filly by him, so did not book him for another year. The average at the RW Sale on 18 and 20 October was £349, almost the same as for 1985. There were no outstanding foals on the sale this year, but many very good mares, 49 of which sold for over 500 gns with the top price of 2,200 gns for Llanfair May Lady. To replenish my section Cs, I bought two mares, the five-y-o Elmead Danielle by Nebo Daniel, and the six-y-o Coediog Catrin by Penlluwch Dafydd out of Penucha Wennol, who was also dam of Coediog Dwynwen, who was first at the RW that year and female champion in 1983. Danielle did not stay long at Ceulan, but Catrin was with us for eight years.

In October, we sold the chestnut section A yearling colt Twycross Cockleshell (son of Rowfant Peacock), the section A mares Ceulan (J) Venna and Forlan Harmony, and arranged the sale of the section C mare Synod Lillie Langtree to Israel. We had sold Weston Rana and her daughter Ceulan Rebecca with Tirmynydd Cream Puff to the same family in 1983, and they had proved a great success. They even managed to get Weston Rana friendly, something which I had failed to accomplish in the eight years that she was at Ceulan. The death occurred in 1986 of the section A stallion Fronarth What Ho at 34 years of age, who had won in harness at the RWS 13 times, the last time at the age of 26 in 1978. Fronarth What Ho cost his owners exactly 75 pence stud fee (15 shillings), paid to me at the 1951 Llanilar Show to have the section C mare Fronarth Queen Bee covered by Dinarth What Ho, with the help of a steep slope!

The World Congress of Agricultural Journalists was held in the UK from 17–22 May 1987 and they spent two days in Wales, with one day on the RW showground, where I was asked to organise a display of Welsh ponies and cobs. I selected one stallion and one mare from each of the four sections, and the display was well received. Owing to ill-health, Mr Tom Roberts, who had been a very good friend to everyone, retired from the secretaryship of the WPCS. Because this was the twenty-fifth RWS on the permanent site, all exhibitors (including myself) who were also exhibitors in 1963 were given commemorative rosettes. In-hand entries for sections A, B, C, D and WPB exceeded 1,000, and there were enormous classes of ridden and driven Welsh.

It was the turn of section A to receive the RW Queen's Cup in 1987, and it was awarded to the mare Cledwyn Seren Goch (f. 1977: Coed Coch Norman x Chieveley Silver), who had been female champion in 1983. She and her year younger full-sister Cledwyn Seren Arian (who was eighth in the same class) were two members of the winning progeny group for Coed Coch Norman. The female progeny group went to three daughters of Nefyn Blodyn – Verdrefawr Oriel, Blodwen and the yearling filly Glenda. We were third in the 51-strong class of yearling fillies with Ceulan Catrin, the first of the palomino sisters Twyford Sprig x Rondeels Cavalla. Also the bay colt foal Ceulan Steffan (Twyford Noggin x Ceulan Sidan) was fourth in a class of 58 foals which were divided into colts and fillies. Synod Roger made his last RW appearance, won his fifth championship and was the HOYS Lloyds Bank qualifier.

With Cui Mi' Lord having gone to Denmark, I leased the bay Synod Captain for the summer, and also bought early in the year a rather immature bay yearling colt, Trefaes Taran (Wynswood Little Acorn x Trefais Tail), on condition that they could keep him to show at the RWS, where he did remarkably well. It was a good thing that I had bought him before the show, otherwise he would have cost more! Taran was one of those ponies that improved every year until middle age and he sired some excellent stock for us. Until Taran was of breeding age, we were short of a stallion to use on the Sprig daughters, and I bought Bengad Rustling Grass (f. 1983: Coed Coch Saled x Bengad Ribbon Grass), the top male on the sixth biennial sale at the Bengad Stud. I had judged Rustling Grass on his first showring appearance the previous year, and had placed him reserve champion, so I thought I should uphold the courage of my convictions, and he proved a good investment.

I leased out the two-y-o colt Ceulan Sentinel to TV producer John Bulmer as a 'teaser' for his Monnington Morgan horses. The whole family looked forward to delivering a colt (Deri Bay Boy in 1988) to Monnington Court, Hereford, to admire the world-famous bronzes sculpted by Angela Connor (Mrs Bulmer) which were spread about the extensive lawns. The thirty-fourth FO Sale was very encouraging, with only a few lots not finding purchasers. Top of the sale at 1,800 gns was the section B yearling colt Brookhall Shuttlecock, and top section A (1,400 gns) was the yearling filly Dryfe Sheer Heaven, who achieved fame later by being the dam of the 1999 HOYS Templeton qualifier Brynodyn Scarlet, who was herself dam of the 2011 and 2012 HOYS ridden ponies of the year, Brynodyn Savannah and Brynodyn Sirius.

My neighbour Mr Viv Thomas of the Trisant Stud got 800 gns for a black filly foal, Trisant Pansy by Yaverland Nero, which augured well for Nero as a sire. When I bought Nero for Viv, it was on condition that I would be given first refusal if he was for sale, and Nero came to Ceulan in 1994. The 1987 RW Sale was a big success story, with the average price increasing from £349 to £504, heralding the start of an explosion in prices to an average of £912 three years later. The nine-y-o mare Talley Wendy (which had been bought on the 1981 sale for 720 gns) broke the record selling at 4,000 gns. Top filly foal at 1,450 gns was Synod Rosary, daughter of Synod Rosemary, whose later progeny Synod Rambo and Synod Robert Black were to sell for 10,000 gns in 1997 and 11,000 gns in 1999.

If I was planning to replenish our section Cs and Ds, we certainly went a good way in 1987 since, in addition to Elmead Danielle and Coediog Catrin in 1986, I bought the section D Persie Nanette (f. 1986: Synod Ranger x Parc Nest, sister of six-times RW champion Parc Rachel), and bought back the cream Ceulan Nyfain, which I had sold as a foal on the Llanarth Sale in 1975. Nyfain was in foal to Ffoslas Flying Rocket, and our advertisement in the 1988 WPCS Journal stated that we were expecting foals from all sections sired by Twyford Sprig (A), Synod Captain (A), Rosedale Mohican (B), Synod Roy Rogers (C) and Ffoslas Flying Rocket (D).

The 1988 RWS was a great success story for Nebo Stud. Nebo Daniel won the George P of W Cup, Nebo Bouncer won the Chetwynd Cup and qualified for the HOYS Lloyds Bank championship. Nebo Brenin groups won both the sections C and D progeny competition, Lisa won the best handler competition with the champion Nebo Daniel, and Owen was second. Brierwood Rocket won the section A championship from the novice mare winner Churchwood Promise, we were reserve for the Gwyn Price progeny competition to the Sunwillow Bernina group (Sunwillow Ofenpas, Sunwillow Monte Rosa and Sunwillow Luzzana) with our Ceulan Seirian group (yearling colt Ceulan Seren Goch, two-y-o filly Ceulan Serch and third prize filly foal Ceulan Sibrwd). Downland Edelweiss was champion section B from Cottrell Amethyst, who had beaten her at the RASE Show. Llanarth Rhun was again champion ridden sections C or D, and Twyford Marengo, one of the first ever to compete at the RW from overseas, won in harness. The Welsh part-bred Meridian Park was champion in-hand hunter and reserve to Nebo Bouncer for the RW HOYS ticket, but got his at the National Hunter Show. 1988 saw the setting up of the Large Welsh Part-bred group by Miss Hilary Legard, and this group is still going from strength to strength today.

With 325 entries, the International Show was held at Groenendaal, Belgium, on 20–21 August, where I judged the sections A, C and D with Mrs Marianne Seidenfaden (Denmark), while the sections B and WPB and ridden were judged by Mrs Robina Mills (UK) and Mrs Anna Svinhufvud (Sweden). The ten championships and ten reserves were well dispersed throughout the competing countries, Holland having seven, Denmark five, the UK four and Germany and Belgium two each. Brierwood Rocket (A) was supreme champion with Llanarth Sally (D) reserve, both from the UK. Mr Jean-Pierre Hachez of the Belgian Ministry of Agriculture attended and presented the rosettes. The whole show ran like clockwork thanks to the wonderful organisation of Miss Isabelle de Moerkerke.

Ruth and I stayed with our good friends Joseph and Maria Ducatelle at Oudenaarde who, the following day, took us to see two of the biggest collections of horse-drawn vehicles and harness in the world, the first with Baron Casier at Nokere and the other with Mr Willy Allo at Kapelle-op-den-Bos. Both these gentlemen often brought their horses and vehicles to compete in the UK, and Mr Allo's daughter drove a team of palomino Welsh ponies in international competitions. The first show ever in Israel was judged by Mrs Jean Houghton, Sinton Stud (whose son and daughter, Mark and Pippa, were working on a voluntary basis at the English hospital in Nazareth). First prize stallion was Foxhunter

Tip (Twycross Cockleshell was third), Twyford Jubilee won the brood mare class (Tirmynydd Cream Puff was third), and Ceulan Rebecca won the barren mare and ridden classes.

The turnover at the FO Sale on 16–17 September was up 33 per cent on the 1988 figure, and the average price was £285. Top price of 2,400 gns was paid for Sunwillow Monte Rosa, who was a member of Sunwillow Bernina's RW winning group, and top section B was the bay two-y-o colt Lemonshill Little Emperor, who sold to Germany for 2,200 gns. We sold the colt foal Ceulan Seryddwr (Synod Captain x Ceulan Serog), who had won at four major shows, to Mme Bocquillon, and his greatest claim to fame is as the sire of Okiwana Daineger (f. 2002), the 2008 European show jumping champion. It is amazing how Sprig progeny to the second and third generation have this jumping ability, which I often learned to my cost when they jumped out of their enclosures.

Early in 1988 I bought back Ceulan Wit privately, and she obliged by producing a very nice filly, Ceulan Wendy, by Bengad Cola Nut. If the FO Sale was the cause of encouragement, then the RW sale on 15 and 17 October caused jubilation – the average almost doubled, and the sale total was three times the figures of the previous five years. The seven-y-o stallion Mabnesscliffe Survivor sold for 10,400 gns, a figure which was not reached again for 11 years (Synod Robert Black 11,000 gns in 1999), and the section C filly foal Synod Romantica sold for 1,500 gns. We sold the filly foal out of Nyfain for 350 gns and Elmead Danielle sold for 650 gns. The first Welsh National Foal Show, organised by the Brecon and Borders WPCA, was held at Llanelwedd. This was an outdoor event which still flourishes today, but is now indoors. The Glamorgan WPCA also held their first foal show at Castellau Farm, home of our chairman Mr David Prichard, and Cariad (Twyford Sprig x Rondeels Cavalla) won from 16 entries.

In January 1989 I gave a talk and film show to the Avon and Borders WPCA, followed on 28 May by judging at the Isle of Wight WPCA, where there were over 20 exhibits in some classes. My supreme was the Welsh cob Gwendraeth Telynor, and reserve the large roan WPB gelding Wylie Pink Panther. The attendance at the RWS reached the magical 200,000 by noon on the fourth day. The WPCS staged a 'Horse World' display every day, which gave me an opportunity to talk about the performance capabilities of the four sections of the WSB. This was done by arranging a team relay of section C and D jumping, followed by a scurry pair of section As and Bs. There were two heats each day, which provided plenty of action, and they performed especially well on the second day in the presence of HRH The Duke of Edinburgh, who was himself an expert team driver. Glamorgan was the feature county, and the president was Mr Idwal Symonds, with whom I am still in touch in 2015. Champion section A was Breachwood Marwyn owned by Mr David Gay, a local, good friend of ours. Marwyn was second in 1984 and 1986 and third in 1987 before finally making it in 1989. My local section B breeder Miss Fiona Leadbitter, who only bought her first Welsh pony in 1980, won the section B championship with her three-y-o filly Thornberry Demelza and the stallion class with Thornberry Gamekeeper.

Gwelfro Tywysog, who had won in harness several times but never in-hand, was section C champion, and Derwen Dameg won the George PofW Cup and reserve for the HOYS qualifier to the WPB champion Starlyte Royal Minstrel – it was the WPB mare Ainsty Merry Maid (g-daughter of Ceulan Minuet) who won at Wembley. Some cob exhibitors became too enthusiastic during the judging of the stallion class, and entered the Main Ring, and I had to announce that judging was suspended until they had all left. Our palomino yearling filly Ceulan Cariad was reserve champion of the palomino section and, joined by her palomino full-sisters, the two-y-o Ceulan Cantores and the three-y-o Ceulan Catrin (which I had sold to Mrs Tchaikovsky of Perth), were reserve for the Gwyn Price Progeny Cup. Sidan, at 11 years, was only shown once in 1989 when she won her thirty-fourth championship at Monmouth. Her three-y-o daughter Ceulan Sulpasc (by Cui Mi'Lord), who won at four shows, had been sold to Vardra Stud, but continued to live at Ceulan. As publicity officer, I assisted with the organisation of a WPCS international conference at Hay-on-Wye on 29 and 30 July, with delegates attending from Australia, Belgium, Denmark, France, Holland, New Zealand, South Africa, Switzerland, the USA and West Germany.

The average of the 310 ponies on the FO Sale on 15–16 September was up from £285 to £393, with the four-y-o section B stallion Cennen Signature Tune top of the sale at 2,400 gns. The sale included the dispersal of Sir Harry Llewellyn's Foxhunter Stud, and the bay section A mare Foxhunter Parakeet topped the section As at 2,200 gns, while a section A colt foal, Fronbach Hello Dandy, broke the sale record of a colt foal at 1,400 gns. We sold a colt foal Ceulan Selog (Bengad Rustling Grass x Ceulan Serog) and a yearling filly Ceulan Cassandra (Synod Captain x Taliaris Calypso) to Ireland. It was a cob stallion, Thorneyside More Magic, which topped the RW Cob Sale on 14 and 16 October at 6,000 gns. A noticeable interest at the 1989 sale was in good cob brood mares, with 67 of them selling for over 1,000 gns with Fronarth Black Diamond breaking the female record at 4,500 gns. This demand was poor in 1980 (only one), and has currently returned to poor (only seven for over 2,000 gns in 2014 with plenty of lovely mares available for under £1,000). 1989 exports were up to 207 from 127, and during the year, we sold for export Ceulan Laddie to Mr Lescanne of France, Bengad Gazania to Mr Rasbach, Germany, Ceulan Venetia and Ceulan Picnic to Ms Blomqvisk, Sweden, and Lisvane Seiriol and Lisvane Leah to Mr Bertil Bengtsson, Sweden.

A new procedure was devised for accepting members onto the panel of judges. Six animals of each section were assembled at two centres, one in England and one in Wales, and the aspiring judges asked to judge them and give their reasons to the 'master' judges who for the initial year were Mr Gwyn Price, Mr Dick Swain and myself. In September 1989 I took early retirement so that I no longer had to rush a visit to Australia into a long weekend, and I could attend all council meetings. Until 1989, my attendance had had to fit in with college duties. For the following 20 years (until the rules changed in 2009 and I was no longer eligible to stand), my attendance was 100 per cent, and I headed the poll every three years.

1990–1999

Although I had written articles on Welsh ponies and cobs for American publications since 1952, it took me 38 years before I actually visited that country to judge at the Penn-Mary-Del (Pennsylvania, Maryland and Delaware) Show on 23–24 June 1990, and at the Welsh of Wisconsin Show on 30 June. My co-judge at the PMD was Morgan horse breeder Mr Lyman Orcutt and, although we judged independently, our placings agreed about 98 per cent of the time. The evening before the show, it was good to meet the directors of the WPCS of America, some of whom I had not seen for many years, including Mrs Gail Morris (president, who attends every RWS), Mrs Carlene Sharples (vice-president, who was with us at Hay-on-Wye the previous year), Mrs Joan Dunning (formerly Mrs Mackay-Smith, who bid against my father at the Coed Coch Sale in 1937), her daughter Mrs Hetty Abeles, who had judged at Vaynor Show in 1956 and Mrs Molly Butler, Glan Nant Farm, who had imported some of the best section Bs from UK. Champion section A with both judges was the brood mare Liseter Reveler's Dream, which had been purchased on the Liseter Dispersal Sale in 1988 when the stallion Liseter Merry Lad sold for $90,000 (£53,000). Reserve supreme was the bay yearling colt Barlys Trois Y Penrhyn, who was also supreme youngstock of the whole show.

Mr Orcutt's choice of stallion winner was Liseter Cadet, while I preferred Severn Sirocco, which had travelled 1,500 miles from Mississippi and was bred by Mrs Iliff, who had imported

Ceulan Serene in 1948. Champion section B was Rotherwood Crown Prince, who had done well in UK shows in 1989, and the same owner (Mr Campbell Lawrence) also owned the section C champion Dawns Dathliad Arian Y Penrhyn. We had different animals for section D champion. Mr Orcott voted for the stallion Llanarth Trustful while I preferred the mare Lidgett Henrietta, two outstanding animals that had held their own in the UK before export. After the show, I gave a talk and slide show, which was a success despite torrential rain pounding on a tin roof. The second day catered for the performance competitions, the most successful of which command enormous prices, often $100,000 for working hunter ponies.

The following day, I was taken to spend three days at Grazing Fields Farm and eventually meet the legendary Mrs Hope Ingersoll, Nebo Fair Lady (the first Welsh cob to fly the Atlantic), Ceulan Shoned (supreme champion at the 1987 Toronto Winter Fair), Synod Rosie O'Grady and many other well-known names. This very special lady, Mrs Ingersoll (who acquired her first Welsh pony in 1909), made an effort to accompany me around the farm, where there were cobs and ponies ridden and driven all day. While I was there, the horse manager Mr Richard Miller (now of Heniarth, Ferryside), got appendicitis and was rushed off to hospital. I had to collect his spaniel from the airport (if he had bitten me, I would have let him go), then get Llanarth Trustful, harness and vehicle loaded up and go off to a driving show. Before flying to Milwaukee, I visited Mrs Cynthia Kirby and her section Bs on Rhode Island.

The first day at Jefferson, Wisconsin, was performance day, where the Canadian-bred cobs Brynarian Brenin and Brynarian Cerys collected most of the awards – they were so well trained that they often beat American Quarter Horses at their own work. Two full-sisters stood out in section A – Asgaard Rhiannon Prydferth (grey) and Asgaard Heulwen (bay-roan). I gave the championship to Heulwen while my co-judge preferred Prydferth. Their extended pedigrees in the fourth generation were 16 animals from the UK. In the third generation was Severn Sure Shot (Eryri Gwyndaf x Ceulan Serene) for which, according to American regulations, E. S. Davies and Son are credited as 'breeders'. Saturday night was time for another talk / film show. The attendance was far greater than expected, and everyone had a jolly evening. The next day was a visit to Asgaard Stud where the owners, the Misses Lapicola, were the editors of *Welsh Roundabout* magazine, to which I was a regular contributor. Then on my last day, there were visits to three more studs, where I saw lots more good ponies and took countless photographs.

My next 1990 overseas visit was to the eighth International Show in Roskilde, Denmark, on 18–19 August, where I assisted with English commentaries. There were 287 entries – 176 from Denmark, 39 from Holland, 35 from Germany, 34 from Sweden and three from Belgium. The judges were Mrs Doreen Jones (UK) and Mrs Theunissen (Holland) (A, C and D) and Miss Isabelle de Moerkerke (Belgium) and Mr Len Bigley (UK) (B and WPB). The champions were Revel Hibiscus (A and supreme), Mollegaards Spartacus (B and reserve supreme), Rookery Full Flight (C) and Menai Sparkling Magic (D). The finale was a pageant of a mounted Danish wedding with Mr Carl Trock in great voice as the parson, while the bride went bouncing around on her Welsh cob with her flowers flying everywhere! Great credit must go to Mrs Marianne Seidenfaden and her small committee for organising such a successful event, where everything ran like clockwork. I was elected an Honorary Life Member of the WPCS of Denmark at a special 25-year jubilee party on the Saturday night for my many visits to Denmark.

Horse entries at the RW were 3,238, of which 1,540 were in-hand Welsh. The bay stallion Waitwith Romance was section A champion. He had spent ten years in a riding school, and was only bought through a local newspaper advertisement two months before the show. Nevertheless, he was a worthy champion, and the three-y-o filly Idyllic Pavlova was reserve champion. Both progeny group winners were from within four miles of each other in Glamorgan. Pentyrch Stud won the mare progeny competition with the two-y-o filly Pentyrch Glory Bee, the novice mare Pentyrch Champagne and the open mare Pentyrch Pearl. We won the stallion progeny group for Twyford Sprig with Ceulan Wit, Ceulan Sidan and Roseisle Ringtime, which we had sold but came back to make up the group, and our two foals, the colt Witty and the filly Sarann, were both placed out of 61 total foals. We had plenty of choice for the Sprig group – Ty'rcapel Sprig, who won 16 first prizes and two championships in 1990, Ceulan Pablo and Ceulan Vivacious were also there. The yearling Lemonshill Limelight was section B champion, Ty'reos Furietta was section C champion, having been champion previously in 1990, and Derwen Groten Goch was champion in 1986 and 1990. Mynach April Shower was WPB champion and qualifier for the Creber (new sponsors after 17 years of Lloyds Bank sponsorship) HOYS championship.

Three section B mares from Baledon were the top consignment on the FO Sale on 14–15 September, with Baledon Czarina, Outdoor Girl and Bronze Poppy selling for 2,600, 2,300 and 2,100 gns. The equal top section A prices (1,400 gns) were received for two mares, Gwynrhosyn Emmerline and Bengad Wallflower. We sold a filly foal, Ceulan Campus (B Rustling Grass x Taliaris Calypso) for 500 gns (equal fourth-highest), and three colt foals including Ceulan Symbol (Trefaes Taran x Ceulan Stella), to Waitwith Stud, and he won eight championships in 1996. Symbol ended up as 'Custard', one of Balanced Horse Feeds' scurry pair (with Rhubarb), who were successful at HOYS in 2006 and 2007. There were 918 entries for the RW Sale on 19, 20 and 22 October, the average was £912 (the highest for forty years including the next 14 years) and the sale total was £531,027, the highest for all sales between 1964 and 2004, and one and a half times the 2014 total. The stallion Leyeswick Daniel sold for 6,000 gns, the mare Calerux Anniversary sold for 6,200 gns, and the filly foal Cathedine April Sunshine for 3,400 gns. The six-y-o ridden mare Gorfelyn Swallow was top section C at 2,600 gns and we were equal third-highest section C colt foal (500 gns) with Ceulan Caradog (Twyford Sprig x Coediog Catrin), who had won at the Glamorgan Foal Show.

We competed at 23 shows in 1990, starting with the stallion Bengad Rustling Grass at Lampeter, Glanusk and Shropshire, then Trefaes Taran, who had developed out of all recognition, won six championships, including a WPCS medal at the United Counties. At the AGM I was elected Honorary Life Vice-President along with Mr Emrys Griffiths, Lord Kenyon, Mr Sam Morgan, Mr Gwyn Price, Miss Barbara Saunders-Davies and Mr Dick Swain. The S4C programme *Cefn Gwlad* on Good Friday 13 April was a half-hour feature with Dai Jones, Llanilar, filmed at Ceulan the previous August. It included a comparison of the four sections with Ceulan Sidan (A), Rotherwood Hollyhock (B), Coediog Catrin (C) and Persie Nanette (D) with me, the show fillies Cariad, Cantores and Sulpasc with David and Jane, a young Trefaes Taran and the 24-y-o Twyford Sprig with David, Bengad Rustling Grass running out with his mares and foals, Ruth with her bucket of cubes and finally some of the horse paintings in the house. This programme has been broadcast several times on S4C over the years.

1991 began with the (1990) AGM on 9 March at Edinburgh, the only time that a WPCS AGM has been held in Scotland, and the evening entertainment must rank amongst the finest there has ever been. Then I had a second Scottish visit to be commentator when twelve Welsh cob stallions were invited to give a daily display at the Royal Highland Show. There was no access to the Welsh national anthem at the finale, so I sang it, and a Scottish newspaper praised the stallions but was not so complimentary about 'Pavarotti'!

The most popular winner at the RWS on 22–25 July was the cob stallion Pantanamlwg Red Fox when his 72-year-old owner / breeder ran him non-stop all the way round the Main Ring. Reserve for the PofW Cup was Fronarth Welsh Model, who won it in 1996. Champion section A and Creber HOYS qualifier was the mare Dyfrdwy Seren Arian. Champion section B was the novice mare Boston Bodecia, who sadly died in 1994, and Glynwyn Diamante was champion section C. The same owners were reserve with their stallion Persie Ramrod, who was the 1990 Olympia ridden champion. We won the colt foal class and reserve overall (from 58 entries) with the bay Ceulan Samswn (Bengad Rustling Grass x Ceulan Stella), and David sold him that day to Mrs Suzanne Glenn of Glenhaven Stud, USA. Taran, at only five years old, was third out of 35 stallions to Dyfrdwy Starlight and Sunwillow Orion, beating Lampeter, Glanusk and Northleach champions and HOYS qualifiers.

I judged at the Summer Show at Leksand, Sweden where the supreme and reserve were two section Bs – Carolinas Foxglove and Mollegaards Suzette. It was good to see many performance winners sired by Kirby Cane Guardsman, which I had exported to Mr Bertil Bengtsson, the original vice-president of the Swedish Society in 1970. I returned to Sweden in November to give a talk at the conference of Welsh breeders at Dalarna, right up in the north of the country. I have never been driven through so much snow and ice, but the Swedish people are geared to such weather conditions, and there was a large attendance of many happy enthusiasts.

Records were broken by large margins at the FO Sale on 20–21 September. The three-y-o colt Colbeach Prince Consort sold for 3,700 gns (the previous record was 2,600 gns in 1990), and the six-y-o mare Lippens Dolly (bought for 200 gns on the 1985 sale) sold for 3,600 gns (the previous record was 2,500 gns in 1985). Her foal Yaverland Delight (reserve overall champion at the 1997 RWS when David judged) sold for 800 gns back to Lippens. We sold the sixth and seventh highest section A foals Ceulan Siani (Yaverland Nero x Ceulan Serog) for 720 gns to Tymor Stud, and Ceulan (J) Bubble (Rookery Rupert x Rookery Bustle) for 680 gns to the USA to go with Samswn, and they were star turns at the Glenhaven Open Day in 1998. The 970 lots entered for the RW Sale on 18, 19 and 21 October were the second highest to date, and the section D female, section C female and foal records were exceeded. Top-priced section D mare was Pantanamlwg Eleri at 6,800 gns, section C, Cwm Lowri at 3,800 gns, and foal Mabnesscliffe Welsh Model at 4,800 gns. We entered two filly foals, Ceulan Ceridwen (Cathedine Flying Express x Coediog Catrin) and Ceulan Nerissa (Bengad Rustling Grass x Persie Nanette), which had won at foal shows, but unfortunately, they were catalogued amongst the last handful in the dark on the Saturday night.

We had received offers of the reserves in the morning from a German buyer, but RB&B regulations did not permit private sales, and the German was leaving at midday to catch his flight. Catching the foals in the dark was a nightmare, and we didn't know until we reached the light in the sales ring whether we had the correct ones or not, by which time everyone had gone home. Although we succeeded in selling them both easily from home over the weekend, the experience convinced me that, after 76 years, there would be no more Cs or Ds at Ceulan. Nanette and her filly Naomi were sold in November 1992 to Mrs Joanna McNamara Jones, where Nanette bred the top sire Twmbarlwm Nimrod and many more. Catrin and her filly Catalina were sold to Popsters Stud in May 1993. Her 1997 foal, Popsters Just Divine, was the dam of Coathamdene Just Dylan, the overall champion M&M WHP at HOYS 2014. Bengad Rustling Grass was again shown at the early shows at Forest of

Dean, Midland Stallion and Lampeter, and then turned out with the mares and foals. Then we showed Trefaes Taran who was champion and supreme of the show at Cothi Bridge (WPCS medal), and was champion another five times, as well as taking second at RASE and third at RWS and Bath and West. We showed the two filly foals for Vardra Stud, Vardra Kismet (B Rustling Grass x Vardra Mi'Lady) and Vardra Serenade (B Rustling Grass x Ceulan Sulpasc), and they did quite well.

Ceulan Sprite died in 1991 aged 27 years. She had produced 20 foals (ten sired by Twyford Sprig), of which eight had been exported, and her progeny had also won the RW progeny group competition six times. Along with Ceulan Cariad (1988–2014), she can be regarded as a true cornerstone of Ceulan, Miskin. We collected at Ceulan for Canada Rhoson Pasiant for Mrs Darlene Morton, and the ridden cob gelding Deytheur Dai from Mrs Ann Jones, Frongoch, to accompany Ceulan Sarann (who was youngstock champion at the Royal Toronto Winter Fair two months after arrival), to Mr Larry Flaska and Miss Anne Marie Morton of Flaska Farms. They bought the roan mare Fieldcote Bridal Veil to live at Ceulan, with her foals exported to Canada annually – Copper Bracken (1992), (ch in Canada) by Cathedine Flying Express, Bronson (1993) by Trefaes Taran (with Caitlan by Pennal Calon Lân x Coediog Catrin) and Bukarah Ddu (1994) by Derwen Railway Express, and then they sold Bridal Veil on the FO Sale.

I thought the 1992 WPCS Journal was a disaster, full of errors and poorly produced, and was persuaded to take over the editorship on condition that it reverted to its previous printers. I continued the work for 12 years until Mr David Blair was persuaded to take over. This is a massive undertaking. It took over the whole house for four months every year, with one room being the 'overseas' room, another, 'obituaries' and so on, with little room for Ruth and me.

Ruth and I began 1992 with a flight to Johannesburg, where I was to judge the National Championships at Bloemfontein on 24–26 March. The day before the show we were taken to a typical farm for the area. Mataffin was over 30,000 hectares, with a workforce of over 7,000 and seven schools for the employees' children. The show had been going for three weeks before the Welsh classes, with nightly parades of horses, Brahmin cattle and sheep. The emphasis was very definitely on performance, with most of the 40 or so in-hand stallions reappearing later in some performance guise. One exhibitor, Jurie Wessels, had 46 ponies (mostly stallions) competing. The champion and reserve stallions, Bukkenburg Nerog and Bukkenberg Vintage (both by Coed Coch Nerog), were good enough to win anywhere in the UK. The Bukkenburg ponies were bred by Mr Myburgh Streicher (he had visited Ceulan several times), who had sold his 175 section As in 1991 and kept about 80 section Cs and Ds. There were not many section Bs present, but plenty of cobs whose exceptional champion was Persie Nimrod (full-brother to my Persie Nanette) and the reserve Parc Crusader.

The harness classes were breath-taking. There were over 50 section As competing in single harness, which mostly reappeared to compete in pairs (some of them being harnessed together for the first time in the collecting ring!), tandems, teams of four and finally spans of eight to a heavy gambo – a truly unforgettable sight. After the judging we were invited to a short AGM, after which I gave them a talk and film show and sang some Welsh folk songs. This was followed by a presentation dinner where some of the trophies were larger than the recipients. A visit to Miss Ida Illingworth (who emigrated from Cheshire to South Africa in 1924) and her Foresyte Stud was a must. She had imported the 1955 RW champion section B Valiant in 1960, and the current stallion, the 27-y-o Foresyte Valiant Cymro, was his son. Miss Illingworth accompanied us for four days in the Kruger National Park (where she was a founder member), which was about half the size of Wales, where we saw large numbers of elephants, giraffes, lions and other animals, and a crocodile blew loud noises at the bottom of the garden all night.

Finally, we were taken down a disused goldmine and to the cemetery at Pilgrims' Rest, where so many of those buried were miners from Wales, and had Welsh poems on their gravestones, which I photographed and sent to their descendants after returning home. Lastly, another talk and showing of some videos to a full house at a large, luxury hotel lecture theatre organised by Shirley and Gerald Sadleir, who stayed with us at Ceulan in the summer and came with us to the United Counties Show. I see in the annual report of the Ceredigion WPCA in the WPCS Journal that the day after I returned from South Africa, despite suffering from jet-lag, I gave them a talk to tell them all about the trip.

The highlight of 1992 was the ninth International Show, held for the first time ever in the UK at Peterborough on 22–23 August under the chairmanship of Mrs Alison Mountain, chief steward Mr Ronnie Mills, WPCS President Mrs Robina Mills and I was commentator. There were 1,033 entries with 94 from overseas: Holland 31, Germany 22, France 19, Belgium seven, Denmark five, Sweden four, Ireland three, USA two and Switzerland one. The champions were Blackhill Picalo (A), Mollegaards Spartacus (B, supreme and ridden), Horeb Fflach (C), Broughton Black Lady (D), Bracon Tara (WPB), Baledon Commanchero (WHP) and Dyfrdwy Starlight (harness). There was an excellent attendance from overseas, and we all enjoyed ourselves at the party on the Saturday night. On the Sunday there was an impressive display of trade turnouts and a musical ride of sections A, B, C, D and WPB. The RWAS had now purchased a publicity exhibition trailer and Land Rover, a big step up from the Ceulan caravan, and greatly admired wherever it went.

Supreme champion at the RWS on 20–23 July was again

Mollegaard Spartacus, winning the first of his three consecutive RW championships. He had already qualified for the HOYS Creber championship at the Bath and West, so the HOYS ticket went to the section A champion Tiffwyl Melodi. Fronarth Red Rose at three years old was section C champion, Derwen Groten Goch was champion cob for the third time and retired at the show, and Mynach Daffodil was champion WPB. Our two-y-o liver chestnut filly Ceulan Lucy (Trefaes Taran x Lisvane Lotus Blossom) won her class of 42 entries and then went on to beat the great Blackhill Picalo (top of the WPCS sire ratings six times) for the two-y-o award – the Main Ring computer screen showing the results displayed 'A winner for Dr Wynn'.

The average prices at the FO Sale on 18–19 September was £489, up 35 per cent on the 1990 figure. Top consignment was from Springbourne Stud, whose two mares Springbourne Cameo and Chorus sold for 4,000 and 3,800 gns respectively, and the filly foal Fronbach Shady Lady sold for 4,000 gns. Two males were top section B at 2,500 gns – the two-y-o Bureside Baron and the seven-y-o Pennwood Milan. Unfortunately, of our 20 foals born in 1992, 14 were colts and only six fillies. Two fillies, Ceulan Lorelei (Trefaes Taran x Lisvane Lotus Blossom), and Ceulan (J) Bounce (Bengad Rustling Grass x Rookery Bustle), were entered for the FO Sale and did not reach their reserves, but both were sold to David and Carol Maurer of California the following spring.

We also entered four colt foals, including Vardra Sun King (out of Ceulan Sulpasc), and they all sold to good homes. One colt, Ceulan Stormus (Trefaes Taran x Ceulan Stella), who was fourth of 59 foals at the RWS, went on to win championships under saddle. We usually have one or two overseas or UK associations visiting us every year, and the South-western Association were shown our FO Sale foals. We had 28 visiting mares at Ceulan in 1992 in addition to our own 20 mares and foals, youngstock and stallions – where we accommodated them all, I do not know. The average at the RW Cob Sale was, surprisingly, down from £870 to £789, but the mare Friskney Frolic sold for 5,500 gns, two males, the 12-y-o Ffoslas Sir Gwynfor and the yearling Thorneyside The Gaffer, both sold for 5,000 gns, and the filly foal Cathedine May Princess sold for 3,000 gns. Top section C was the mare Persie Rosaleen at 3,200 gns. Our last entry ever at the cob sales was the colt foal Ceulan Cynfelin (Cathedine Flying Express x Coediog Catrin). He was shown a fair bit from his new home, and always looked very well with them. We competed at 27 shows and five foal shows. Taran was overall Best in Show at Blaenavon, champion five times including Swansea (WPCS medal), reserve champion at the Bath and West and second at RASE. Lucy, in addition to the first at the RW, was first at Gower, and Caryl (yearling filly: Bengad Rustling Grass x Taliaris Calypso) won a WPCS medal at the Vale of Glamorgan.

My first talk in January 1993 was to the Gwent WPCA at the Bailey's Arms, Cwm, Ebbw Vale, where I was always guaranteed a large audience and a warm welcome. Then the Glamorgan WPCA held a 'teach-in' at Thornberry Stud in April, where the master judge was Mr Len Bigley, who had examples of the five sections to demonstrate with. The section C was Ceulan Copper Bracken, and her co-owner Miss Anne-Marie Morton came over from Canada to present her. *Horse and Hound* of 11 March featured an article by Adella Lithman on my contribution to the RWS where she describes me as 'one of the stars of the Welsh world'!

On 24 June, Ruth and I flew to Switzerland where the National Show was being held at Kloten. Ruth was recovering from a broken leg and was on crutches, but she was offered every assistance. A talk was arranged for the previous evening which about 50 Welsh breeders attended. Among the audience members was the top Scottish breeder Mr Dougal Dick, who was there to judge the

Shetlands. The sections A and B were a bit thin on the ground, but the cobs turned up in droves and were of a very high standard, some of them having won at Peterborough the previous year, and it was good to see the mares competing under saddle with their foals standing contentedly at the ringside. The dun cob mare Platinarth Fidelity was overall champion, with the Dutch-bred section A Valkenhof's Whitney reserve. The following day we were taken sightseeing including (by four-wheel drive) to the top of a ski resort where vehicles are not normally allowed. When we entered the restaurant Ruth, on her crutches, was given a loud congratulatory cheer, because they thought she had climbed up all the way! We also saw the luxurious showground at Frauenfeld, site of the following year's International Show.

We excelled ourselves at the RWS by winning both the Pennell (stallion) progeny group for Bengad Rustling Grass and the Gwyn Price (mare) progeny group for Taliaris Calypso. We had won the Pennell Cup twice before and the Gwyn Price Cup five times, but never both in the same year. Our group consisted of the yearling colt Ceulan Caredig, the two-y-o filly Ceulan Caryl and the three-y-o filly Ceulan Campus, which we had sold and bought back. There were 37 stallions including previous champions, and standing top (with Trefaes Taran second) was Gredington Calon Lân, owned by 80-year-old Mr Gordon Jones. I announced congratulations to octogenarian Mr Jones on his success, but when I met the judge the following day, he said he was just about to have a second look at the top two, but couldn't very well after I had announced the winner! Making their debut at this show were the novice mare Dryfe Sheer Heaven and her filly foal Brynodyn Scarlet, who were both winners. Calon Lân qualified for the HOYS Creber, where he ended up fourth. Reserve champion at Wembley was Mollegaard Spartacus, who was champion at the RW for the second year. Nebo Bouncer was champion section C for the fourth time, and

Horeb Euros was champion cob and reserve for the Creber. Taran had a very good season, winning the championship and supreme at Barry, Cathedine Cup (overall Welsh) at Brecon, champion (WPCS medal) at Swansea, three more championships and reserve champion at the Royal Bath and West.

Cariad returned to Ceulan at the end of July after two seasons under saddle, and was champion (WPCS medal) and supreme at Vaynor, and reserve champion at Pembroke County. A mare that we had at Stud to Taran in June 1992 was Synod Nutmeg (dam of Yaverland Nero), and she was sold on the 1992 FO Sale with a covering certificate for 3–4 June. The purchaser was not happy since, on getting her home, she was covered by his cream stallion Cennen Herriot, and he had wanted a Taran foal. Nutmeg had a chestnut filly (later named Grenham Melody Rose) on 14 May 1993, but would not let it suckle, so the filly was bottle-reared successfully. Then on 25 September, Nutmeg had a cream colt foal (named Grenham Park Royal) which she allowed to suckle naturally. The DNA of both foals corresponded to Nutmeg, Taran and Herriot, so Nutmeg created veterinary history by producing two foals within the space of four months.

The WPCS held its first ever performance show on 25 September at Felin-newydd, Llandefalle, with hunter trials, and the following day on the RW showground with riding, dressage, show jumping and harness. The FO Sale on 17–18 September returned the highest average figure in 58 years (1954–2002) of £526, with the top figure of 3,700 gns for the section A stallion Silvester, 1991 RW male champion, followed by 3,600 gns for the section A mare Springbourne Carmine and 3,200 gns for the section B mare Ashwell Diamond. We sold the bay filly foal Ceulan Siskin (out of Sprite's last daughter Swan Song) to Perthshire, and the chestnut colt foal Ceulan Sionyn to Homeshill Stud, where he spent the rest of his life and sired some very good foals. Despite 926 lots catalogued for the RW Sale on

15, 16 and 18 October, the average (£853) was the third-highest. Equal top at 5,000 gns were two 11-y-o stallions, Leyeswick Daniel and Cathedine Express. The Glamorgan WPCA Christmas party was a surprise, well-kept secret, the 'Wynne Davies, This is your Life'-style presentation. The writers must have requested details from my family of events long since forgotten. At the AGM, I was very honoured to be presented with a Life Membership Badge and Certificate of the WPCS of Australia for my publications in their journals.

Starting with the Lampeter Show on 23 April 1994, it was the first time that the supreme award went to a section A, Gredington Calon Lân. It was first presented in 1989 to Cottrell Pendragon (B) then to three cob stallions Nebo Daniel, Cathedine Express and Horeb Euros (twice). Ruth was president of the Glanusk Show on 7 May and awarded the trophies to the champions, but the supremes were judged by Mr Mostyn Isaac, who selected the section C Nebo Bouncer with the three-y-o section A champion Blanche Mimic reserve.

The glorious weather on July 18–21 attracted a record attendance of 229,712 to the RWS, where the HOYS Creber qualifier was Dyfrdwy Seren Arian (who had qualified previously in 1991) and the reserve was the section C champion Synod Roy Rogers. Mollegaard Spartacus won the last of his three RW championships, other overseas-owned section B prize-winners were Dubbel Ll's Swifty (Belgium), Shamrock Mr Oliver (Holland) and Simberg Hobnob (Sweden). Nebo Hywel was the third 'Nebo' stallion to have his name engraved on the PofW cup. The Pembrokeshire-bred WPB Copybush Catchphrase was Creber champion at HOYS with Mollegaard Spartacus third. The other qualifiers, in addition to Seren Arian, were Waxwing Reward (Royal Highland) and Cottrell Faberge (RASE), and the lead-rein Pony of the Year was Lechlade Melissa (daughter of Ceulan Siwan).

I attended the tenth International Show at Frauenfeld, Switzerland, on 27–28 August as commentator, and also took photographs. The champions were H-S Bambi (A, Germany), Krogengaard Bunny (B and supreme, Denmark), Oakvale Rhion (C, Belgium), Valhallas Emily (D and reserve supreme, Denmark) and Giglbergs Outsider (WPB, Germany). Swiss exhibitors excelled in the performance competitions on the second day, and won all the top awards in working hunter and showjumping, and put on a pageant with all the riders in Welsh costumes.

We had a very good show season, starting with Bengad Rustling Grass who was champion at West Midlands and Ponies (UK), and reserve champion at Swansea. Then Trefaes Taran took over and was male champion at RASE, champion (WPCS medal) at Bridgend plus another five championships. Cariad was champion at Gower (WPCS medal) and United Counties, and also won the barren mare class at the RWS (after an exciting last-minute reversal of first and second with Dryfe Sheer Heaven), where she was also a member of the winning Twyford Sprig progeny group, joined by the yearling colts Ceulan Lloyd and Forlan Humdinger. It was a fitting climax to the career of Twyford Sprig, who died later in the year aged 29 years. The three-y-o filly Ceulan Caryl was youngstock champion at the Vale of Glamorgan, and in the top three at another eight shows, including the RASE and Royal Bath and West.

After the record prices at the 1993 FO Sale, the average at the 1994 sale on 16–17 September was reduced to £492, but prices for the top lots remained as firm as ever. A new section A record of 4,500 gns was obtained for Sunwillow Quest, and equal top with 1993 of 3,200 gns for the section B Cottrell Celebration. Quest was bought by Heniarth Stud, and her g-daughter Heniarth Yum-Yum was RW youngstock champion in 2005 and overall in 2012. Quest had been a member of the 1985 RW champion female progeny group when we won the male progeny group for Twyford Sprig. At the FO Sale, we sold Fieldcote Bridal Veil for Mr Larry Flaska and Miss Anne-Marie Morton who had decided that they had sufficient of her progeny in Canada.

We sold for export privately to the USA the filly foal Ceulan Rhiannon (out of Bengad Rainbow) to Mr Jack Craig of Ohio, the filly foal Ceulan Miranda (out of Newpriory Mirabelle) to Mrs Suzanne Glenn of California, and the colt foal Ceulan Lwcus (out of Lisvane Lotus Blossom) to Carol and David Maurer of California. In the USA, Lwcus has won the American Legion of Merit, the Award of Excellence and twice the Order of the Dragon, and he was American top section A sire 2008–2014. At the RW Sale on 14, 15 and 17 October, the top price was 5,000 gns, paid for the mare Bronfoel Boneddiges Mai, and 4,200 gns for the filly foal Ffoslas Lady Model. The AGM was held under the presidency of Miss Rosemary Philipson Stow, who presented WPCS mementos to Mrs Alison Mountain and to me for our contributions to the WPCS over 50 years, and for having been members of Council for over 40 years. At the request of the Inland Revenue and Charity Commission, a WPCS trading company was set up to be responsible for items which were sold at shows and sales, and to be distinct from the main society activities. Mr Brian Foster was the very efficient chairman of this committee, and I served with him as publicity officer. On 6 May I received the sad news of the death of my great friend of almost fifty years, Mrs Dinah Griffiths of the Revel. I had so many happy memories of her kindnesses to me when I stayed there over a period of four years. We had two Area Associations visit Ceulan – the Brecon and Borders WPCA in June and the Severn Valley WPCA in September.

1995 included my life-time high point. In May, a confidential letter arrived from 10 Downing Street stating that the Prime Minister was recommending to Her Majesty The Queen that I be appointed a Member of the Order of the British Empire in the Birthday Honours List. Ruth, David, Jane and I attended the investiture at Buckingham Palace on 25 October. We stayed near Buckingham Palace the previous night and, during our walk to the Palace, called in at the Horseman's Bookshop, Lower Buckingham Palace Road to meet the sprightly nonagenarian Mr Joseph Allen, who had published five of my books and was to publish another three. During my investiture, I was amazed at how much Her Majesty knew about the WPCS, and that she was interested to know how the exports and registrations had kept up. I received many letters of congratulations from all over the world, and one American breeder, Mrs Suzanne Glenn, took out a full-page advertisement in an American magazine.

Trefaes Taran spent four weeks in April at the AI Centre with Mr Ron Williams MRCVS, who organised the transport of frozen semen to Mrs Helen Bandy of Oregon, USA, and in 1996 the first two Welsh section A foals conceived by AI were born in the USA – a colt, First Knight, out of Roblyns Sheena and a filly, Caris Love Story, out of Pontllys Tamsin. Nebo Bouncer, who had been section C champion at Lampeter five times, went a stage further this time and won the supreme on 22 April. Supreme at Glanusk on 6 May was Criccieth Arwr (A) and the reserve was Thorneyside Flyer (D). Champion section B was the two-y-o colt Simberg Hobnob, son of Rotherwood Hollyhock, which I had sold to Sweden.

The RWS had glorious weather again on 24–27 July, which helped attract an attendance of 234,897. Tiffwyl Melodi was champion section A and Templeton HOYS qualifier, Cottrell Aurora (who was sold to Australia in 1998) was champion B, Neuaddparc Rowena champion C, Gellifach ap Dafydd champion D and Duntarvie Catamount champion WPB for the third time. HRH Prince Charles was present on the second day and spent some time in the Main Ring discussing the Welsh breeds with the judges.

Entries for the FO Sale on 15–16 September reached the highest

(801) since 1974 and have never been as high since, and the averages plummeted from £492 to £406. There were no record-breakers, but the better animals still found a good trade. The section B stallion Priestwood Oberon topped the sale at 2,500 gns, followed by the section A filly foal Fronbach Velvet Lady at 2,400 gns. We entered four filly foals and two colt foals, and were very pleased with the result. Ceulan Linda (out of Ceulan Lucy) was sixth-highest filly foal, and Vardra Secret (out of Ceulan Sulpasc) was top colt foal, selling to Mr James Ashman of Utah, USA. We also sold another three foals privately to the USA – the fillies Cerys and Lydia (out of Rondeels Cavalla and Lisvane Lotus Blossom) to Carol and David Maurer of California, and the colt Ceulan Cadog (out of Cariad) to Mrs Diana Fischer, also of California.

There were 133 ponies and cobs competing at the 1995 American Welsh Nationals (of which 27 were imported), and for the second year in a row I received a special award for Ceulan, having bred the greatest number (six), with two American studs being second and third. Average prices on the RW Sale on 13, 14 and 16 October also fell considerably, from £788 to £715, but the section C filly foal Dyrfal Red Rose sold better than any Ds at 4,500 gns, and top D was a three-y-o filly, Abergavenny Welsh Model, which sold for 4,000 gns.

We had a visit from the Southern WPCA to Ceulan in July. Kevin Townsend, publicity officer of the WPCS of New Zealand, was staying at Ceulan and helped with the showing of the ponies. We had a busy and very successful showing season starting with Bengad Rustling Grass, who was reserve champion at Ponies (UK) then ran out with the mares and foals. Trefaes Taran was champion at Gwent WPCA (WPCS medal), won another five championships and was reserve champion at the Royal Bath and West and Gower (to Cariad). Cariad was champion at the National Palomino championships and Gower (champion overall Welsh and reserve supreme to the champion Shire), plus another three championships, and Ceulan Lucy (novice mare) was reserve champion at the Vale of Glamorgan. We also did quite well at the foal shows with two fillies which we were keeping, Ceulan (J) Ruby (Trefaes Taran x Bengad Rainbow) and Ceulan Mariah, daughter of New Priory Mirabelle, the last ever Sprig foal, who is now the senior mare at Ceulan.

The first event of 1996 was the opening of the WPCS's new refurbished offices at Chalybeate Street, Aberystwyth, on 20 February. The RW HOYS Templeton qualifier was the section B champion Cwrtycadno Cadfridog, owned by my local breeder Mrs Pat Johns-Powell of Cottrell Stud, with the WPB Rotherwood Peter Pan reserve. On the first weekend in August, I travelled with Mr Emrys Bowen to judge at the Danish National Championship Show at Roskilde, where we had some very large classes.

My next overseas trip was to the eleventh International Show held at Compiègne, France, on 24–25 August where I was co-commentator (English and a bit of Welsh) with Mr Thierry Clement (French), as well as assistant photographer and, when one section did not have a steward, I was given that task as well! The champions were Cuppers Morning Mist (A, Holland), Hoekhorst Nikita (B, Holland), Fronarth Rascal (C, Belgium), Llanarth Mererid (D and supreme, UK) and Bannut Secret Melody (WPB, Germany). It was a brilliant achievement for a ridden Welsh section A to be mini-champion at the Ponies (UK) Summer Show. This was the dun gelding Ceulan Champagne (f. 1992, Twyford Sprig x Rondeels Cavalla) ridden by Chloe Willett.

The average price at the FO Sale on 20–21 September was £481, with top prices of 3,800 gns paid for the section A filly foal Fronbach Simply Red, and 3,600 gns for the section B Cottrell Rose of China. We entered three filly foals and two colt foals and experienced the best trade for many years. The filly foal Ceulan Salome (Yaverland Nero x Ceulan Sidan) at 1,200 gns was the fourth-highest foal on the sale to Fronbach, Friars and Synod fillies. Salome was bought by the Hon Mrs Sheila Monck, and we bought her back in 2005 when Mrs Monck was downsizing. Ceulan Prattle (Nero x Foxhunter Pratincole) sold to Jim and Melody Ashman of Utah to join the colt Vardra Secret, which they bought on the previous year's sale, and Ceulan Rhoslyn (Bengad Rustling Grass x Ceulan Romance) sold to Boreton Stud. She subsequently won a lot in good company in youngstock classes, and later, under saddle.

The average on the RW Sale on 19 and 21 October was £702, very similar to the previous year. The nine-y-o section D stallion Mabnesscliffe Advisor sold for 5,100 gns and the filly foal Synod Maggie Poppins topped the Cs at 2,700 gns. The auctioneers RB&B offered a new award to celebrate their one hundred and fiftieth anniversary given to an animal, individual or stud for outstanding services to the Welsh breeds. This was awarded to me at the AGM in recognition of my contribution to publicity and sale reporting.

We had coachloads of visitors, from Germany on 6 May, the Isle of Wight on 21 June and the South-eastern WPCA on 29 June. A member of the German party, Mrs Schierholter of Glandorf (manufacturer of Schierhölter Wildschehe liquor), bought New Priory Mirabelle and her filly foal Ceulan Maglona, sired by Bengad Rustling Grass. Later we had a visit from French driving expert Mr Daniel Pillet, who drove teams of dun section As, and he bought the dun mare Ceulan Cavalcade (f. 1991, Twyford Sprig x Rondeels Cavalla) and her dun colt foal Ceulan Constable, sired by Bengad Rustling Grass. In the 1997 Journal, Mr Kevin Morris wrote that I struggled through snowdrifts in my Land Rover in February to give a talk and slide show to the Trefil WPCA, 2,000 feet above sea-level. He was particularly pleased that I managed to get there, since I showed a photograph of his late father showing Revel Joker at Glanusk in 1961, a photo which neither he nor any member of his family had ever seen. We had a competition to recognise ponies and people, and one person that I had not seen for many years and assumed had passed away brought loud applause, and when I looked up, there he was standing at the bar, looking very proud to see himself on the screen! Shortly after I took this photo, the other stallion in it, Revel Playbox, got away from his owner Mr Brian Roberts, Pinetree Stud, and swam across the river Usk. He was caught on the other side making his way towards Crickhowell. Trefaes Taran missed winning a WPCS medal by being reserve champion at RASE and another six shows, but eventually succeeded at the Vale of Glamorgan Show.

In March 1997, I started my visits away with a trip to Gleneagles, Scotland, to conduct a seminar with plenty of animals present, which included driving, working hunter, lead-rein and vaulting, and for the slide presentation in the afternoon it was standing room only. Mr David Blair in the WPCS magazine reported that 'Dr Wynne was on cracking form'. 1997 included the climax of our showing experiences. With David judging the section As at the RWS (the youngest RW Welsh breeds judge to date), we did not exhibit under any judge who was a section A exhibitor. Taran competed at only four shows in 1997. He was champion section A and reserve supreme to Blaengwen Brenin (D) at Lampeter, overall champion at the RASE, champion section A and supreme at the City of Swansea, then at the Royal Bath and West, after being section A champion under Mrs Egerton, the thirteen in-hand champions competed for the Templeton HOYS qualifier with hunter judge Mr Peter Hobbs. He awarded it to Taran, with the in-hand hunter champion Mrs Jane Thornton's Corbally Magic reserve.

So we all went to Wembley in October, and Taran was reserve pony champion to the riding pony brood mare WPB Huttons Ambo Camelia, the best section A result for fourteen years since Winneydene Satellite was champion in 1983 and Mollegaards Spartacus (B) reserve in 1991 and 1993. RW entries for 21–24 July for section A (540), B (272) and WPB (84) were the highest of the century. With section A exhibitors aware that Ceulan Stud kept only bays, chestnuts, blacks and palominos, these colours turned up in strength at the RWS, and the top four senior stallions (led by Betws Fflach) were bays with a black fifth, although a grey (out of 24 entries) occupied sixth position! It was also a grey – Synod The Colonel – that won the junior stallion class and he was male champion. My commentator colleague Mr Christopher Jones asked me to place these 35 stallions from the commentary tower, and was very impressed when I selected five out of 35 the same as David later placed them. Announcing the results, he said that I had judged them and got one wrong, to which I replied that the judge had got them all correct apart from one!

The barren mare winner Fronbach Carys had the advantage over the young brood mare winner Yaverland Delight when they reappeared for the championships on the second day, and Carys was overall champion with Delight reserve. Both were g-daughters of Brierwood Rocket, and I reminded David afterwards that he was under-bidder on Delight when she was bought by her current owner as a foal on the 1991 FO Sale. The male champion Synod The Colonel and reserve Betws Fflach were Brierwood Rocket sons, and when I judged at the RWS 26 years previously, my champion was Brierwood Rosebud, g-dam of Brierwood Rocket. The yearling filly Friars Posy (supreme champion at the 2005 International Show), who had won a class of 79 entries, was youngstock champion, and the yearling colt winner Heniarth Quip (from 55 entries) and the three-y-o filly winner Sunwillow Bellona (from 52 entries) were a son and daughter of Sunwillow Quest. The senior brood mare winner was Mr Lewis Edwards' grey Neuaddfach Skylark. Three of her grand-parents – Revel Carlo, Revel Choosey and Revel South Drift – were all sired by Twyford Sprig, who was only at the Revel for one year (1967) as a two-y-o. Lady Evans-Bevan's choice for

HPYS Templeton qualifier was the riding pony breeding champion Cusop Dimension, and reserve the section C champion Ty'reos Lowri, who had won at the RW as a foal, two-y-o filly, barren mare and now as brood mare. The other Welsh champions were Carwed Charmer (B) and Trevellion Giorgio (D).

My 1997 overseas trip was on 9 August to Sweden to judge at the Molstaberg Show. The weather was superb, very different from my previous visit to Sweden in the dark and deep snow. There were 65 Welsh ponies and cobs entered. Supreme was the four-y-o section B Simberg Hobnob, whose only section B rival was the 28-y-o Coed Coch Targed. There was an abundance of section As, where the champion was Ekbackens Saga, and the reserve a palomino mare Verona, bred in Sweden from the mare Ceulan (J) Venetia, which I had exported in foal to Twyford Sprig, and Verona was that foal. The presentation of some animals left a lot to be desired, and I was asked to comment on every exhibit. The report of the show in the Swedish Journal said: 'There were many laughs around the ring, and the owners took the comments in happy spirit.' The following day, I took photographs of the 34-y-o mare Deri Joy (which I had exported in 1965) with Per and Margaretta Aschen.

Section As made the top prices at the FO Sale on 19–20 September, with the mare Springbourne Carmen selling to Denmark at 3,100 gns and the filly foal Synod Juliana to the Hon Mrs Monck for 1,800 gns. Top of the RW Sale at 10,000 gns on 17, 18 and 20 October was the chestnut cob stallion Synod Rambo, who had been champion at Glanusk and the Royal Bath and West – it was a great shock to his purchasers to find him dead in his field in May 2000. Top section C at 3,100 gns was the filly foal Neuaddparc Dancing Queen, daughter of the 1995 RW champion Neuaddparc Rowena. We sold the colt foal Ceulan Cadfael (Penual Mark x Ceulan Cariad), who had won locally as well as the RASE, privately to Mr Henrie Leeuwenhaag (Holland), and he was reserve junior champion at the International

Show the following year. We also sold the yearling colt Ceulan Cariadog (Yaverland Nero x Ceulan Cariad) to Germany, from where Mr Leeuwenhaag bought him to be later a preferent stallion and top sire of Holland.

Our other exports were three filly foals to Mrs Betty Chambers of Wisconsin, USA, two by Rustling Grass, Rhamant out of Ceulan Romance and Rhosyn out of Bengad Rainbow, as well as Ceulan Carisma by Trefaes Taran out of Taliaris Calypso. Included in the 1998 WPCS Journal is a photograph of Mrs Alison Mountain and me with our birthday cakes at the AGM, which had been made by Mr Owen Jones, Nebo Stud – mine had Trefaes Taran in icing on it. Also, to commemorate Mrs Mountain's retirement from the chair of the WPCS Council, she was presented with a bronze of her favourite dogs, border terriers. This bronze is now in the Mrs Alison Mountain memorial cabinet at the WPCS offices, Bronaeron.

I made three overseas visits in 1998 – to the International Show in Belgium in May, Sweden in August and the Glenhaven Open Day in the USA in September, and David judged at the fifth international Merlod Show, Holland in June. There were 137 entries at the Belgian Fan Club Show held at Putte, near Brussels, on 14 May, and this was the first time that medals from the parent society were awarded. Supreme champion was the cob stallion Tyhen the Best, and reserve supreme was the section B stallion Dubbell Ll's Swifty, who was the sire of the foal at the show, Liezelhof Macho, who became the overall section B champion at the 2009 RWS. The largest class was that of fifteen section A brood mares won by Withof Shana, who was reserve champion to the Belgian-bred filly Voermanhof Delight, sired by Springbourne Claret.

The twelfth international WPCS Show was held at Gothenberg, Sweden, on 8–9 August. The organisers were afraid that exhibitors would find Sweden too far to travel, and indeed, only 17 entries had been received two days before the closing date. But over the following few days, entries increased to over 350. Supreme champion was the eight-y-o section A stallion Burhults Toy, bred and owned by Gunn Johansson, who has over fifty Welsh ponies and cobs in her local riding school. The section B champion Mollagaards Spartacus was well-known to UK breeders, since he was three times RW champion between 1992 and 1994. The Danish-bred palomino stallion Rytterbjergets Imperial was section C champion, section Ds turned up in droves with Menai Sparkling Magic as champion, and Fairley Alicia was WPB champion.

The second day was performance day, and despite most of the ridden exhibits being sections A and D, champion was the Danish-owned section C gelding Badentoy Villeam, bred in Aberdeen. The well-known section A stallion Kasper from Holland won the pony driving class and Dimbeth Sion, all the way from Wales, won the cob driving. The WPCS publicity vehicle, driven by Emma Edwards of Frongoch Stud, had also travelled all the way from Aberystwyth. After missing the planned ferry from Harwich to Denmark due to engine problems, and driving through Holland and Germany instead, they still managed to arrive in good time for the start. The photograph of the commentary box which appeared in the WPCS magazine was captioned: 'Dr Wynne perched precariously on his ivory tower', but I can assure you that it was not me on the roof, and that I was safely inside. Ingrid Andersson, Swedish Press Officer, wrote in the WPCS Journal that it was 'a special feeling to see Mrs Alison Mountain, Mrs Ann-Charlotte Svinhufvud (who started the Swedish WP Society) and Dr Wynne Davies at the same occasion', and she supplied a photograph captioned 'The Three Musketeers'! It was altogether a very happy event. The organisation was exemplary, thanks to chairman Miss Gunn Johansson and her large band of helpers.

To celebrate ten years of being the largest breeder and importer of Welsh ponies and cobs into the USA, Mrs Suzanne Glenn and her family held a field day at their Glenhaven Stud, Santa Ynez, California on Sunday 6 September, to which I was invited as commentator. The parade began with the in-hands, five section A mares, three section A stallions, five section B mares (all Downland) and three section B stallions, including the famous Downland Rembrandt, five Derwen cob mares, then the cob stallions Tuscani Aramis, Derwen True Grit, Derwen Denmark and Powysvalley Trooper York, handled by his breeder Mr Phil Pugh of Adfa, Newtown. The cobs then reappeared ridden English and Western style and finally a harness display of Ceulan Sirius and Ceulan Samswn and the cobs Derwen True Grit and Derwen Denmark, all driven to the most magnificent two- and four-wheeled vehicles.

On the home front, to celebrate the fortieth anniversary of the first Glanusk Stallion Show held at Glanusk Park, Crickhowell in 1958, a field day was organised on the same site (although the Glanusk Show has been held at Llanelwedd since 1968). It was a very pleasurable and nostalgic experience for me to commentate at this unique event. It began with a parade of 80 ponies from sixteen Improvement Societies, followed by ridden and driven displays, discussions on judging and trimming for the showring, registration advice, a parade of personalities and veterans and finally a parade of section A and B Royal Welsh champions. Amongst the personalities were Penual Mark (A) and Rotherwood State Occasion (B), two stallions which had topped the sire ratings numerous times but had not appeared in the showring since their youngstock days, 31-y-o Betws Glenys, Ceulan Sidan and the RW champions 24-y-o Winneydene Satellite (also HOYS champion 1983), the local 11-y-o Eppynt Victoria (champion in 1996) and the reigning four-y-o Eppynt Skyline. The Dowager Viscountess de L'Isle (who lived there in 1958, and mother of the current resident, the Hon Mrs Shân Legge-Bourke) attended, and she was joined by three members of the 1958 committee – Messrs David Reynolds, Emrys Griffiths and Gwyn Price. A historic photographic display of premium stallions was organised by Mrs Pam Evans, who had been on the WPCS staff for forty years.

The two 'royal' shows were very successful for us. At the RASE on 8 July, the yearling filly Ceulan Sali (Yaverland Nero x Ceulan Sidan) won her class and the female championship, David won the stallion class and the male championship with his pride and joy, Trefaes Taran, and when it came to the overall championship, David advised me not to bother taking a little sapling up against his 'giant'. But having travelled her a long way, I ignored the advice, and much to David's surprise, Sali was proclaimed overall champion and, later in the day, reserve breeders supreme. At the RWS on 20–23 July, with the worst weather conditions since 1954, Sali was fourth out of 83 entries and Sulpasc sixth senior brood mare out of 32 entries, and her foal Vardra Serenity second and reserve champion foal from 59 entries. Sali and Sulpasc were then joined by the two-y-o Salome, who travelled back specially from the Isle of Wight, and they won the Gwyn Price female progeny group. This was the eleventh time that Ceulan had won this competition (which was discontinued in 2000), seven times with three out of the same mare and four times with three by the same sire. The four-y-o Eppynt Skyline, section A champion, had never been caught, running out on the Epynt mountains until three weeks before the show. Section B champion Paddock Picture had her name engraved on the Coed Coch Trophy, the stud at whose dispersal sale Paddock Stud bought her g-dam. Ty'reos Furietta, section C champion, had won as a barren mare and as junior brood mare. Ebbw Victor, at 19 years of age, finally won the PofW cup (and the Tom and Sprightly Cup), having been male champion here four times over fifteen years, and the three-y-o gelding Aberbrwynen Superman was WPB champion (his dam, Forge

Sarita, had qualified ridden for HOYS four times before going to stud).

There was no HOYS Templeton qualifier offered at the RWAS in 1998. In addition to the royals, Taran was overall supreme at Glamorgan WPCA, and won his WPCS medal at Barry. Sali was youngstock champion at the City of Swansea, the yearling colt Vardra Sirius (Trefaes Taran x Ceulan Sulpasc) won at Aberystwyth and Pembroke County, Ceulan Lucy won at the United Counties, Cariad won the brood mare class at the Three Counties, reserve champion to Taran at Barry and champion and WPCS medal at Pembroke County, and her filly foal Ceulan Cusan (who is still a regular breeder at Ceulan) was champion foal at the Wales and Border Counties Show.

I judged section Bs at the Shropshire and West Midland Show on 16 May, where there were very large classes, including 21 yearling fillies. My champion was the grey three-y-o colt Millcroft Riviera and reserve champion the dark dun brood mare Farchynys Rhianwen, who had travelled all the way from Surrey. Next, I judged section As at Cheshire County on 24 June, where the champion was the bay stallion Friars Super Ted and reserve the grey, good-moving mare Crumpwell Helena. Again, they were enormous classes – 29 brood mares, 27 barren mares and 37 yearling fillies. I am told that my section A number of entries (225) is the highest total ever in the history of the show (David had 204 when he judged there in 2006), a figure which has not since been equalled. The big classes took so long to judge that by the time I went for refreshment, the marquee had been dismantled, and I was on my way, hungry, to judge at the other side of Britain to the Western WPCA at Cottenham, near Cambridge, on the Sunday. Mr Daley, chief steward at Cheshire, has increased the 'Welsh' entry numbers to be the second highest (next to the RW) in Britain – they were 865 in 2014, a far cry from a total of 21 when I first visited Cheshire County in 1949. My champion at Cottenham was the liver chestnut stallion Synod Strongbow, son of Brierwood Rocket. Joined by the other judges, Messrs John Batt and Dewi Evans, our supreme was the Welsh cob mare Thorndonpark Pride with Synod Strongbow reserve.

Prices at the FO Sale on 18–19 September were the lowest for a decade (average of £375), with a top price of 2,500 gns for the section B colt Priestwood Punchinello (to Germany), followed by 2,200 gns for the section A mare Friars Sweet Rose. The average price at the RW Sale on 16, 17 and 19 October (£618) was also the lowest of the decade and a section C six-y-o mare, Synod Nutkin, topped the sale at 6,000 gns. One of the most influential mares ever at Ceulan, Rondeels Cavalla, died at the age of 26 years. She had four foals at Mynd Stud before coming to Ceulan in 1979, after which she had a further seventeen – eight colts and nine fillies, five of which were exported.

I received a letter from the WPCS of America informing me that since there was no provision in their articles to award honorary membership, their members had collected $400 to make me a Life Member in appreciation of my contribution over many years. On 16 December, Ruth and I travelled to London to a party given by J. A. Allen and Co to celebrate the sale of 10,000 copies of my book, *Welsh Ponies and Cobs*. To commemorate the occasion, I was presented with an engraved glass goblet. The 1999 WPCS calendar was produced, which featured Ceulan Mariah winning the Edgar Herbert trophy at Lampeter, with our grand-daughter Leah, on the front cover.

January 1999 found Ruth and me heading off to the New Zealand North Island's twenty-first anniversary show with a stop-off at Los Angeles, USA, for a brief visit to Carol and David Maurer's Gaslight Farm at Orba Linda to catch up with Ceulan Lwcus, Bounce, Cerys, Lorelei and Lydia. Because the New Zealand

Show (140 entries) was a special anniversary event, the WPCS had allocated a bronze medal for the supreme in-hand championship, and this was won by the 17-y-o section A brood mare Glynmawr Petunia, sired by Twyford Gendarme out of Nattai Bluebell, who was bred at Lady Creswick's Nattai Stud in Australia. Bluebell, who died later in the year at the remarkable age of 35, was descended from Coed Coch Proffwyd (imported in 1955), Ceulan Comet (imported in 1934) and Greylight (imported in 1911). Section A male champion was the imported 19-y-o Bengad Cedrus, who won the progeny competition for the sixth time. Youngstock champion was the yearling filly Punga Irma la Douce owned by Mrs Robin Collier who, as Miss Robin Elliott, imported her first Welsh ponies into New Zealand in 1950.

Champion section B was the yearling filly Greenlee Windflower by Carolinas Blue Moon, champion WPB was another yearling filly, Glenwood Mandalyn, sired by the Australian-bred Glenmore Brigadoon, and champion cob was the three-y-o filly Nesscliffe Ronda owned by Mrs Jenny Davidson, a New Zealander by birth, who bred Welsh cobs in Sussex for many years, then returned to New Zealand in 1998. There were 61 classes on the second day for ridden and driven Welsh ponies and cobs, and rosettes were presented by Kathleen and Colin James of the Highland Stud, Uckfield, Sussex, who were guests at the show. Ruth and I stayed on for another two weeks and two open days / talks / stud visits had been organised. We visited Kevin Townsend's Drayton Stud, Ngaire Crockett's Ngalaire Stud, Mrs Dorothy Barler's Nanteos Stud and Mrs Robin Collier's 4,000 acre Punga Farm, which rises to 2,700 feet at the foot of Mount Ruapehu volcano, which last erupted in 1996. We also spent time sightseeing in famous places such as the hot water springs at Rotorua. We had a tremendous welcome throughout our stay, caught up with many friends of long standing and made new friends.

After the exciting 1998 events such as the Glanusk Open Day, it was feared that 1999 might be somewhat of an anti-climax, but the president, Mr Will Jones of Towy Valley Stud, had some surprises up his sleeve. On 16 June, the president and members of council were invited by Lord Geraint of Ponterwyd to a reception at the House of Lords, and we had the opportunity to discuss matters of importance to the society with many members of the House of Lords and Parliament, including Baroness Symms, Under-secretary of State at the Commonwealth Office, my school colleague Lord John Morris, the Attorney General and Lord Gwilym Prys-Davies, who was a student with me at Aberystwyth and now lived near us, in Llantwit Fardre. On Sunday 25 July, the president invited everyone to an unforgettable afternoon tea-party at his home in the Towy Valley, near Rhandirmwyn. There was an attendance of over 500, including several overseas members who had stayed on after the RWS. We were entertained by a male voice choir, various competitions and an auction, where I bought the president's specially commissioned plate. Again we had two successful 'royal' shows – at the RASE, Taran was male champion for the fourth time with Blackhill Picalo reserve, and he was also reserve overall to the bay three-y-o filly Shacklebridge Street Angel.

At the RWS, Mariah was fourth out of 55 barren mares, Cariad was fourth out of 42 senior brood mares, her foal Cerian was reserve champion foal out of 69 and the two-y-o colt Vardra Sirius (Trefaes Taran x Ceulan Sulpasc) was first out of 31, having also won first prizes at Glanusk, City of Swansea, Ponies (UK) Wales (also champion), the Three Counties, United Counties and Pembroke County. At the RWS on the Monday afternoon, the Welsh Books Council launched my book *The Welsh Cob* at their stand.

Cariad was also champion at Barry (WPCS medal) and at another four shows, including Pembroke County. Taran was shown only a few times and was champion (WPCS medal) at Bedwellty.

Mariah and the yearling filly Ceulan Cusan were shown from David's base at Blaen Nant Goch Farm, Hermon, Carmarthen. Both won first prizes at four shows and Cusan won a WPCS medal at Nevern. At Teifyside, Ceulan Swyn (f. 1994, Bengad Rustling Grass x Ceulan Seirian) won under saddle. We had several overseas visitors at Ceulan, including groups from Australia, Spain, Holland and Sweden. In April we exported two mares – Vardra Charisma and Brynvane Alys – to the Golan Heights Riding for the Disabled Centre to replace Ceulan Rebecca and Tirmynydd Cream Puff, which I had sold them in 1983.

Trade at the FO Sale on 17–18 September was more encouraging, with the average of £418 (up from £375) and top price of 3,700 gns for the four-y-o mare Springbourne Clara (to Holland) and top section B the yearling filly Leucarum Poppy at 3,000 gns. We sold the colt foal Ceulan Simwnt (Yaverland Nero x Ceulan Sidan) to Holland, and bought the stallion Synod Birthday Boy (f. 1991, Brierwood Rocket x Synod Miss Pinkie), who had spent his life at Rhydyfelin Stud, where he left some good stock. Also on the sale was Ceulan Pablo (f. 1988, Twyford Sprig x Revel Phillipa), who had been a premium stallion in the Dowlais area, and he was sold to the Orpons Stud, Enfield, Middlesex. The average price at the RW Sale leapt from £618 to £683, with a new section D record of 11,000 gns for the stallion Synod Robert Black, with his son, the colt foal Synod Rumpus, selling for 4,200 gns. Top section C was another 'Synod', the filly foal Synod Rose of Tralee (4,000 gns). The Synod consignment of one stallion and seven foals totalled £34,175, which guaranteed Synod receiving the RB&B Champagne Moment trophy at the AGM. At this AGM, I was presented with the Brodrick Memorial trophy for my work as publicity officer. My father had received this award in 1971, and this trophy has been awarded to two generations of the same family on only two other occasions – to Mr Arthur McNaught as the breeder of Clan Pip in

1964 and Mrs Alison Mountain in 1976, then to Mr Gwyn Price in 1992 and to Mr and Mrs Cerdin Jones in 2014. Of the 92 section A stallions listed in the 1999 sire ratings list, we had three stallions that qualified, each one with only four progeny competing. Taran was tenth with 46 points (equal fifth in 1998), Sprig was twentieth with 35 points, and Yaverland Nero was thirty-fourth with 19 points, with the winner Springbourne Caraway, with 133 points, being represented by 17 progeny.

This period was my busiest for reporting for *Horse and Hound*. In 1999, I reported 29 shows and sales, five obituaries (including Sir Harry Llewellyn) and took 17 photographs. In my last year of reporting in 2011, the new editor restricted the Welsh reporting to seven shows, and changed the brief to report 'what the judges said' rather than informative comments on the animals. Admittedly, it was very much easier submitting reports by email rather than the old reliance on first-class post and same-day film processing, but the deadlines still had to be met, which meant attending the RWS from Monday to Thursday, then typing continuously for three days in order for the copy to reach London by 9 a.m. on the Monday morning. I was glad to retire in 2012 after sixty years.

2000–2009

Many of the functions during the millennium year were geared towards raising funds for the 2001 WPCS centenary events and the show, which had to be postponed until 2002 owing to the foot and mouth outbreak. The main event was the open day at Llanllyr organised by the Ceredigion WPCA on 27 August, where I was commentator. There were 162 ponies, cobs and part-breds, all from Cardiganshire, shown in-hand, ridden, driven, giving dressage displays and being used as shepherding ponies. There were several RW winners and champions within sections A, B and C and when it came to the cobs, what has never been assembled before and probably never will again, five RW PofW champions all from the same county – Cyttir Telynor, Nebo Daniel, Gellifach ap Dafydd, Fronarth Welsh Model and Fronarth Boneddiges – and three reserves: Gwenllan Sali, Fronarth Victor and Elonwy Shooting Star. There were three other open days held to raise funds, at Telynau Stud on 1 July, at Waxwing Stud, Scotland, on 6 July, and at the home of the president Mr Elwyn Davies, Eppynt Stud, on 31 July.

The National Eisteddfod was held at Llanelli from 5–12 August and the Rural and Agricultural Area featured Welsh breeds from Carmarthenshire, a Welsh Black cow, a Welsh mountain sheep, a Welsh pony section B, Cennen Amorette, and section A Ceulan Cusan from Ceulan, Carmarthen. At the Glanusk Show on 6 May, the show president Mr Gwyn Price presented me with an engraved goblet for having been commentator for 42 years, and it was hinted that the committee would like me to write the fiftieth anniversary history for 2008. The RWS again did not offer a HOYS qualifier for the in-hand championship (which had changed from Templeton Horse and Pony divisions to Breeders Challenge with youngstock and senior divisions) but the RWAS' own Welsh championship was won by Danaway Flashjack (D) with Carwed Charmer (B) reserve, the other champions being Dyfrdwy Seren Fwyn (A), Hywi Moonlight (C) and Rosevale Only Fun (WPB). At the RW we had Ceulan Lieutenant (Yaverland Nero x Ceulan Libby), who was fourth of 58 yearling colts, and we sold him to Twyford Stud, where he was a good sire for many years before being exported to Germany. Vardra Sirius was second to the International Show junior champion and 2003 RW male champion, Gartconnel Shooting Star. We sold Sirius to the Templeton Show team, and he won many ridden championships for them. Cariad was fourth of 54 senior brood mares, and her filly foal Ceryl third of 81 colt and filly foals.

I was the English commentator at the thirteenth International Show held at Ermello, Holland, on 12– 13 August, where there were 413 Welsh ponies and cobs from seven countries competing. From 334 in-hand exhibits on the first day, the supreme champion was the Welsh cob mare H-S Image from Germany (who had won at the RW two weeks previously and whose parents were both bred in Cardiganshire), with the reserve supreme going to the section B yearling colt Mollegaards Don Pedro (Denmark). The six-y-o stallion Winneydene Gwyn-Emrys was section A champion and Rhosymeirch Sian section C champion, both from the UK. There was a most spectacular driven display on the first day of singles, pairs, tandems, three abreast and four-in-hands, with all drivers and passengers dressed in traditional Dutch costumes. At the Saturday evening party, the Welsh contingent took to the stage and was in very good voice! The second day was devoted to performance classes, and Carwed Charmer displayed his superb temperament amongst all the ladies, and was overall ridden supreme with Pentrepiod Duchess (D) supreme in harness.

There was a last-minute change of date for the FO Sale from mid-September to 6–7 October due to the fuel crisis, and with many overseas purchasers having arrived at Hereford in September, it was feared that they might not return. However prices were good – £4,000 for the section B mare Rhoson Carmen was a record, as was £2,300 for the section B foal Waxwing Princess Royal. Top section A price was £2,800 for the 15-y-o mare Fronbach Carys, and the filly foal Synod Mirth sold for £2,000. I bought the cream filly foal Cui Elenor (Waxwing Victory x Cui Elle) at Hay-on-Wye, but over the winter she turned grey, so I sold her. Elenor developed into the most superb mare – ridden by Sophie Harvey, she was in the front row at the 2007 HOYS and she was second of 70 barren mares at the 2008 RWS, beating mine! It just shows we can all make mistakes.

Mr Emrys Griffiths of the Revel had passed away at the age of 91 years, and his remaining 28 ponies were sold at Tal-y-bont-on-Usk on 18 October for £21,357 which was an exceptional figure, considering that these included three filly and eight colt foals. A record was broken at the RW Sale on 20, 21 and 23 October when £5,000 was paid for the section D filly foal Fronarth Elin, and a record equalled when the 12-y-o section C mare Synod Athina sold for £6,000. Exports increased significantly to 458 (from 383 in 1999) with USA exports increased from 34 to 51. From Ceulan to the USA we exported two filly foals – Ceulan Lynette (Yaverland Nero x Ceulan Lucy) to Gaslight Farm, California, and Ceulan Roma (Yaverland Nero x Ceulan Romance) to Mrs Elizabeth Utting of Pennsylvania. Having purchased Synod Birthday Boy, we sold the two stallions Yaverland Nero and Bengad Rustling Grass to Denmark, and the colt foal Vardra Santos (Trefaes Taran x Ceulan

Sulpasc) went to Mrs Inger Becker, Sweden, in the same load as the RW winning yearling colt Heniarth Mr Milligan and the entire 2000 Downland foal crop of five fillies and four colts bought by Mats and Cecilia Olsson.

Show reports in the 2001 Journal included the Isle of Wight WPCA, where I judged with Mr Robert Manchip and the Southern Counties WPCA, where I judged with David (B and WPB), Mrs Val Robinson (C) and Mr Rob Robinson (D), and we awarded the supreme to Trefaes Golden Pearl (D). We showed Cusan at Lampeter, where she won the Edgar Herbert trophy and first at Aberystwyth and Bridgend, Taran, who was champion (WPCS medal) at Bridgend and Cariad, who was champion (WPCS medal) and supreme Welsh at the Vale of Glamorgan. Ceulan Caryl was NCPA Ridden Pony of the Year for the Shacklebridge Stud in Derbyshire. The WPCS Performance Competition, where I was Master of Ceremonies at the presentation, had increased so much in popularity and participants that it had outgrown the facilities available at the Hare and Hounds Hotel, Tetbury (after over twenty years), and was moved to the larger Chesford Grange Hotel at Kenilworth. The supreme champion of the 2000 competition (9,775 points) was the section A gelding Cammac Dracma, ridden by Samantha Roberts who, six weeks after being bought unbroken at Northampton market, was winning ridden championships.

2001 got under way on 27 January with a centenary dinner dance at the Holiday Inn, Newport, which was attended by the deputy president, the Hon Mrs Shân Legge-Bourke, representing the incoming President HRH The Prince Of Wales. Because of the foot and mouth outbreak, the AGM had to be postponed and Mr Elwyn Davies' presidency extended, which included the visit of HRH to Aberystwyth on 20 July to the launch of my book *One Hundred Glorious Years*, which included the preface written by Prince Charles. I also produced a commemorative visitor's book / desk diary of 52 paintings of Welsh ponies and cobs, of which eleven are at Ceulan. Her Majesty The Queen wrote a thank you letter and supplied a photograph, both of which were printed in the diary and, as patron, sent her congratulations to 'the Society with which I and my family have been pleased to have been associated for many years.' These were soon sold out, and demand big prices if ever they appear for sale now.

We managed a few early shows before they were all cancelled. We had leased the bay stallion Joiners Kilkenny (f. 1996, Penual Mark x Ceulan Perl), but had to buy Perl back before we could lease Kilkenny, and he was reserve champion at the Midland in-hand and third at the Three Counties. The fact that the shows were cancelled did not seem to affect the sales – at the FO Sale on 5–6 October, the 10-y-o section B mare Downland Eventide topped the sale at £4,000, with the grey three-y-o colt Sarum Cadw Mi Gei top section A at £3,200. We sold the chestnut filly foal Ceulan Romany, who went to join her sire, Yaverland Nero, in Denmark.

Six hundred and fifty-one sections C, D and WPB sold at the RW Sale on 19, 20 and 22 October for £358,938, which gives an average of £719, the highest since 1994. Synod Stud topped the sale for a staggering fifth year, this time with the section C filly foal Synod Relegance at £11,000, almost treble the previous record. It was also a foal that topped the section Ds – Fronarth Valmai, at £7,500. Sitting near me was pop star Peter André, who bought a filly foal, Fronarth Cymraes Ddu.

David and Carol Maurer of California asked David to go to look at the Synod section C filly foal crop early in the year and buy one for them. He bought the chestnut Synod Aurora by Synod Gabriel, and when the Maurers were told that Relegance sold for £11,000, they thought they had an astounding bargain in Aurora! Aurora turned out well in the USA, and her performances under saddle are a good advertisement for Welsh section Cs. I judged at the Danish

Foal and Youngstock Show, Funen, on 1 September, where my champion foal was Valhallas Cherry (D), reserve was Fakla Gerald (A), and youngstock champion was the chestnut two-y-o colt Brierdene Napoleon bred by Mrs Wendy Dobinson in Tyne and Wear. I stayed on in Denmark for a few days and visited studs and took photographs. Because only ten of the usual HOYS qualifying shows were held in 2001, the Breeders Challenge (sponsored by Gail Chapman) champions and reserves were allowed to compete at the NEC, Birmingham. The youngstock champion was the WPB colt Greenbarrow Mr Smee, and adult Rosslyn Sweet Repose, who had qualified six times, and she was retired that day. To celebrate the centenary of the WPCS, a special one-off competition for the Supreme Welsh, sponsored by Brightwells Auctioneers was offered, judged by WPCS President HRH The Prince of Wales' representative, the Hon Mrs Shân Legge-Bourke, and it was won by the lead-rein section B Colne Heiress, ridden by three-year-old Charlotte Dent. Reserve was the section A lead-rein Roseisle Tudyr Melody, ridden by Ryan Homfray-Jones.

HRH Prince Charles and the Duchess of Cornwall hosted a reception in October for WPCS Council members and their husbands and wives at Vaynor Park, between Newtown and Welshpool, Powys. Ruth and I had difficulty locating the venue, and when we asked a local resident for directions, he pointed to the sky and said, 'Follow that royal helicopter.' There was tight security around the mansion, and every car was checked and mirrors placed underneath them. The police officer in charge was brought up in Tal-y-bont, and his father was one of my friends, so when he recognised me, I was allowed to jump the queue. HRH enquired about the sales of *One Hundred Glorious Years*, and was very impressed when I informed him that over 2,000 copies had been sold in three months. He had a laugh when I suggested that people didn't read the book, only the preface, which he had written.

Because live cattle, sheep and pigs were not allowed to compete at the RW Winter Fair held on 4 December, the organisers extended it to include junior classes of Welsh ponies and cobs and sport horses. The section champions were Maesgwyn Highball (A), Rosedale Oberon (B), Hywi Rhian (C) and Fronarth Dafydd Ddu (D). The supremes were judged by the Prince of Wales and Mr Emrys Bowen, who awarded the youngstock championship to Maesgwyn Highball (RW champion in 2010) and the foal championship to Sianwood Bayleaf, a daughter of Abercrychan Antonia, whose g-dam was Antonia (by Reeves Golden Lustre), and I collected two of her daughters from Mr Tovey, Oxfordshire in 1972. The RWAS awards normally presented at the summer show were awarded at the Winter Fair. The All-Wales Silage Competition winners were Dai and Gwen (my niece) Davies, Gwarffynnon, Lampeter. Dai won the Grassland competition in 1995 and 2002 and the Sir Bryner Jones award in 1984, and Gwen was UK Lady Farmer of the Year in 1988. With Starcrest Discovery (C) winning the Olympia M&M Ridden Championship in December, it brought the Welsh total up to an impressive ten out of a possible 23 against all other native breeds. The other champions were Criffel Casper (B, 1978), Norwood Principal Boy (B, 1981), Wiston Llwynog (D, 1986), Marston Monsoon (B, 1988), his son Harwel Wizard (B, 1998), Persie Ramrod (C, 1989), Verwood Roger (D, 1990) Kentchurch Cloud (D, 1994) and Kentchurch Request (D, 1996).

After all the problems of 2001, we thought events would have returned to normal, but 2002 started with another crisis when, after everyone had arrived in Aberystwyth for the AGM on 2 March, legal advice prevented it going ahead, and it was eventually held on 9 May at Llanelwedd, where I was presented with the 'Pride of Wales' print for having been publicity officer for 25 years. I was also congratulated for the £48,000 surplus which *One Hundred Glorious Years* had generated. The next event set the climate for a most successful year ahead – an exhibition of paintings and live pony displays on Saturday, Sunday and Monday 30 March–1 April at Glanusk Park, home of the Hon Mrs Shân Legge-Bourke, deputising for WPCS Centenary President HRH The Prince of Wales once again.

Featured on the front cover of the catalogue was the exhibition logo, a Welsh cob head by Sir Kyffin Williams RA, and on the back cover, Welsh mares and foals at Tan Lan by C. F. Tunnicliffe RA, OBE, on loan from the royal collection. There were 242 paintings and sculptures in a large marquee, including Debbie Dunbar's painting of a Welsh mountain pony stallion commissioned by the WPCS to be presented to Prince Charles, and two other centenary paintings, *Pride of Wales* by Philippa Porley and *Three Kings and a Queen* by Anne Thompson. Fifteen ponies and cobs put up a ridden display on the Saturday, ten each of section C and D in-hand on the Sunday and twenty sections A and B, including premium stallions on Monday. These ponies included many RW champions.

On 27 April at the Lord Mayor of Cardiff's Mansion House, Mrs Legge-Bourke, on behalf of the WPCS, presented the riding pony Highland Jinks to Catherine Zeta Jones for her 20-month-old son Dylan. HRH The Princess Royal attended the RWS (22–25 July) on the first day, and presented me with the Sir Bryner Jones Memorial Award awarded to 'the person who has made an exceptional contribution to the Welsh pony and cob breeds'. The Welsh breed in-hand champions were Fouroaks Reanne (A), Eyarth Windflower (B), Ashgrove Abigail (C), Gwynfaes Culhwch (D) and Duntarvie Cat Burglar (WPB). There was a centenary display every afternoon organised by Mrs Anne Roberts, the theme being 'Grace, pace and power', and the Welsh participants included event horses, dressage horses and show horses, and were a credit to the WPCS.

The WPCS Centenary Show postponed from the previous year took place on the RW showground on 1–2 August, and was a resounding success. Visitors were present from all over the world, and there were winning owners from Australia, USA, France, Holland, Sweden, Germany, Norway, Belgium and Denmark. The handlers included Mark Brown, a member of the Australian Olympic athletics team. Before the show there was a reception for more than 500 overseas visitors sponsored by *Horse and Hound*, and a dinner for 600 people on Thursday, sponsored by Thistledown Stud, including harpists, a male voice choir and soloists performing traditional Welsh music. The show ended with fun classes, bringing the total entries to 1,680.

The competitions ran like clockwork thanks to the small committee of five members – Mrs Robina Mills (chairman), Mrs Doreen Jones, Mr David Jones, Mr Len Bigley and me. Champions and reserves were Brynodyn Scarlet and Blackhill Picalo (A), Douthwaite Signwriter and Wedderlie Mardi Gras (B), Parvadean Renegade and Synod Rum Punch (C), Rotherdale Magic Princes and Blaengwen Brenin (D), Small-Land Extremity and Hollybush Bolero (WPB ponies), Llanarth Swansong and Penstrumbly Our Lulu (WPB horses), ridden Heniarth Quail (A) and Sydenham Forget Me Not (D) and harness Donys Llawen (C) and Gwynfaes Shon (D). We won the section A junior stallion class with Joiners Kilkenny. Every WPC Area Association was allocated space to put on a display, and there was judging for the best stand, which was won by the Scottish WPCA with Gwynedd second and Severn Valley third. Judges at the Northleach Show on 6 July were Mr Benno Crezee (Holland, A), Mr Kevin Townsend (New Zealand, B), Mr Carl Trock (Denmark, C) and Mrs India Haynes (USA, D).

Other centenary events included the Clwyd and Gwynedd WPCA Open Days, the visit of HM The Queen to Powys, and the Aberaeron Festival on 11 August, where the president was the TV presenter Ms Sara Edwards. The WPCS Journal featured a photograph of 'the president with her Uncle Wynne'. At the shows,

Joiners Kilkenny was champion at Pembroke County and Bridgend (WPCS medal) where Ceulan Mariah was reserve, and Synod Birthday Boy was champion locally. David bought three blacks – a yearling colt, Pentyrch Tom Sawyer (second at RW Winter Fair, Wilcrick Baron x Tanlan Tomosina), a colt foal, Fairstoke Spring Solo (champion at Wales and Border Counties, Fairstoke Count Domino x Ceulan Spring Song) and a filly foal, Courtway Flair (top filly at Hay-on-Wye, Heniarth Quip x Cusop Flutter).

After holding the FO Sale at Hereford for 48 years, due to the site being redeveloped, the sale was moved to Llanelwedd, and it was feared that the atmosphere would be lost. However, this proved to be unfounded, and the average price increased from £418 to £543. The ridden section A mare Drumphin Trinket was top of the sale at £3,200, and the top section B was the 14-y-o stallion Lemonshill Royal Flight (£2,200). All records were broken at the RW Sale on 18, 19 and 21 October, and the average of £911 was equal to the previous highest of 1990. Top of the sale at £14,500 was the four-y-o section C stallion Uphill Tom Thumb, with a section C filly foal, Synod Ruby Gem, selling for £4,800. Top section D was the gelding Mowcastle More Magic (£6,500), with £6,200 for the stallion Fronarth Telynor Yr Ail and £5,300 for the mare Glantraeth Red Heather. The 7 November issue of *Horse and Hound* featured a list of 'The 200 most influential people in the British horse world today' and, to my great surprise, I was included, alongside such as David Broome, Harvey Smith and Dick Francis!

When David Blair took over as editor of the WPCS Journal from me, he publicly thanked both Ruth and myself in the 2004 Journal, acknowledging the major part which Ruth had played in typing the mainly hand-written articles and putting in many hours of proof-reading. Making up for no shows in 2001, we started off the 2003 shows with extra enthusiasm and three reserve championships – Kilkenny at Swansea, Tom Sawyer at Wales and Border Counties, and Ceryl at Barry, where Mariah and her foal Menna also both won. At the RASE, Cariad was second brood mare, her foal Carwyn was fourth and daughter Ceryl (three-y-o) also fourth, then for a special progeny class of mare and two progeny, they won a further £100! At the RWS, Spring Solo was eighth, Ceryl was seventh, Cariad was fourth and Kilkenny third. There were a massive 97 yearling fillies entered. We had sold a foal, Ceulan Lena (Joiners Kilkenny x Ceulan Lucy), the previous year to Stephen and Sarah Dickmeyer of California, and she had been left in UK with Barry Shepherd to show. The Dickmeyers also bought Menai Seren Las privately, and the foal Randan Absolutely Gorgeous on the Randan Sale on 27 July for £1,800 (they also bought her dam Randan Absolutely Fabulous for £1,700). All three were in this class, all three were in the final fifteen that were kept in, and Menai was fifth, Randan seventh and Ceulan eighth. What an achievement for overseas owners.

David was also in the last fifteen, and when he came out of the ring, he told me that he had beaten the black Mynyddtarren Hermia (sired by the 2010 HOYS Riding Pony of the Year Mynyddtarren the Maverick), but should not have, so he had bought Hermia and instructed me to go and pay for her! We have had exceptional successes with Hermia and her daughter Ceulan Hannah (f. 2011 and sired by Pendock Bridegroom). Without my prior knowledge, the WPCS of America had arranged with the RWAS to present to me on the Wednesday afternoon in the Main Ring the Legion of Merit plaque won by my Lisvane Lotus Blossom for her three progeny, Ceulan Lorelei, Lwcus and Lydia, all three owned by David and Carol Maurer of California. The presentation was made by Mrs Gail Thomson, director of WPCSA. It is not often that one gets an award without having to do anything! It was fitting that the award was given in 2003 since Lotus died that year aged 24 years, having produced fourteen foals at Ceulan.

The RW champions were Springbourne Elly (A), Eyarth Windflower (B), Tyngwndwn Daylight (C), Gwenllan Sali (D) and Broadgrove Chatterbox (WPB). The HOYS Cuddy qualification at the RW was reinstated. Chatterbox won it and ended up overall champion in the final. The First Ridden Pony Of The Year was Lowland Bronwen Cariad, whose dam Ynyscrug Bronwen was sired by Ceulan Sentinel (full-brother to Sidan who won 28 championships and seven WPCS medals and died in 2003 aged 25). Another connection was that Wesley Hill, breeder of Ynyscrug Bronwen, had been a pupil of mine at Porth County School almost fifty years previously!

An innovation in 2003 was the National Welsh and Part-bred Championship Show held at Shrewsbury on 3 August, organised by Mesdames Jocelyn Price, Ann Bigley and Lorraine Partridge and Messrs David Blair and Robert Jones, and sponsored by Brightwells, Rhydspence Stud, Mrs Kath Panayiotou, Mrs Ceri Fell and Mr and Mrs John Geddes. The champions were Friars Posy (A), Paddock Northern Lustre (B), Tyngwndwn Daylight (C), Fronarth Model Lady (D), Talponciau Heavens Above (WPB), Starcrest Discovery (ridden) and Parvadean Lotta Bottle (driven). We were section A reserve champion with Joiners Kilkenny.

The fourteenth International Show was held in Aachen, Germany on 23–24 August. The champions were Blackhill Picalo (A and reserve supreme), Douthwaite Signwriter (B), Nebo Rachel (C and supreme), Felinmor Triple Crown (D), Golden Highlight (WPB) and Naomi Ballerina (WPB, ridden). I judged at the National Show, Orivedella, Finland on 12–13 July and gave a slide show on the Sunday afternoon. My supreme champion was Waitwith Delight (A), with Polaris Jonquil (B) reserve and Cathael Lisa champion section D.

The fiftieth celebration FO Sale held on 26–27 September included a Friday evening party with a gala auction of 28 selected lots, and presentations to 'a select band of people who, over the years, have been instrumental in the Fayre Oaks success'. These were the Countess of Dysart, Miss Laura Hutchins, Mesdames Robina Mills, Doreen Wyatt, Joyce Wilding-Davies, Jocelyn Price, Rosemary Rees, Doreen Jones, Mr Gwyn Berry and myself. The ridden Orielton Beamish (B) topped the gala auction at £10,500, followed by two section A stallions, Synod The Colonel (£7,000) and Friars Superman (£6,000). The filly foal Synod Sugar Candy topped the usual day FO Sale at £4,300, and the seven-y-o mare Friars Welsh Doll sold for £4,200. The section A stallion Littlestones Red Fox sold to Brierdene Stud for £3,300, and we bought his son, the colt foal Wernderris Caramel, who lived at Ceulan for eleven years until half of our mares were his daughters, and then he went back to Wernderris in 2014. We also sold the eighth-highest section A filly foal Ceulan Sws, and Synod Birthday Boy, who had spent his time at Ceulan, went to Lippens Stud. At the RW Sale, 542 lots sold for £530,100, creating a new record average of £978. The Fronarth / Blaengwen family sold both top section D male Blaengwen Wayne Rooney and female Fronarth Esther for £9,500 and £8,500 respectively, and the seven-y-o mare Synod Rosie's Angel from Synod was top of the Cs at £6,500.

Photographer David Hurn's book *Living in Wales* was launched in Cardiff on 27 November. It consisted of 101 portraits of people who 'have enriched my [David Hurn's] life and that of Wales', and included poets R. S. Thomas and Owen Sheers, opera singers Dame Margaret Price and Bryn Terfel, rugby legend Gareth Edwards, Peter Hain MP, broadcaster Vincent Kane, President of Plaid Cymru Dafydd Wigley, boxer Joe Calzaghe, rock singer Bonnie Tyler, harpist Catrin Finch and historian Dr John Davies. I was very surprised and honoured to be subject number 97 alongside Colin Jackson, our greatest ever sprint hurdler.

In readiness to be broadcast in June 2004 to celebrate 100 years of the Royal Welsh Show, four one-hour programmes were filmed by Teledu Telesgop at the Lion Royal Hotel, Rhayader, in August, to portray the history of the RWAS. Present-day members Sir Meuric Rees, Dr Emrys Evans, Messrs Robin Gibson-Watt, Albert Lewis, Picton Jones, four others and I were dressed in costumes to represent the 1904 council members the Earl of Powis, Lords Tredegar and Penrhyn, Sirs Richard Green Price and Pryse Pryse, and the final production was quite realistic. I judged at the Ceredigion WPCA Foal Show on 20 September at the new venue of Lampeter Market, and my champion was the filly Cefnfedw Sophie and reserve the colt Frongoch Trysor, which had travelled from West Yorkshire.

To start 2004, we leased the five-y-o Frongoch Cardi from my niece Mrs Ann Jones of Frongoch Stud. He had been three times male champion at RASE and was RW male champion later, in 2007. We showed him only once, at the Glamorgan WPCA Show where he was section A champion and reserve supreme, and then he ran out with our mares and foals. Having been chairman of the Glamorgan WPCA for ten years, I thought it an appropriate time to hand over, and Mr Robert Manchip, Ffald Stud, was elected chairman and I became vice-president to Mrs Serena Homfray. HM The Queen, Patron of the RWAS and HRH The Duke of Edinburgh visited the RWS (19–22 July) on the Wednesday, when Her Majesty spent some time inspecting the Welsh ponies and cobs and discussing the animals with the judges and owners. Prince Charles, in his introduction to the show catalogue, wrote: 'There can be few, if any agricultural shows in the world which can boast an equally superb display of animals,' and as Centenary President, he opened the show in the Main Ring on the Monday morning.

There was a centenary cavalcade staged every evening, coordinated by Major Sir Michael Parker, which included pit ponies, mail coaches (complete with highwaymen), cockle pickers, 'shot-gun marriage' and scores of young people riding and dancing – several hundred participants in all, a most magnificent spectacle. The champions were Friars Goldilocks (A, a wedding gift from Siân Morris' father and first time championship for Friars Stud), Mintfield Songthrush (B and HOYS qualifier), Tremymor Sportsman (C), Blaengwen Brenin (D) and Penstrumby Lulu (WPB). We showed Ceulan Soffia (three-y-o, Yaverland Nero x Ceulan Sidan) who was sixth of 46, and we sold her to jockey Seb Sanders as a riding pony for his daughter. Ceulan Mariah came sixth of 64 senior brood mares, and her filly foal Ceulan Mai fifth of 46. David had sold Mariah's previous year's foal Menna (sired by Joiners Kilkenny) to John and Bev Batt of the Abergavenny Stud, and she was fourth of 80 yearling fillies to Friarly Siaradus, Synod Sugar Candy (the £4,300 FO foal) and Springbourne Claudia.

Professor David Howell's book *Taking Stock*, the 100-year history of the RWAS, was launched at the show, and he thanked me for assistance with the Welsh pony and cob sections. The Welsh Government magazine *Gwlad*, issued during Royal Welsh week, featured a photograph of Dinarth What Ho and me (1952) on the front cover. Mynyddtarren Hermia was first and youngstock champion at Swansea and first at the United Counties, Ceulan Lucy was champion (WPCS medal) at the Vale of Glamorgan, and her colt foal Ceulan Lucius (sired by Joiners Kilkenny) was also first, and we sold him as a yearling to Switzerland. We lent Ceulan Swyn as a riding pony for Catrin Reed of the Tyngwndwn Stud, and she won a ridden championship two weeks after her arrival at Nebo, with sister Lowri reserve, riding Pica Primrose. Their Journal advertisement stated that they won 129 rosettes between them.

Because the celebration gala auction of 2003 was so successful, Brightwells decided to continue with this event within the FO Sale held on 24–25 September, and 27 ponies were catalogued as 'high flyer' lots, including five from Yaverland Stud, two of which, Yaverland Cherry Blossom (which spent the 1999 summer at Stud at Ceulan) and Castellau Valeta sold for £7,000 each to top the sale. Fortunately, we had bought Ceulan Salome back privately from Yaverland before the sale! Top section B at £5,300 was the three-y-o colt Moelgarnedd Calypso by Carwed Charmer who had died in 2002. Excluding the 'high flyer', 390 ponies sold for an average of £719, and the additional facilities for ridden ponies at Llanelwedd compared with Hereford paid dividends, with the ridden gelding Putwell Golden Boy (A) selling for £3,800 and Gorfelyn Honey Roan (A), a consistent performer in WHP competitions, selling for £3,000. The three-y-o colt Griashall Valentino was top section B at £3,300. We sold the section A foal Ceulan Lorna (Joiners Kilkenny x Ceulan Libby) for £1,300. During the year we sold privately the 1998 RASE overall champion Ceulan Sali and the colt foal Ceulan Cariadwr (Joiners Kilkenny x Ceulan Cariad) to Mrs Ceri Fell of the Brynseion Stud. Cariadwr sired some very good foals at Brynseion before being sold to the Coffee-Pot Stud and, out of the many hundreds of section A stallions at stud in the UK in 2014, Cariadwr was equal ninth in the WPCS sire-ratings.

The 2004 RW Cob Sale was re-organised onto three consecutive days without having a Sunday break in between, on 15–17 October. The average figure exceeded £1,000 for the first time, with 579 selling for £620,128 and 58 geldings selling for an average of £1,772. Top of the sale at £13,000 was the nine-y-o section C stallion Parvadean The General. Parvadean also had top section C mare with Parvadean Pom Pom (£4,000), and equal top section C foal Parvadean Denise at £3,200. The two top cobs at £9,000 each were the stallion Brynithon Royal Diplomat and the mare Thorneyside Lady Boss. Two major studs were involved in weddings during the year. Amanda Price Jones of Synod married Marc Harries in August, and Cerys Reynolds of Springbourne married Stephen Brook in September. David judged the RW Winter Fair on 29 November, where there were 43 colt foals, 73 filly foals, 16 yearling

Thank you both

It is hard to think that Dr Wynne Davies is no longer Journal Editor. For the last twelve years he has worked tirelessly to see the Journal earn its place alongside the best on the equestrian bookshelf. At times the task has not been easy and surprisingly his efforts not always appreciated by those who should have supported it best.

However, the Society and its members have always been foremost in his mind and he clearly saw 'The Green Book' as an effective tool to promote the Welsh Pony and Cob Society. Most people will agree that he has done a fantastic job. Each year the anticipation of its arrival in February is clear testimony to the value that the members place on the Journal.

Thanks, Wynne and Ruth for a job very well done.

David Blair

Article from the WCPS Journal 2004

Presenting a copy of *The Welsh Pony* to HRH Princess Anne, 2006

Announcer at the WPCS Performance Competition Presentation 2006

At Ceulan (from left): Jane, Wynne, Leah, Ruth, Miriam, Joseph and David

Mr David Williams, vice-chair of WPCS Council, makes a presentation to Ruth and me at the AGM in 2009

At the launch of *Sixty Years of Royal Welsh Champions* with Ruth and Royal Welsh Lady Ambassador Lucinda Dargavel, RWS 2009

Signing *Ceredigion Champions* – an author rises above his surroundings

Launching *Ceredigion Champions* with Ruth, RWS 2010

Top: Ceulan foals and handlers October 1992 (from left) Ceulan Suran, Rhydian; Ceulan Bounce, Gareth; Ceulan Lorelei, Jane and Ceulan Caredig, Allen. Below: Colts for Fayre Oaks Sale 1992 (from left) Vardra Sun King, Rhydian; Ceulan Stormus, Gareth, Ceulan Syndod, Jason and Ceulan Syniad, Allen

The same handlers 20 years later in 2012 (from right, Gareth, Allen and Rhydian. With them (from left) are Aled, Ryan and Megan, Gareth's daughter. Ryan wasn't born in 1992 when the previous photos were taken!

Ceulan Hannah with David, 2012

A family photo from 2012: my older sister Kathleen (left) with daughter Janet and grandson Jonathan; younger sister Ann (centre) and husband Gwilym with their four children Mair, Gwen, Enoc and Dafydd and their families

Receiving the Lifetime Achievement Award at the Horse of the Year Show 2012 with grandchildren Joseph and Leah

With David and Ceulan Corona at the Fayre Oaks Sale, 2013 (Photo: Mike Daley)

With leading trainer Ed Dunlop at Newmarket, 2013

Ceulan Cariad (1988–2014) producer of 15 foals, six of them exported

Weston Distinction, the current main sire at Ceulan   *(Photo: Emyr Young)*

colts, 18 yearling fillies, sixteen 2–3-y-o colts and 20 fillies entered. His champion was the three-y-o colt Flydon Wyn by Nerwyn Cadno, the reserve the yearling filly Hengwys Cherry Blossom by Windleway Shogun, and his champion foal was Islyn Hafoc by Lacy Brigadier, who was later proclaimed overall foal champion, and won the Brightwells section A championship at the Welsh National Championships the following year.

The main event we were planning in 2005 was our daughter Jane's wedding to Simon Field in Miskin Church on 3 September. They bought a marquee, and we had the reception in the paddock in front of our house. David's three daughters Rachel, Leah and Miriam were bridesmaids, and their son Joseph a pageboy. Jane graduated from Exeter University in 1986, and in 1988 was awarded a Rotary International Scholarship for two years to study for a Higher Degree at Boston and Virginia universities. She visited many American Welsh pony studs while she was there. From 1990–1999 Jane visited primary schools all over Wales, assisting teachers on aspects of health and wellbeing, and she co-wrote the Welsh Government resource on health education. Jane has worked in the Education and Skills Department of the Welsh Government since 1999, and she and Simon have three sons, Jamie, Mathew and Oscar, who are very happy to be with the ponies. At the wedding, WPCS members made up a large proportion of the guests. When our foals were paraded for all to see at the reception, one of them remarked, 'This is the only wedding that I have attended where we have had a foal show!' Perhaps this helped to advertise the foals since, at the FO Sale, two daughters of Frongoch Cardi, the chestnut Cassie (out of Cariad) and the bay Sharonn (the first foal out of Santes, Synod Birthday Boy x Ceulan Sali) sold for £1,050 and £1,000 respectively.

We leased the six-y-o Powys (NL) Shon (Blackhill Picalo x Lacy Sable) from Mr Harold Zoet, Ysselvliedt Stud, Holland, for two years, on condition that we prepared him for the 2006 FO Sale. He had a most successful showing year – champion at Swansea, champion (WPCS silver medal) at the Royal Bath and West and stood fourth for the HOYS Cuddy qualifier there. In order to keep the Vardra prefix in the public view, we showed the yearling filly Vardra So Charming (Synod Birthday Boy x Ceulan Sulpasc), and she won at Glamorgan WPCA, youngstock champion at Swansea and second at Pembroke County. The three-y-o Mynyddtarren Hermia also had a few outings, took reserve champion at Wales and Border Counties, first at United Counties and youngstock champion at Pembroke.

I was awarded Honorary Life Governorship at the RWS for having exhibited there for 58 years and commentated for 29 years. Another RW honour went to Charlotte Clarke of Manchester, who was champion young handler. She was showing Popsters Just Rosie, daughter of Coediog Catrin that we had had at Ceulan for ten years and sold to Popsters. David and Mrs Jill Williams (Glebedale) assessed the young judges at the National Championships, where the overall winner was Samantha Roberts, currently the most successful producer of ridden M&M ponies in the UK. David also judged in Holland in April, where his supremes were H-S Adrian (A) with Hoekhorse Joelle (B) reserve, and the section As at the Royal Highland in June, where his champion was the yearling filly Waxwing Pimms with reserve the brood mare Tullibardine My Fair Lady.

The fifteenth International Show was held in Belgium, where the supreme was Friars Posy (A) and reserve Pentrepiod Welsh Flyer (D), with Moorkieker Gawain champion B, Gweunydd Sionyn champion C and Moelgarnedd Myrddin ridden supreme. We had our best ever successes at the foal shows. Ceulan Mia (Frongoch Cardi x Ceulan Maria) was first of 58 and champion at the Welsh National Foal Show, and reserve supreme to Blaengwen

Freddie Flintoff (D). Ceulan Shem (Pentyrch Tom Sawyer x Vardra Solitaire) was second of 34 at this show, first at Glamorgan WPCA, champion at Gwent and second of 51 at the RW Winter Fair.

Since we had Powys Shon for another year, and Wernderris Caramel started limited stud duties at the age of two, Pentyrch Tom Sawyer and Fairstoke Spring Solo were surplus to our requirements. Tom Sawyer was sold to Sweden and Spring Solo to Messrs Hodge and Walters of Okehampton, who bought five black mares and fillies on the FO Sale to go with him. There were 27 lots entered for the 'high flyer' FO Sale. Twenty of them sold for £61,600, with top prices of £10,000 for the section B stallion Heaton Romeo, followed by £7,000 for the section A mare Pendock Jade, who had qualified for the lead-rein class at HOYS. Mrs Betty French of the Forlan Stud had three on the 'high flyer' and another thirteen on the sale which sold for a total of £18,200. The top two, Forlan Harebell (£2,300) and Forlan Honey Girl (£2,000), were daughters of Forlan Honeybee by Twyford Sprig. The top section A outside the 'high flyer' was the palomino yearling filly Rookery Sound of Music, sold to Holland for £6,000, and the top B was another palomino, the three-y-o filly Stoak Tanya, sold for £4,400. There was a new female record at the RW Sale when the eight-y-o Tardebigge Estelle sold for £17,000, and the filly foal Fronarth Telynores Goch for £12,000. Top male was the three-y-o colt Kallistalodge Assasin, sold for £7,000, top section C was the mare Hardys Decorum (£4,500), top WPB was the piebald stallion Trixies Cappuccino (£5,100) and top gelding Townies Fenman (£4,100).

Over 2,000 visitors turned up at Glanusk Park on 14 May 2006 for an open day organised by the Hill Ponies of Wales Society to raise funding for their biennial newsletter. Most of the premium areas had brought groups of their ponies and stallions which had been awarded premiums at the Glanusk Show, Llanelwedd, the previous week. There were other displays, such as a parade of foxhounds and a mounted pageant of the Rebecca Riots. Mr Aneurin Jones had donated a print of nine mares on the Preseli mountains which was raffled, and his painting of Mr Emrys Griffiths was presented to Mrs Betty French in recognition of her work collating statistics of ponies on the Welsh hills. The weather was glorious, and the Society benefitted financially extremely well due to the generosity of the hosts Mr William and Mrs Shân Legge-Bourke.

My tenth book, *The Welsh Pony*, covering sections A, B, C and WPB was launched at the Royal Welsh Show. The *Western Mail* supplement the week before the show featured a double-page article on the 'Voice of the Show', which guaranteed good sales of the book at the launch. Also available were cards of an amusing cartoon. At the RWS, I welcome as many named overseas visitors as I know are present. One such wrote in the WPCS Journal how important it made them feel, and others often wrote to Mr David Walters, secretary of the RWAS, expressing their appreciation. The week following the show, I presented a copy of the book to HRH The Princess Royal at the NPS Centenary Show at Malvern. I made certain that the book opened on the page which featured a photograph of HRH in 1951 with Kirby Cane Greensleeves, and her comment was: 'A lovely pony to ride, but she had a habit of galloping and stopping suddenly, when I would fall off.' I didn't think that Welsh ponies did such tricks!

The book was very well received worldwide. The WPCS Journal contained a photo of Mr Edwin Prosser presenting a copy to Mrs Hetty Abeles, a senior director of the WPCS of America and her mother Mrs Joan Dunning who, as Mrs Mackay-Smith, had bid against my father at the Coed Coch Sale seventy years previously. Rhoson Shem (B) qualified for the HOYS Cuddy In-hand at the RW, and the other champions were Eppynt Silver Locket (A), Tyngwndwn Moon Lady (C), Llamri Lausanne (D) and Woodview Ianthe (WPB). At the HOYS, the Cuddy champion was Waitwith

West Wind (A), who qualified at the South of England Show, Nebo Rachel (C) was fourth, Stoak Tuscany (B) fifth, Rotherwood Peek-a-Boo (WPB) seventh, Pennal Free Dancer (D) eighth and Rhoson Shem (B) ninth.

Our shows got off to a good start. Powys Shon won a bronze medal at Carmarthen WPCA, then a week later a silver medal and supreme Welsh at Cothi Bridge, where Shem also won a class of 15 yearlings. We did well for WPCS medals in 2006. In addition to the two for Powys Shon, Vardra So Charming won a bronze medal at Barry as did Mynyddtarren Hermia at Nevern. David was busy judging at Devon County and Cheshire County, and was chief steward to Australian judge Mrs Suellen Deane at the National Championships. United again with Mrs Jill Williams (who was without her luggage for a week), the two judged the Danish Grading and Show in heavy rain, but were very pleased with the standard of the ponies and cobs.

Our entries for the FO Sale were a yearling filly, Ceulan Shanny (Fairstoke Spring Solo x Ceulan Swyn), that had won at Wales and Border Counties and the Vale of Glamorgan, and she sold well on the 'high flyer' in addition to three filly foals and two colt foals. Ceulan Salimali (Fairstoke Spring Solo x Vardra Solitaire) was the eighth-highest section A foal, Ceulan Megan (Powys Shon x Ceulan Mariah) sold to Waitwith Stud, though I bought her back two years later. Our time was up with Powys Shon, who sold for £3,000 to Julmar Stud, and to replace him, we bought the bay five-y-o Sunwillow Irving (Knodishall Gwillym x Sunwillow Berenice) for the same price. He was the twenty-second bay stallion / colt to stand at Ceulan since we came here in 1962. Top of the 'high flyer' sale at £11,000 was the eight-y-o chestnut mare Friars Tears of Gold (A) followed by the WPB yearling colt Small-Land Tapdance at £9,800. Outside the 'high flyer', the nine-y-o section A mare Springbourne Cleo sold to Holland for £9,000, and altogether,

477 lots sold for £476,490, averaging £1,000. We were the under-bidders on the bay colt foal Weston Distinction (Cwmhendy Buster x Weston Lady Lace) bought by a neighbour breeder, but we later leased him then bought him. He won the colt foal class out of 37 entries at the RW Winter Fair, where we also had fourth of 68 with the palomino filly foal Ceulan Cara. Distinction's RW winnings include first in 2009 and second in 2012. At the RW Sale, the cob mare Pennal Calon Mai, schooled to perfection by Jane Weller, sold for £14,500, the filly foal Cascob Powys Princess sold for £11,000, the dun yearling filly Caebryn Surreal sold for £8,500, the stallion Pentrefelin Jake (just returned after two seasons in Holland) sold for £8,000 and top of the Cs at £4,500 was the palomino filly foal Popsters Lalique. Finally, during 2006 I received a congratulatory card from the President of the Royal Society of Chemistry for having completed fifty years of membership.

2007 was a comparatively quiet year for us on the pony front, but we still had ten foals. Unfortunately, six were colts, but they were nice colts, sired by Wernderris Caramel and Powys Shon. In February, Ceulan Cariadog was awarded the Preferent Stallion of Holland title, and I received a certificate as breeder. One daughter of his, Shamrocklake Silk Hortensia (f. 2001, out of Fronbach High Society), came to the RWS and won a class of 41 junior brood mares, a very nice mare and an exceptionally good mover. We had Ceulan Shem gelded at two years of age, and he was sold to the Southworth family of Warrington, Cheshire who owned Mynyddtarren The Maverick, sire of Hermia. Shem has turned out to be the most successful ridden section A ever bred at Ceulan.

At the RWS, the champions were Glyncoch Hyfryd (A), Paddock Northern Lustre (B), Fronarth Robben (C), Fronarth Model Lady (D) and Llanarth Kitty (WPB). Glyncoch Hyfryd went on to win the Tom and Sprightly competition with Paddock Northern Lustre reserve, and Hyfryd won HOYS Cuddy qualifier, with the two-y-o riding pony breeding champion Bradmore Celebration reserve. Glyncoch Hyfryd did the Welsh breeds proud at HOYS, where she was champion pony and reserve overall.

The FO Sale on 15–16 September went off very well again. The fifth 'high flyer' was the best to date with 21 lots selling for £77,150, an average of £3,674, with top price of £10,500 for the section A yearling colt Colne Turbo, followed by £9,500 for the WPB two-y-o colt Small-Land Mooncoin and £6,000 for the ridden 15-y-o stallion Bengad Rumex. We had plenty of the 'S' family at Ceulan, and sold the 11-y-o mare Ceulan Salome, which went to Carmarthenshire for £1,750. The top of the 'outside high flyer' came from Cascob Stud. This was the 13-y-o section A stallion Winneydene Gwyn-Emrys, who had won at the RW and been international champion. He sold for £6,000 to Rhydyfelin Stud, where Coed Coch Siaradus was bred 65 years previously. My neighbour breeders, Jo Claes and Jane Bugler, bought a filly foal, Eppynt Sequel, for £32 at Brecon Market and sold her seven years later on this sale to Finland for £4,000. We sold the colt foal Ceulan Cynnan to Mr Leeuwenhaag, owner of the preferent Cariadog (same dam), and he has been a very successful sire in Spain for five years. The section B stallion Eyarth Caliph at 14 years came back from Holland at £3,500, and the Dutch-bred two-y-o filly Hoekhorst Juliet sold for £3,400 – she was ridden champion at Glanusk in 2009. The RW Sale total was £60,000 up on the previous year at £791,490, averaging £1,193, with 104 selling over £2,000 and 37 over £3,000. For the first time ever, one vendor sold two animals for over £10,000 – Thorneyside Magic Lady at £11,000 and Thorneyside Tradition at £10,000. Within section C, the two black stallions Synod Request and Parvadean The Gigolo sold for £6,000 each, and the chestnut filly foal Synod Angelica also sold for £6,000.

I gave a talk to the Ceredigion WPCA at the Grannell Hotel, Llanwnen, on 1 October. I must say this Association always seems to be able to rely on a good attendance. The most exciting 2007 event for me took place at the HOYS on Sunday 7 October, when I was invited to judge the £1,000 supreme ridden horse and £1,000 supreme ridden pony of the year with co-judge show and TV commentator Mr Mike Tucker. This competition took place to a packed audience under spotlights, and I treated myself to a new dinner suit for the event. There were nine champions eligible for the pony division and twelve for the horses. Supreme pony was the M&M mini champion, the first-ridden Waxwing Thumbs Up, ridden by Oliver Shuttleworth, and the reserve, the show hunter pony Yealand Angelina, ridden by Jack Starkie. Supreme horse was the Large Riding Horse of the Year Broadstone Doulton, ridden by Robert Walker.

2008 began early with a talk and film show at the Hotel Darthuizen at Leersum, Holland, for the Dutch WPCS Vereniging on 12 January. There was a very good attendance, and afterwards I was taken to visit the nearby historic city of Dordrecht. This was followed by a talk on 'Animals in Carmarthenshire History' at the day school of the Carmarthenshire Antiquarian Society at the National Botanic Garden of Wales on 16 February. The other speakers were Dr Morfydd Owen ('Welsh poetry of the twelfth century'), Cledwyn Fychan ('Wolves in Wales'), Mr Roger Davies ('Balwen sheep), Mr John Pratt ('Welsh Black cattle') and Lord Dynevor ('Dynevor White cattle'). My talk, with accompanying photographs, was published in the *Carmarthenshire Antiquary volume XLIV*. Glanusk held their fiftieth anniversary show at the Royal Welsh Showground on 3 May, and to celebrate the event they published an article which I wrote on Glanusk Show 1958–2008 in their special, gold-covered show catalogue. The 2009 WPCS Journal published a series of colour photographs which I had taken at Glanusk shows every year from 1958 to 1963. Supreme of the 2008 show was Eppynt Shot (A) with reserve Trevallion Stepping Jack (D).

Sunwillow Irving started off the showing season well at the Glamorgan WPCA Show at Pencoed College where he was champion (WPCS medal), and then he was sent to Mr Wayne Isaac to break into harness, and entered for the RWS to be driven by Mrs Emma Edwards who, as Miss Emma Lewis, had won at HOYS driving the Welsh part-bred mare Twilight II. Irving won second prize in the harness class at the RW, and the report in *Carriage Driving* read: 'Dr Wynne Davies reappeared as a harness exhibitor after an interval of 55 years, and it is hoped the good doctor will not leave it so long before competing again'!

At other shows we were three times reserve champion – Vardra So Charming at the City of Swansea, Mynyddtarren Hermia at Bridgend and Ceulan Cara at the Vale of Glamorgan. The yearling filly Ceulan Lodes, from David's Crymych base, won first prizes at Cardigan, Fishguard and Nevern. The Ceredigion WPCA held their inaugural Summer Show at Llanllyr on 29 June, and I was appointed president and judge of the supreme, which I awarded to the Welsh cob mare Nebo Miss Maple, and reserve supreme to the section A champion Brynrodyn Sioned.

The autumn sales were conducted in the wake of one of the most traumatic periods in the world financial markets, and understandably, prices were down. At the FO 'high flyer' Sale, the average was down to £623, but two geldings excelled – Rosemarche Huckleberry (A) sold for £11,000 on the 'high flyer', and Akadame Scimitar (B) topped the remainder at £4,800. By the time of the RW Cob Sale, things were not so gloomy, and 654 animals sold for an average of £1,016, with a top price of £12,000 for the filly foal Abergavenny Princess Yasmin (D) to Holland, and £9,200 for the 11-y-o mare Mathfred April (D). The 12-y-o stallion Parvadean Golden Glory was top of the section Cs at £7,200 to Norway. Two rather special foals which we bred in 2008 were the palomino colt Ceulan Calon Lân (Wernderris Caramel x Ceulan Cariad) and the palomino filly Ceulan Clara (Wernderris Caramel x Ceulan Cusan, daughter of Cariad). We sold Calon Lân to Bethan Hooper and Rhydian Donati (one of my helpers since 1990), and Clara won many prizes, and is one of our best young brood mares.

Calon Lân went on to win five foal championships (16 championships in total to date), including the Royal Cornwall 2011 where he was also reserve for the HOYS Cuddy qualifier to the in-hand hunter Rocklodge Rhapsody from 18 champions. Following on from the success of Glyncoch Hyfryd in the HOYS Cuddy Championships in 2007, 2008 heralded the start of a run of successes for the Welsh, when the champion was the section A stallion Pinewell Bucks Fizz, who qualified at the Midland Counties and had not long returned from standing at stud in Holland. Second to Bucks Fizz was Cottrell Lara (B) with Parvadean Delight (C) fourth. Bucks Fizz repeated this championship in 2009 and Parvadean Delight herself was champion in 2011, starting a run of successes for section Cs with Glebedale Ding Dong (C) champion in 2012 and Synod Lady Lilian (C) champion in 2013. I judged the Supreme Welsh at the RW Winter Fair on 2 December, which I awarded to Llanarth Delilah (B) with Friars True Love (A) reserve, and the other Welsh champions were Karnarth Rocky Balboa (C) and Thorneyside His Majesty (D).

The 2008 AGM was held at Llandudno in March 2009 with the retiring president Mr Len Bigley (Llanarth) handing over to Mr William Lloyd (Geler). Mr David Williams presented Ruth with a bouquet and me with an engraved vase for having been publicity officer for 35 years. In the evening party, a copy of my book *Sixty Years of Royal Welsh Show Champions* sold by auction for £600.

The first 2009 event for me was judging the section As at the forty-eighth Lampeter Show on 18 April. The weather was glorious, and entries were at a record 176 – 39 yearling colts, 47 yearling fillies and 20 stallions. I was very impressed with the winning chestnut three-y-o filly Runshaw Heulwen, a beautiful filly that moved as if on air, which was not surprising since she was a double g-daughter of Coed Coch Bari, one of the greatest movers of all time. There were some very promising youngsters, with bays and chestnuts appearing in droves. However, the reserve champion to Heulwen was the grey stallion Dukeshill Darcy, who had a most impressive walk.

At the Royal Bath and West on 29 May, Clara won the yearling filly class from 15 entries, and Weston Distinction was second 2–3-y-o to Sarum Rembrandt, who was second HOYS Ridden section A Pony of the Year in 2014, when he and Ceulan Shem had the highest ride marks of all. Mr Eddie Tamplin was the nominated judge for section B, but he was taken ill the previous night, and I ended up judging in a borrowed bowler and a rather untidy suit. The Dyfed WPCA members visited Ceulan in June, and we were lucky to have extra helpers to show off the stallions Sunwillow Irving, Wernderris Caramel and Weston Distinction. I was President of the Northleach Show and judge of the supremes, which I awarded to two 'Scrumpy Jacks' – the champion section D Danaway Scrumpy Jack, and the ridden, section C Lychfields Scrumpy Jack. The weather at the RWS on 20–23 July was atrocious, and the main ring was a sea of mud. But judges, stewards and exhibitors battled on valiantly, and Distinction won the three-y-o colt class from 26 entries, and Clara was eighth out of 83 entries in the yearling filly class. The *Sixty Years* book was officially launched at the Welsh Books Council stand, and there was a good attendance despite the mud outside.

The International Show was held in Holland on 22 August to coincide with the fiftieth anniversary of the Nederlands WPCS Stamboek. There were over 400 entries from nine countries, and the supreme was Llanarth Seldom Seen, the section D youngstock champion. Over 600 people, including coachloads from Glamorgan,

Carmarthen and Gwent turned up for the Danaway Stud Open Day on 16 August, where I was co-commentator with Mr Geraint Davies, the highlight of which were the five stallions, Trevallion Valentino, RW champion Danaway Flash Jack, Danaway Harry, Danaway Samson and Danaway Tango. The 12-y-o section A stallion Lacy Buzbee topped the FO Sale ('high flyer') at £9,200 on 26–27 September, with two section A mares, the 13-y-o Heathside Honey Bee and the eight-y-o Dryfe Sibrwd-y-Gwynt, both selling for £6,500. We had one of our best FO Sales ever, with the palomino filly foal Ceulan Carol (Wernderris Caramel x Ceulan Cariad) selling for £1,550, and the bay filly foal Ceulan Lilly (Sunwillow Irving x Ceulan Libby) for £1,500, the second and third highest section A foals on the sale.

Having arranged to lease the black Pendock Bridegroom for 2010, we sold Sunwillow Irving to Ireland from where he returned to Dukeshill Stud, only to be sold on to the Czech Republic in 2013. We also sold the ridden mare Ceulan Lotus to Ms Cecile Sparfel of France, who had bought the colt Ceulan Logan in 2008. At the RW Cob Sale on 16–18 October, two three-y-o fillies, Fronarth Fonhesig and Fronarth Model Supreme, sold for £11,200 and £10,000, the four-y-o stallion Harrowclough Talisman sold for £8,000, the mares Cascob Wardance and Lagonda Starlight both sold for £7,000 and the filly foal Rhydelian Orchid sold to Holland for £7,500. Within section C, the 11-y-o stallion Synod Apollo was top at £5,500. The final 2009 event for us was the RW Winter Fair on 30 November, where the colt foal Ceulan Supersonic (Wernderris Caramel x Ceulan Stella) was second from 54 entries and we sold him to Cheshire, and the filly foal Ceulan Caryn (Wernderris Caramel x Ceulan Cusan) was tenth out of 101 entries, and she was sold to another of my helpers, Ryan Wilson, and they have had some outstanding successes, including eighth out of 89 barren mare entries at the 2014 RWS.

2010–2014

2010 events began in January for us with the wedding in Anglesey of Emma Jones, Frongoch Stud, to Gwyndaf Edwards, Fronbach Stud, so the pony interest was set to continue. A photograph in the 2015 Journal shows their son Huw, already with several wins in lead-rein classes. A signed copy of *Sixty Years* which was auctioned at the AGM of the Australian WPCS fetched $650, and their Board of Management decided to award six Ceulan sashes with $100 to each of the champions at the six state shows. I was told that five of the six recipients had Ceulan in their pedigrees but, not to be outdone, I found a Ceulan connection in the sixth!

Ceredigion was the feature county for the 2010 RWAS, and many fundraising events were held. The RWAS President was the well-known TV presenter Dai Jones MBE, who had been to Ceulan to film the *Cefn Gwlad* programme. His niece Margaret is married to my nephew Enoc of Tynygraig Farm, Tal-y-bont. The RWAS AGM was held on 16 June at his Berthlwyd Farm, Llanilar, where two books were launched, published by Gwasg Gomer Press – *On With The Show* (Charles Arch and Lyn Ebenezer) and the book which I wrote, *Welsh Ponies and Cobs, Ceredigion Champions*, featuring Ceredigion RW champions from 1904. HRH The Princess Royal became Patron of the NPS in 2010 and all nine native breed societies were invited to stage displays at the NPS Summer Championship Show at Malvern in June, where I presented HRH with the book *Ceredigion Champions* when she visited the WPCS display.

On 19 June, three Ceredigion studs held an open day, with an attendance of over 500, including many groups from overseas. It started at Dai and Siân Harris' Pennal Stud in the morning, going on to Huw and Carys Davies' Trefaes Stud in the afternoon, and ending up at Peter and Ann Jones' Menai / Friarly Stud for the evening. I was commentator, and at Pennal there were 23 cobs, all looking as if they were about to enter the RW showring, with star turn Pennal Brynmor, the only youngstock recipient ever of the RW PofW Cup. At Trefaes, there were 37 mountain ponies and cobs, the result of sixty years of selective breeding which has resulted in RW champions, RW section A progeny group winners and record-priced cobs at the sales. The last visit began with a musical ride with Richard and Thomas Jones on their section As, and Gemma Paxford riding Menai Cardi Llwyd, to which I had awarded the Overall Supreme Championship at Cothi Bridge Show on 29 May, then large groups of section A ponies all loose with a stallion, section Cs and finally the cobs, which included many RW champions – a perfect end to a perfect day.

Conditions at the RWS on 19–22 July were dreadful, but in spite of this, there was an attendance of 230,766. The Main Ring resembled a ploughed field, but competitors struggled on bravely in the mud, and Welsh Assembly Member Mr Brynle Williams selected the section D champion Haighmoor Glain as HOYS Cuddy qualifier. The Ceredigion fund-raising events raised over £400,000, which was earmarked towards the construction of a new equine facility on the showground.

On 14 August I went with Mr Edwin Prosser to judge at the Dutch Welsh Dragon Show, held at Oldebroek in conjunction with the Oldebrook Agricultural Show, which included competitions for cattle and sheep and an auction of agricultural machinery. The weather was glorious, and the large attendance were obviously intensely interested in the placings. There were some very large classes, especially the harness classes, where some of the competitors had swept the board at the RWS. Supreme of the show was the section B yearling filly Stougjeshoeve Enjoy, and reserve supreme the section D brood mare Cuneras Morwena Sian. The champion section A was the palomino mare Powerfuls Clarissa by Ysselvliedts Special Edition. She was a very beautiful mare, and a spectacular mover. A copy of *Ceredigion Champions* was auctioned in the main ring and bought by Mrs Byma for 85 euros.

Because the Shropshire showground was no longer available, the Welsh National Championship Show was held at the Three Counties showground in Malvern on 29 August, where Distinction was second out of 12 in the stallion class. In August, the WPCS moved their offices from Chalybeate Street, Aberystwyth, to Bronaeron, Felinfach, Lampeter, and Ruth and I spent a day there setting up the museum. Following the death of Mrs Alison Mountain in January 2013, I have also set up a Mrs Alison Mountain memorial cabinet within the museum. The Chalybeate Street premises were purchased in November 1973 for £13,500 and the 2010 valuation was £500,000.

Three hundred and eighty-six lots were sold at the Brightwells FO Sale on 27–28 September for £258,925, with the average down to £671, but the top price was as good as any. £11,000 was paid for the ridden section A gelding Glenwood Sionyn, who had qualified for HOYS, and the top section B was the palomino yearling filly Laithehill Concerto, sold for £6,000. We sold Ceulan Coron Aur (Cariad's fourteenth foal) privately to France. Five hundred and thirty-five lots sold on the RW Sale on 15–17 October for £396,020, which was an average of £740, with top section D price of £7,800 paid for the palomino stallion Janton Philanderer, and £5,200 for the palomino foal Synod Red and Gold. The black filly foal Popsters Puddles was top section C at £6,000. The RW average figures have followed a consistent pattern, reaching £900 in 1990 then down every year to £600 in 1998, after which they increased every year to £1,000 in 2004–2008, dropping to £700 in 2011. Mynyddtarren The Maverick (sire of our black mare Mynyddtarren Hermia) won the title Ridden Section A of the Year at HOYS having qualified at Cheshire County Show, and the same owner's Ceulan Shem was fifth after qualifying at the North of England Show.

Welsh author Owen Sheers (whose mother breeds Welsh cobs near Abergavenny) wrote a novel called *Resistance* (Faber and Faber) about Germans winning the war, taking over Britain in 1944, capturing the Welsh farmers and the farmers' wives of the Llanthony valley (near Abergavenny) and staging an agricultural show on 10 April 1945. It was decided to make a film of this book, and Amanda Faber visited Ceulan to ascertain from photographs how the 1940s horse exhibitors were dressed, the type of headwear used for the animals and the format of a Breconshire Show catalogue. Faber also asked for suggestions of people who were familiar with horses to act as judges, stewards and spectators. Filming of the horse show took place at Forest Coal Pit farm near Abergavenny on a very damp and muddy Saturday in October, and many WPCS members were dressed in 1944 attire and mingled with famous film stars such as Michael Sheen and Sharon Morgan. The show catalogue cover stated: 'Held at Llanthony Priory Farm by kind permission of Wynne and Ruth Davies'. I did not appear in the film myself. My duty was to assist a worried Sharon Morgan to hold the cob stallion Llanarth True Briton, who was a perfect gentleman throughout, and my name appeared amongst the credits at the end as 'Horse Consultant'.

Finally, on 29 November at the RW Winter Fair, with deep snow in the lorry park and outside the horse marquee, the palomino colt foal Ceulan Cappuccino (Friars Rupertino x Ceulan Cara) was second of 53 entries to the Swedish-owned Forlan Honey Supreme, and Casey (Wernderris Caramel x Ceulan Ceryl) was seventh of

66 filly foals, having previously been reserve champion foal at the Glamorgan WPCA and champion and overall supreme at the Wales and Border Counties Show.

2011 started with a talk and digital presentation on 'Conformation of Welsh Ponies and Cobs' at a teach-in held at the Lion Royal Hotel, Builth Wells on 29 January, where there was an enthusiastic audience who asked many questions. The WPCS AGM on 5 March was held at the Celtic Manor, Newport, when the presidency was handed over from Mr Terry Court of Brightwells to Mrs Kathleen James of the Highland Stud, and I gave my thirty-fifth publicity officer's annual report. Over 600 members attended the evening party sponsored by Brightwells Auctioneers, and the entertainment was fantastic, with comedian Max Boyce, the Pearly Kings and Queens from London, male voice choirs, singers Eric and Endaf Jones of Llanidan Stud, all compered by TV personality Dai Jones, Llanilar.

On Saturday 2 April, Ruth and I celebrated our golden wedding at the Miskin Arms, and we were delighted to have in attendance family members and the bridesmaid and best man who were there on the day. The fiftieth Lampeter Welsh Breeds Show was held on 23 April, and because I supplied a list of every champion from 1962 to 2011, and many historic photographs which appeared in the gold-covered catalogue, I was presented with an anniversary clock by the show chairman, Mr Daniel Morgan. Mr Peter Jones was the show president, and awarded the supreme championship to Marged Simons riding Yrallt Mayday Surprise (C).

I was President of the Glanusk Show, and awarded the supreme championship to Trefaes Black Flyer (D) with Moelgarnedd Derwyn (B) reserve. There were 3,073 horse and pony entries at the RWS held on 18–21 July of which 1,709 were Welsh. Stonedge Samuel (A) was awarded the HOYS Cuddy qualification. HRH The Duke of Kent visited the show on the Wednesday, and senior commentator

Mr Charles Arch introduced him to the commentators in the Pembrokeshire Main Ring control tower. Because 2011 was the hundredth anniversary of the mountain pony stallion Greylight being sold to Mr Anthony Hordern of Australia for £1,000, Mrs Tina Taylor (daughter of Lady Creswick and grand-daughter of Mr Hordern, Nattai Stud) came to the RWS and awarded a framed photograph of Greylight to Stonedge Samuel. The next Welsh stallion to be bought by Mr Hordern (in 1934) was four-times RWS champion Ceulan Comet (f. 1926), and after the show we were delighted that David and Tina Taylor visited us at Ceulan to see the many descendants we have of Seren Ceulan (f. 1910), dam of Ceulan Comet.

The first ever International WPCS Show to be held in Wales was on the RW showground on 6–7 August, where I was commentator. There were 1,104 entries from 11 countries and 10 overseas judges. Many first prizes went to overseas exhibitors, but the supremes (judged by all the judges holding up their marks as in ice-skating competitions), all stayed within the UK, going to Lacy Buzbee (in-hand), Nebo Julie Ann (ridden) and Croniarth Keltic Starlight (harness). Three hundred and ninety-four ponies sold for £256,290 (an average of £650) on the FO Sale on 24–25 September. The top was Amesbury Dolly Mixture (WPB) at £10,300, and next highest was the section B three-y-o colt Thistledown Arctic Fox (who was section B champion at the International Show) at £9,000. We sold the palomino yearling colt Ceulan Cappuccino privately to David and Carol Maurer, who had moved to Oregon by this time, as an outcross on their Ceulan Lwcus daughters. An S4C television crew had filmed him as a foal in the snow at the RW Winter Fair, and went to Oregon to film him and the other Ceulan ponies at Gaslight Farm for *O Gymru Fach*, a series of programmes dealing with exports from Wales. This series has been broadcast several times by S4C, most recently in May and June 2015. Five hundred and eighty Welsh section C, D and WPB sold on the RW Sale on 21–23 October for £404,325, the lowest average (£697) for thirteen years, with a top price of £6,500 for the section C stallion D'Abernon Sugar Ray. Mynyddtarren The Maverick qualified for HOYS at Midland Counties and Ceulan Shem at the NPS Summer Show, but this was not their year for winning – the supreme ridden pony (£1,000) was the section B mare Crystal Vision, which had been purchased on the FO Sale the previous year for £600.

Most of my WPCS publicity officer work during these years was spent supplying material for the society website. The website's monthly visits were around 15,000, with over 60,000 page views averaging five pages per visit, and a breakdown is available showing the countries of the visitors. Permission had been given to overseas societies to publish these articles (often translated), provided that the WPCS website was acknowledged. It is very gratifying to receive impressive annual journals from the overseas societies containing these articles. In addition, our own WPCS Journal contained 41 pages of reports I had written on shows and sales in addition to four historical articles.

I celebrated my eightieth birthday on 19 March, and received many congratulatory emails from all over Britain and abroad. I don't follow Facebook, but I was shown a Dr Wynne Davies Appreciation Society group with over 150 members, though I must admit that many names were unknown to me. Having reported shows from Wales for *Horse and Hound* for 60 years, and with my birthday looming, I thought it was a relevant time to retire. *Horse and Hound* showing editor Nicola Swinney wrote: 'Wynne is going to leave some very big boots to fill. His comprehensive knowledge of the Welsh pony and cob is second to none. It really does feel like the end of an era for me.'

After many months of continuous rain, the weather for the RWS on 23–26 July was glorious, and Llanarth Delilah received the

HOYS Cuddy ticket. On Sunday 2 September I was commentator at the Thorneyside Stud, Windsor, promotional and sale preview day. Here, there were 11 mares and foals which were entered for the RW Cob Sale on 20 October, 13 mares not entered, 17 sale fillies, seven non-sale fillies and nine sale colts, followed by a ridden display of four, a harness display of eight, three sale stallions and eight non-sale stallions, including the 29-y-o Thorneyside The Boss and his full-brother, the 27-y-o Thorneyside Flyer and finally, nine Thorneyside stallions brought home for the day. A copy of *The Welsh Cob* which I donated to charity sold for £380 by auction. There was a large attendance, with several from overseas, many having decided on which lots to bid on 20 October. Three hundred and twelve lots were sold on the FO Sale on 29–30 September, where the average was £660 and, for the first time, an unbroken three-y-o gelding, Cosford Challenger, topped, the sale at £7,200. The palomino section B colt foal Laithehill Wild Wind sold for £3,400 to Oregon.

As expected, the inclusion of the 43 from Thorneyside at the RW Sale on 19–21 October boosted the average from £668 to £908. The Thorneyside cobs averaged £3,511, topped by the two-y-o dun colt Thorneyside Golden Boy at £22,000, and the colt foal Thorneyside Royal Command, which sold for £16,000.

I was invited by *Showing World* magazine to attend the HOYS on 5 October – to present an award, I was told – but to my great surprise, it was a presentation to me of Lifetime Achievement Award. I was accompanied by my grandson Joseph and grand-daughter Leah, who lived within easy travelling distance of the NEC in Birmingham. David has four children: Rachel, born in 1988 who graduated from Lancaster University and works at Blue Coats School, Liverpool; Leah, born in 1990, who graduated in Law from Birmingham University in 2013 and works at an estate agents' office in Wolverhampton; Miriam, born in 1993, who graduated from Cardiff Metropolitan University with first-class honours in Fine Arts and the prize for best student in 2015, and Joseph, born in 1996, who was the top pupil of his Wolverhampton School at A-level, and is reading Physics for an MSc degree at Birmingham University.

David studied Agriculture at the Welsh Agricultural College, Aberystwyth 1980–1983 and graduated with honours in Agriculture at the University College of North Wales, Bangor in 1986. Since then, he has been lecturer in Agriculture at Coleg Sir Gâr (Carmarthen College of Technology and Art) and is currently curriculum head of the land-based studies.

Sadly, 2013 started on a sombre note with the news of the death in January of Mrs Alison Mountain, who had been a very good friend of our family for over sixty years. Twyford ponies have been very successful at Ceulan and, likewise, Ceulan ponies at Twyford. It was only a week previously that she had phoned me, full of plans for acquiring a new section C stallion. A service in celebration of her life was held in a large marquee at Twyford Farm on 20 May, and a very large gathering of friends attended, many having come over from overseas. I was very happy to present a eulogy at the service and hope that I got across Mrs Mountain's great sense of humour and loyalty. I was very honoured that she bequeathed me the painting of Twyford ponies by Barbara Waller (1958) which I had always admired when staying at Twyford, and had been tested to see whether I could name the six mares with foals. One foal was easy for me, since it was Twyford Matador, that we had at Ceulan until 1968. I don't claim that it is a particularly valuable painting, but to me, it is priceless.

On 6 March I gave a talk to the Art Appreciation Group of the Cowbridge Branch of U3A (the University of the Third Age) on 'Horse Paintings in Wales'. I was able to buy on eBay two Dyoll Starlight WPCS medals (presentation medal 1912 and Royal

Lancashire 1914), which had been 'lost' since the death of Mrs Raleigh Blandy in 1992. Twelve Dyoll medals had been bought by an antiques dealer at Chilcotts Auctions, Tiverton, and I had to pay more for one than he paid for all twelve. However, they are now safe (most of the others went overseas), and I talked about them on the S4C programme *Prynhawn Da* on 6 April, the day before the AGM at Aberystwyth, and many members told me how relieved they were that the medals are safe in Wales.

The weather for the RWS on 22–25 July was glorious, which helped to attract an attendance of 241,741. This was the fiftieth show to be held on the permanent site, and HRH The Prince of Wales and the Duchess of Cornwall attended, and spent much time in the Main Ring with the Welsh ponies and cobs. One section D filly foal which the Duchess particularly admired was subsequently registered as Llwynhywel Lady Camilla! The Olympic gold medallist Carl Hester judged the HOYS Cuddy qualifier and awarded it to Synod Lady Lilian (C). We had many overseas visitors to Ceulan over the period of the RWS. The Danaway Stud, Sittingbourne, Kent, held an open day on 8 September, where I was commentator. The RW George PofW Cup has only left Wales eight times in 105 years, and three of those recipients were present that day – Danaway Flashjack (2000), Danaway Crackling Rose (2012) and Trevallion Black Harry (2013). The Glamorgan WPCA spent three days in September visiting racing stables at Newmarket – I was particularly interested in the 440 paintings at the National Horseracing Museum. I had attended the official opening by HM The Queen Mother on 2 April 1986, invited by Mrs Stella Archer Walker, co-founder of the British Sporting Art Trust who was art correspondent for *Horse and Hound* from 1962–1987.

Three hundred and eleven ponies were sold on the sixtieth FO Sale on 28–29 September for £190,930, averaging £614, with the ridden section B stallion Mynach Orsino (who had qualified for

HOYS) top at £9,000. We sold the dun colt foal Ceulan Hannibal (Ceulan Calon Lân x Mynyddtarren Hermia), who had been placed third at the RW, and the palomino filly foal Ceulan Corona (Wernderris Caramel x Ceulan Cusan). The yearling filly Ceulan Hannah (Pendock Bridegroom x Hermia) had a successful showing season, winning at Cothi Bridge, Cardigan and Nevern, and placed at Northleach and the Royal Bath and West. We collected the bay stallion Ysselvliedts Highwood (A) in September for showing and stud duties in 2014. Overall supreme ridden pony at HOYS 9–13 October was the lead-rein champion Nynwood Fantasia (A), ridden by five-year-old Henrietta Rogers. Ceulan Shem qualified at the NPS summer championships and was placed seventh.

The Welsh hit the highs at the Olympia Ridden Championships, with Bronheulog Harvey (B, champion), Cadlanvalley Sandpiper (B, reserve champion), Menai Thomas (C, fourth) and Thistledown Scotch Whisky (A, fifth). Our foal show exhibits were the black filly Ceulan Mona Lisa (Weston Distinction x Ceulan Mariah) and the large WPB gelding foal Crosswell Rio (Abergavenny Armani x the Quarter-horse mare Crosswell Roxanne), bred by David and Carolyn at Crosswell. I gave a talk on the history of Welsh driving horses and ponies to the Dyfed Carriage Driving Group on 4 November, which was easy, since the Welsh breeds can usually hold their own against all other breeds when it comes to driving.

Mrs Mary Redvers, whose mother Mrs Nell Pennell was WPCS President in 1937 and 1954, and whose grandfather Mr Gwynne Holford was a founder vice-president in 1901, took over the presidency at the AGM on 5 April 2014 at the Mercure House Hotel, Cardiff. On 18 May, Mrs Redvers invited everyone to an open day at her home, Tweenhills Farm, Hartpury, where her son David has a world-famous thoroughbred breeding establishment. The parade of stallions began with the world champion Makfi, who had covered 250 mares at a stud fee of £25,000, then we saw the mares and foals, some of which were sold on the autumn sales for over £1m. Tweenhills bought the colt foal Galileo for Qatar Racing for 2.5m gns in 2013. The Northleach Show celebrated its fiftieth anniversary, held on the magnificent Cirencester Park on 28 June where, for the first time ever, the overall supreme was a working hunter champion, Wyken Lady Jasmine (C).

The RWS was held in glorious weather on 21–24 July, when the attendance reached 237,694, and there were classes with enormous entries, including 89 in the section A barren mare class. The star of the show was the section C two-y-o colt Rhoswen Guardsman, who was the HOYS Cuddy qualifier. Our junior stallion Ysselvliedts Highwood was third out of 28 entries, having previously been third at the Royal Bath and West, and champion (WPCS bronze medal) at the Three Counties.

I judged at the Brecon County Show on 2 August, where my champion section A was the bay stallion Tryfel Triumph, and reserve another bay, the brood mare Cilmery First Edition, who has the same dam (Cilmery Springtime by Trefaes Taran) as Cilmery Hot Chocolate, champion at the RWS the previous week. Champion and reserve section B both came from the 2–3-y-o class, Sianwood Celtic Gold and Maybrock Vanity Fair. The following day we had an open day at Ceulan, where the main visitors were Carmarthen WPCA members who filled a large coach, plus many who travelled individually, some having come from as far afield as Cornwall. We were glad of the many helpers who came to trot out the ponies and assist with the refreshments. We were also very lucky with the weather – the following weekend at the National Championship Show at Malvern, the weather was atrocious and the secretary's marquee blew into the middle of the ponies in the main ring.

On 19 August at Pembroke County Show, our senior stallion Weston Distinction was champion section A (WPCS silver medal), and went on to be Overall Supreme Welsh. The following day, the

Abergavenny and Glebedale Studs held open days in aid of the Gwent 2015 RW feature county fund. The first was at Abergavenny, where 30 section Cs and Ds were presented in show condition. Star of the Cs was Abergavenny Bayleaf, twice RW female champion, and within the Ds were the George PofW Cup winner Abergavenny Morning Queen, and the exquisite Abergavenny Sally. At Glebedale, there were twenty section A, B, C and D mares with their foals in the fields, then the youngstock were shown individually and finally Glebedale Savannah, twice champion section A and overall best mare at the NPS summer championships.

Three hundred and three ponies sold on the Brightwells FO Sale on 27–28 September for £210,590 averaging £695, which was about consistent for the last five years after the £800–£900 of 2003–2007. Top section B was Thistledown Arctic Monkey at £8,800, and top section A Uphill James Fox at £8,100. We sold a bay colt foal, Ceulan Louis (Weston Distinction x Ceulan Lodes), to Nova Scotia, the first time that one had been sold from the FO Sale to Canada for eleven years.

Because we had so many Wernderris Caramel daughters and only one other non-related mare, we sold him back to Wernderris Stud. Ysselvliedts Highwood was required back in Holland, and we leased Ysselvliedts Irresistible (Vechtzicht Hywel x Hafdre Ithwen) for 2015. At HOYS on 8–12 October, the WPB Rendene Royal Charm was Cuddy in-hand champion, and another WPB, Barkway Moonfairy, won the £1000 supreme ridden pony. Ceulan Shem had his best ever marks in the ridden section As and was placed third. Four hundred and thirty-eight section Cs, Ds and WPB sold on the Brightwells Cob Sale on 17–19 October for £361,461, an average of £850 with a top price of £20,000 for the palomino section D stallion Thorneyside Gold Dust, and £14,600 was paid for the ridden section D stallion Renvarg The Mystic, who had done well at HOYS. A celebration of the life of Mrs Robina Mills was held on the

RW showground on 15 November. Mrs Mills had been chairman of the WPCS International Show committee, and the first chairman of the National Foal Show, and had continued for 23 years. Our favourite mare, Ceulan Cariad (f. 1988: Twyford Sprig x Rondeels Cavalla), died in December. She had been a prolific winner and produced 15 foals, two of which went to the USA, two to Holland, one to Spain and one to France. We kept her last daughter, Ceulan Ceirios (f. 2012), who was youngstock champion at the Vale of Glamorgan Show, and g-daughter Ceulan Cressida (f. 2014), who was champion at the Glamorgan WPCA Show and second at the National Foal Show, and two other daughters.

POST-SCRIPT: TODAY

2015 finds Ruth and me still living at Ceulan Farm after half a century, and although we have downsized to about twenty ponies and breed fewer foals, with 65 acres, the ponies, the shows, the sales and the family, there is always something to do! David converted four stables into a bungalow, and he now does most of the showing, buying and selling, though I still have to pay my share of the bills!

His children are frequent visitors, and with the birth of Leah and Josh's baby, Anya, we are looking forward to welcoming the next generation. Jane and Simon and their three boys are also often found at Ceulan, and Ruth's brother Roger and his wife Margaret live in Porthcawl, so they and their families are also frequent visitors. We still visit my family in Tal-y-bont whenever the occasion arises, and my niece Janet and her son Jonathan live conveniently nearby in Cardiff.

We have marvellous friends all over the world through having been a member of the WPCS for 68 years, and we have constant streams of visitors to Ceulan – we are now on our third visitors' book! In addition to my contribution to the WPCS through my publications, I have received many communications from breeders stating that it was through reading my books and my 58 years of writing for such as *Horse and Hound* that they became interested in the Welsh breeds. On a local level, Ruth has a circle of friends, former Soroptimists and members of St David's Church, Miskin, who meet regularly, and I meet up with former college staff on a monthly basis. We have had a regular supply of helpers with the ponies over fifty years, some of whom, with no previous equine experience, now have their own studs (and sometimes beat us!), and we have even had marriages amongst them.

Ruth and I consider that we have a wonderful life. We are part of a lovely family, we have known so many super ponies and cobs and the people associated with them. We have a lot to be thankful for, and owe so much to so many.

ACKNOWLEDGEMENTS

I would like to thank Mr Tom Best for very valuable suggestions during the compilation of this book. In such a massive undertaking covering such a long period of time, there will inevitably be some errors, hopefully very few. They are my sole responsibility.

Many thanks to the following for their kind permission to use their images: Tom Best, Lesley Bruce, Mike Daley, Maud Farghen, Carol Gilson, David Maurer, Stuart Newsham, Arvid Parry Jones, Anthony Reynolds, Aniek Rolf and Ryan Wilson.